Dr. Jacquelyn Bobien-Blanton

Dr. **Jacquelyn Bobien-Blanton** is a distinguished educator with nearly three decades of educational experience. She currently serves as the Executive Director of Early Learning for Orange Township Public Schools, and holds a doctorate degree from Walden University, as well as a master's degree from Montclair State University and an undergraduate degree from Louisiana State University. Certified in Preschool-Third Grade, Elementary Education, Supervision, and Principalship, Dr. Blanton oversees early-learning education, professional development, curriculum programming, budgeting, and coordinates governmental mandates.

Recognized as an Exemplary Elementary Educator, she contributed to early childhood education protocols and revised teaching standards for the New Jersey Department of Education; and was also recognized by the Senate and General Assembly for dedication to scholastic achievement. Actively engaged in professional organizations, including the National Association for the Education of Young Children, Dr. Blanton is committed to educational advancement.

Among many other efforts, her dedication extends to community service, having assisted in creating the Shiloh Rainbow Academy in Newark, NJ. Beyond her professional achievements, "Jackie", a devoted wife and mother, values family closeness and believes in the transformative power of education for a fulfilling life.

It Takes a Village to Raise a Reader

A Vital and Essential Resource to Unlock a Student's Success

by Dr. Jacquelyn Bobien-Blanton

Based on the disseration "Reading Fadeout"

by Dr. Jacquelyn Bobien-Blanton

PUBLISHED BY
LIGHTHOUSE MANUSCRIPTS
August 2024

Lighthouse Manuscripts™

It Takes a Village to Raise a Reader
August 2024

Published by Lighthouse Manuscripts LLC
PO Box 2181
Reston, VA 20195

ISBN: 978-1-7358723-2-2
EBOOK ISBN: 978-1-7358723-4-6
Library of Congress Control Number: 2024906281

Printed in the United States of America

For more information, email: info@lighthousemanuscripts.com

Dear Students,

In the words of the late President Emeritus of Morehouse College, Dr. Benjamin Elijah Mays:

"It must be borne in mind that the tragedy in life doesn't lie in not reaching your goal. The tragedy lies in having no goal to reach. It isn't a calamity to die with dreams unfulfilled, but it is a calamity not to dream. It is not a disaster to be unable to capture your ideal, but it is a disaster to have no ideal to capture. It is not a disgrace not to reach the stars, but it is a disgrace to have no stars to reach for. Not failure, but low aim is sin."

To all young beautiful, gifted, and talented young people: Believe It, Receive it, It's Yours....Dear to Dream Big...You Can Do All Things!

- Dr. Jacquelyn Bobien-Blanton

Dedication

This book is dedicated to my mom, my guardian angel in heaven, My A-1 from Day-1. My rock. My everything! Thank you God for sending me your best to guide me through life. Because of my mother's sacrifices, I am who I am today.

Second, this book is for all who struggle to read and for family members struggling to help. Don't give up, stay the course. The race isn't given to the swift, but to those who can endure. Just think about the metamorphic process of a butterfly. The process does not begin pretty, rather the caterpillar must go through several stages, and some can be tough. However, in the end, a beautiful butterfly emerges. When the time is right, it will spread its wings and soar high into the sky for all to enjoy and admire. Wait for it. Your time to soar will soon come!

Acknowledgements

I would like to thank God from whom all blessings flow. Your Grace and Mercy brought me through!

Tomm Boyer and the Lighthouse Manuscripts Team, thank you for this platform to turn my message into a movement and my passion into a purpose to benefit others. This was truly a labor of love. To whom much is given, much is required. Thank you for allowing me to Dare to Dream and to bring this project to fruition.

To the educators in my focus group, thank you for your time, honesty, and for sharing your experience and knowledge with me. You are Superheroes without a cape!

John, my wonderful and supportive husband, thank you for being a significant presence in my journey. Your unwavering love and constant support pushed me to the finish line.

To my sons Khaalis, Gyasi, and Jahir, and my D-Love Sharee, I can't imagine life without you. You are the wind beneath my wings. I am not sure what I did to deserve such a beautiful crew. Your support and encouragement mean the world to me. I love you all unconditionally. I have had many titles in life, but none more precious than Mom/Momma J. You are the reason why I do what I do.

To our grandchildren, you are the reason why we should have grandchildren before children. You make my heart skip a beat. If I could change the world for you, I would, but I would not change you for the world. Remember, you were not born to fit in, you were born to stand out.

To my brother Donald, my nephews DJ and Xavier, and my beautiful niece R'Kaiya, we are Joe's legacy. Keep making her proud. Always remember to let her smile warm our hearts.

Thank you to the Bobien-Blanton Crew for the support, love, and encouragement. Family matters! To my third-grade teacher and all my track and field coaches, thank you for being my Champions in Life. You taught me that I had everything I needed inside of me to win.

To the Orange Township Public Schools, the greatest little district around, thank you for making a difference in the lives of our students and for the clear vision for early learning. We are Moving into Greatness!

To my awesome friends, classmates, and teammates old and new, near and far, thank you for your inspiring words and your motivation. I truly appreciate you.

Acknowledgements (cont'd)

My LSU Tiger Family, I am so glad blood does not always make you family, and family does not always mean blood! We have a bond that will never be broken. Geaux Tigers!!

Montclair Child Development Center, thank you for my humble beginnings. You are true women of power, my first mentors, and true Champions for Children.

Last but certainly not least, to the Dynamic Divas of Delta Sigma Theta Sorority, Incorporated, thank you for representing sisterhood so effortlessly and for showing me that it's ok to share your light with others and still be lit yourself. To my 82 Fabulous F.L.A.M.E.S. and forever sisters; step by step...all we do is win, win, win! Thank you for always showing up and showing out no matter what. I am my sister's keeper.

Table of Contents

Conclusion   286

References   294

Images

Figures

Introduction

The impetus for writing this book was to shed light on the historic and ongoing concerns about children struggling to read by the third grade, particularly children of color. Third grade is a good barometer for later school success because children switch from learning to read, to reading to learn. If children do not read proficiently, they are far less likely to understand what they are learning as they move from grade to grade. Early reading skills lay the foundation for future academic success. Without these skills in place, knowledge will be stalled, and children may begin to struggle with anxiety, stress, and low self-esteem. The economic implications for non-readers are significant.

In full transparency, I am not a reading specialist, a reading coach, or a reading supervisor. I am not a neurologist, pediatrician, or politician. I am a long-time educator, contributing member of society, taxpayer, former struggling reader, social change agent, and champion for children. This book is about social justice for those who have been and continue to be marginalized, skipped over, disregarded, disenfranchised, and left without a voice. It is about social justice for young Black and Brown children and correcting the systems that have failed to see their beauty, their worth, their value, and their possibilities.

This book is for families who may not have an educational background but want the best for their children. I am a lifelong educator and I have yet to meet parents who aspire for their children to grow up and become gang members, drug dealers, high school dropouts, or criminals. No, they want what's best for their children and that begins with a good education. The problem is many parents may not know or understand the qualities of a "good education." My mother thought that sending my brother and me to school every day and insisting that we earn good grades were enough. She left the "schooling" to the teachers and the school. We had to be quiet, listen, and learn from the teachers. According to my mother, if the teacher said the sky was yellow, we had better paint it yellow because the teacher was right. My mother would say, "They went to college, and they are smarter than children." This was how the world turned, according to my mother. My mother was unaware of the elements of a good education; therefore, she did not challenge the system or hold anyone accountable. But what are the elements of a good education? When does learning begin? Who are the individuals responsible for providing a good education? What does it mean to be educated? I will attempt to explore these questions and more.

This book is not about throwing blame at any one person or any one system as there is plenty of blame to go around. It is not about teaching reading per se but about a child's ecosystem that either hinders or promotes reading proficiently by third grade. Building readers is a multifaceted approach and to fully understand the significance of our current reading problems in the early grades, we must examine what occurs before children enter elementary school as well as what occurs during the first few years in elementary school. This book gives a glimpse of what children are exposed to either directly or indirectly that impacts their growth and development. I explore the systems (past and present) that impact our children's ability to read proficiently by third grade. Journey with me through this researched-based book that explores real issues and concerns that impact young readers. While this book is heavy with research, many of the chapters have an added section labeled "Practically Speaking" that provides professional and personal commentary to help readers better connect with the research and the subject matter.

We are all responsible for the proper growth and development of children and providing them with equitable learning opportunities and experiences. The educational system has come a long way in the United States, but we have a long way to go. Moving from equality to equity in education is a start but we must continue towards liberation and remove the historic barriers that kept Black and Brown children from receiving a quality education in the first place. This concept will be further explored in the chapters ahead. Currently, we have states like Arizona and California using fourth-grade reading scores to determine future plans for the prison population, furthering the preschool-to-prison pipeline mentality. In the book, *Why Kids Can't Read: Challenging the Status Quo in Education* by Blaunstein and Lyon, it was pointed out that 25% of young adults lack the basic literacy skills needed for a job. Sixty percent of adolescents who abuse drugs also have a reading problem. Seventy six percent of children living in poverty cannot read at a proficient level and more than 60% of young prisoners are functionally illiterate. The fact of the matter is these statistics can change. We know the steps children need to improve reading outcomes in our schools, close the achievement gap, and transform every child into a proficient reader. However, we continue to engage in the same practices year after year, because it is either too hard, too controversial, or too much of a hassle to change from what has always been done. Whatever the reason, children are caught in the crossfire.

As a social justice change agent, it is incumbent upon me and anyone who cares about children to continue to advocate for quality education for every child. Social change means having the courage, confidence, and knowledge to address challenges and issues that hinder justice and equality for all. It means taking a stand to be a catalyst for making life better for others through resources, education, and deeds. Social change means using education in practical ways to effect change, which is sometimes motivated by deep emotions and/or personal experiences that drive an individual to make a conscious commitment to make a difference in the lives of others. It also means that we must acknowledge injustice, inequality, discrimination, and other disparities, and take action to create a more equitable place for everyone. Many of our major social change reforms were born from people having an emotional connection to the issue. Reading is emotional for me and thus a social justice issue worth fighting for. The content in this book is meant for those privileged enough to have the opportunity to touch the lives of children.

It is my hope that this book will open hearts and minds for real talk about early reading. We need pediatricians, families, educators, daycare center workers, legislators, and community members to pause and think about what can be done in our own spaces to collectively ensure that we are providing rich opportunities, experiences, and quality environments for children. The educational system cannot solve this problem alone. Rather, it will take a village, a multifaceted approach, true commitment, time, and money to help put our young scholars on a path to becoming successful and confident readers. Yes, It Takes a Village to Raise a Reader.

Prologue

Reading proficiently matters. The economy is enhanced when reading levels are high. Reading proficiently opens the doors to more educational and employment opportunities and reduces poverty and chronic underemployment. A long-term study by the Annie E. Casey Foundation found that children who were not proficient in reading by the end of third grade were four times more likely to drop out of high school than proficient readers. Additionally, 88% of children who failed to earn a high school diploma struggled to read in third grade. Our children must be able to compete in a global society. This means that they must develop critical thinking skills, must be creative, and must learn how to collaborate and communicate effectively with others. Additionally, children must have media and technology skills. These essential skills are intended to help our children keep up with the fast-paced markets of today and to compete in a 21st-century global economy.

According to the National Assessment Educational Panel (NAEP), only 34% of fourth graders are reading proficiently. Unfortunately, this has been the narrative for decades. The research is clear: if children do not read by the third grade, there is a strong possibility that they may struggle in the later grades and fall behind their peers who are proficient readers. Once children fall behind, it is almost impossible for them to catch up. Missing the mark for proficient reading has major implications for children, including higher incidents with the law, higher incidence of juvenile detention, higher rates of gang membership and activity, and a higher rate of drug and alcohol abuse. In fact, there is an urban myth that says prison planners use the results from third grade reading scores to plan the size of prisons. Although this may be a myth, the criminal justice system has always linked the reading performance of children to crime. The reading struggles that plague many of our children should be a national epidemic, but sadly, it is not. Our educational system was not created to educate all children. For decades, the current educational ecosystem has failed our children, but this has been the case historically.

According to historians, during the antebellum period in the United States or the time between the formation of the U.S. government and the outbreak of the

American Civil War, anti-literacy laws were a major strategy used by southern plantation owners to prevent the enslaved population from learning to read in any form. Reading fluently back then was a sign of intellectual development and the possibility for social mobility both of which were seen as a threat to plantation owners. Therefore, learning to read was out of the question for African Americans. Despite anti-literacy laws, the Black community found multiple strategies to learn how to read. The irony is that people of color have struggled to read for a very long time, and the struggle continues today although the reasons for the struggles are different…perhaps. Since the anti-literacy laws, Black and Brown children have had to deal with segregation, desegregation, inequality, inequities in learning experiences, and underfunded schools. These issues made it difficult, if not impossible, for children to receive a quality education. Decades later, we continue to fight for quality education, but who determines quality, and what does it look like? Does quality look the same from school district to school district and from state to state? My retort is a resounding no.

Practically Speaking

When I was in high school, I received good grades and graduated within the top 30% of my small graduating class. I felt confident academically and thought that college would be a smooth transition for me. During the registration process at the university I attended, I learned that I could not take specific first-year courses because I needed remedial courses. I could not understand why I needed remedial courses when I was a good student in high school and earned high grades. In retrospect, the "A" that I received in many of my courses did not have the same weight and did not mean as much as an "A" in more affluent school districts. I realized that it did not matter what grades I received in high school; I was ill-prepared for college.

Looking back, I can remember being in an Honors English class as the teacher announced essays that were exemplary and had the students read their essays out loud to the class. As my classmates read their essays, I remember following along word for word in the book. The English Literature book had pictures of various contributors to English Literature, and under each picture was a narrative about the person's life and accomplishments. As I reflect, I wonder how was that exemplary, when it was memorized. No fault of my classmate; the teacher placed more emphasis on memorization instead of memorable learning experiences that required critical thinking skills. Even in this situation, I cannot blame the teacher, rather it was the educational ecosystem as a whole that failed me coupled with my limited experiences outside of the classroom. Teachers are supposed to make learning meaningful and impactful so that it endures. Providing children with learning experiences that are hands-on, exciting, meaningful, relevant, and interesting will be impactful and long-lasting. I did not realize it at the time, but many of my educational experiences before college were not impactful, rather they were filled with memorization, compliance, busy work, and one-right-answer experiences. However, I was so excited to be on a college campus and was so proud to be the first in my family to attend college. I soon realized that it was not going to be easy because I was not prepared for the academic rigor that I was about to face. How was this possible? It was possible because we have an educational system that is built on inequality, and inequitable experiences and opportunities, which was made crystal clear during the COVID-19 pandemic.

The COVID-19 pandemic did not create our broken educational system or the inequalities that exist in the healthcare system. The pandemic did not cause disparities in living conditions, insurance benefits, employment opportunities, or food access. COVID-19 simply exposed what was already there. Many people knew that these inequalities existed, but they existed with other people and in other communities. The severity of the pandemic was not real for some until it hit middle America. Suddenly, there was no hiding from the lack of technology and connectivity (internet service) for many school-aged children forced into virtual learning or the issues with the distribution of wealth, or the widening gap between those that have and those that have not. The pandemic unveiled so many of our country's deepest woes.

However, despite the issues, we cannot allow the pandemic to continue to rob our children of the education they deserve. We cannot buckle under and dwell on all the negative media coverage that continues to inundate us about the devastating effects the pandemic had and continues to have on our children who are overwhelmingly Black and Brown. We cannot allow the pandemic to become yet another excuse to mis-educate our children, lower educational expectations, and water down the curricula. Many researchers are weighing in on the impact of the COVID years and predicting a bleak and dark future for children. Many of our children did experience "unfinished learning" but they also picked up different skills that they would have picked up in a higher grade. The phrase "learning loss," which has been used frequently during the pandemic, assumes that children had the skills to begin with. However, if they had the skills and lost them, I wonder if they ever had them (the skills) in the first place. Unless children had some sort of medical or mental conditions, how can learning just disappear?

I prefer the term unfinished learning because our children learned a lot, some skills were learned out of order, some were interrupted, and some were placed on hold because of the learning conditions. How we view the pandemic years will ultimately determine how we move forward with our children and how our children view the learning process as a whole. If we view those years as "learning loss," we will see children spending an enormous amount of time in remediation, compliance, and rote learning, with limited access to grade-level content. If we view the pandemic years in terms of unfinished learning, we have a different perspective and will see teachers capitalizing on the skills that children picked up during remote learning. We will see teachers leveraging those skills to support more advanced skills, and we will also see teachers empowering children to become partners in the learning process while making learning exciting, interesting, and meaningful to them. This isn't to say that I am not concerned about the learning trajectory of children, because I am. Specifically, I am concerned about the social and emotional development of young children who have been exposed to mask-wearing during the COVID years.

I am concerned about the impact of mask-wearing on social and emotional development, especially for young learners who rely heavily on facial expressions for socialization and enculturation according to Herba and Phillips (2004), Glanville and Nowicki (2002), and Matsumoto and Hwang (2011). The COVID-19 pandemic necessitated the use of masks as a preventive measure, but it has also affected how people communicate with each other. Mask wearing limits the visibility of facial expressions, which include the seven universal emotions: anger, contempt, disgust, fear, happiness, sadness, and surprise. Children missing these skills may have a harder time with the enculturation process (Matsumoto and Hwang, 2011). Merriam-Webster defines enculturation as "the process by which an individual learns the traditional content of a culture and assimilates its practices and values." Through enculturation, children learn what behaviors, values, language, and morals are acceptable in society. They learn by observing other members of society, including parents, friends, teachers, and mentors. Enculturation is more than facial expressions, and we know that it is possible to use other nonverbal cues such as body language, tone of voice, and context to understand someone's emotions and intentions; however, young children may not have enough experience to be able to decipher these social cues successfully. I am concerned for young learners because socialization is a major part of the learning process and difficulty with obtaining these skills may make teaching and learning a little more challenging. Children may end up with behavior concerns because of the limited amount of time spent learning and observing cultural norms, which may impact learning in general. Advocates for children must provide alternative ways for children to develop these skills to reduce the chances of children needing special education.

To help children in this area of development, teachers and parents can use alternative methods to teach social and emotional skills, such as role-playing, storytelling, and social games. These activities can help children learn how to identify and express their emotions, understand other people's perspectives, and develop empathy and cooperation. Encouraging open communication and active listening can also help children feel understood and supported, even if they cannot see each other's full facial expressions. While masks may present some challenges for social and emotional development, there are other ways to support children's development in these areas. We must hit the "reset" button and think outside of the box to help our children develop these critical skills otherwise we will see a significant number of children needing special educational services.

In addition to social and emotional learning, I am concerned about children who are in the early grades (first and second grades), which are the most important grades for learning to read. Key predictors of reading success are phonemic awareness and the alphabetic principle. Phonemic awareness is the ability to identify and manipulate individual sounds (phonemes) in spoken words. The alphabetic principle is the understanding that there are systematic and predictable relationships between written letters and spoken sounds. If young learners spend a considerable amount of time in virtual learning or learning behind a mask, it becomes very difficult to teach letter sounds.

When teaching letter sounds, children need to see the movement of the teacher's mouth and how the mouth moves when making the sound of a letter as well as the position of teeth, the tongue, and the jaw. For young learners, it is very hard to tell the difference between the letters, "B", "C", "D", "Z" or "P" behind a mask, even if there is complete silence in the classroom. Children do not have the ear to decipher like adults at such an early stage in their learning process. This is true for adults who have mastered this concept. For example, how many people have ever been on the telephone and had to ask the person on the other end to repeat a name or a phrase or ask the person to spell it phonetically? It is difficult for adults, just imagine how hard it is for young learners who have just begun their journey toward reading. Just the same, when children try to match letters to sounds, teachers may not know if they are correct because they cannot see the movement of the mouths of the children behind the masks. Children could, inadvertently, make the wrong letter sound correspondence and teachers may not even know.

If children do not master these early foundation skills, learning to read will be very challenging, almost insurmountable. Therefore, teachers should wear a shield or a clear mask that does not fog up when explicitly teaching letters and letter sounds. These skills are far too important for reading proficiency to leave it by chance. Again, we must hit the reset button in our instructional practices to combat the impact that COVID had on our children.

As a result of the COVID experience, teachers must be ready to revise their instructional practices according to the needs of their children. Zaretta Hammond, author of *Culturally Responsive Teaching and the Brain: Promoting Authentic Engagement and Rigor Among Culturally and Linguistically Diverse Students*, says that the mistake that is happening far too often is that struggling children, and in particular children of color, are exposed to a pedagogy of compliance where teachers do all the talking and the heavy cognitive lifting and where classroom work lacks complexity and real-life context. It is crucial to ensure that all children, regardless of their background, receive equitable and culturally responsive instruction that is engaging, rigorous, and meaningful. This means that teachers must be intentional about creating an inclusive learning environment that recognizes and values diversity, and supports children's cognitive, social, and emotional needs.

As Hammond (2015) suggests, teachers should avoid a pedagogy of compliance that focuses solely on maintaining order and control, and instead prioritize complexity and real-life context in their classroom work. This means providing children with opportunities to think critically, solve problems, and engage in collaborative learning experiences that are relevant to their lives and interests. By doing so, teachers can ignite children's natural curiosity and foster their intrinsic motivation to learn. Providing meaningful, stimulating, and cognitively interesting learning opportunities are crucial in maximizing children's potential. Teachers must be intentional about creating an inclusive and culturally responsive learning environment that prioritizes complexity, real-life context, and student engagement.

I have seen reports about the "COVID Generation" of children and how they stand to face diminished economic opportunities and as much as a half year to a full year of missed instructional hours. I have also heard that children will never recover from the "lost" COVID years. I would ask everyone to be cautious about the words used to describe not only children but their future. Words hurt, they have a lasting impact, and they tend to be self-fulfilling. If we keep pumping these negative and dreadful words and images into our children's heads, why would they even try to work hard to overcome the barriers, or why should teachers waste their time teaching if there is no hope? Words matter. The old phrase 'Sticks and stones may break my bones, but words will never hurt me' is simply not true.

Practically Speaking

Words can cut like a double-edged sword and can build or tear a child down. I am still living with the words of my high school guidance counselor today. I remember sitting down with her and discussing my plans for after high school. She asked me about my plans, and I told her where I thought I was going to attend college and she gave me a look that I would never forget. She looked me in my eyes and said, "I think you might need to reconsider, that's so far from home. I have seen so many people go far from home, only to return home in debt." The words cut me like a sharp knife. She continued and said, "You are pretty good at typing and steno. Have you ever thought about technical school? You would be great as a secretary or office manager one day; they make a pretty good dollar." I still remember her face, the office, the words, everything on the office walls, and how small and unworthy I felt. After that, I blacked out. I could hear her, but I blocked out what she was saying.

I told her that I was offered scholarships and would not have to pay for school. She stated, "That's all the more reason for you to think about this. That's a lot of money to waste if you don't really know if it's for you." Those words hurt me so badly that I memorized them and left high school with an attitude and a chip on my shoulder because I knew she was not the only one who felt as such. Others never said it out loud to me in the manner that she did, but their actions or in-actions spoke volumes. She knew my circumstances, but she did not know me, my heart, my drive, or my determination. Failure was not an option, and giving up was not a part of the plan. I sometimes wonder if her comments also reflected the level of confidence she had in the school system where I spent 13 years and whether it had prepared me for higher learning. If educators do not have high regard for the educational system they are a part of, it will show up in the decisions that are made for students, in the interactions with students, and in the type of teaching methods and strategies employed in the classrooms, all of which impacts students' learning.

My mother believed that school staff members and officials were credible resources, and they are. Since they were the experts, she felt they were right all the time. She often stated, "They went to school for this, they know best." My issue was that if my guidance counselor had met with my mother and pitched technical school to her and filled her mind with me being a great secretary or office manager, my mother would have been extremely happy and would have encouraged me to do what my counselor wanted me to do. There is nothing wrong with being a secretary or office manager, that is not the point; rather, it was not what I aspired to do in life. The fact that my guidance counselor could not hear me, did not believe in me, and could not see my potential, hurt me to my core. She placed me in a box that was labeled by society as 'most likely not to succeed' because of my family dynamics. My mother gave birth to me when she was very young. She was single and had to drop out of school to take care of me. To top it off, my stepfather had a history of alcohol and drug abuse. Therefore, my guidance counselor wanted to put me in a box that represented my upbringing because she saw my family dynamics as a deficit rather than a strength.

The deficit type of thinking that plagues school systems across the country are hurting children. Rather than placing them in a box, we should encourage them to think outside the box and to think big. More importantly we must give them the tools they need to go after their dreams. We must help children believe that they were not born to fit in, but to stand out. My guidance counselor wanted me to stay in my place and blend in. She never took the time to get to know me. She only saw my circumstances and tried to place me in a box that fit my background. If the term Adverse Childhood

Experiences (ACEs) was popular back then, I would say she only saw my score and wrote me off. ACEs are potentially traumatic events or experiences in a child's life that can have negative and lasting effects on health and well-being. These experiences occur before the age of 18 and are remembered by that child as an adult. You get one point for each type of trauma. The higher your ACE score, the higher your risk of health and social problems. As your ACE score increases, so does the risk of disease, social and emotional problems, poor school performance, unemployment, and nicotine and drug use. An ACE score of four or more is serious. If ACEs were around back then, I would have scored more than a four. I respect what my counselor tried to do for me, but the box that she tried to put me in, wasn't for me.

There is an old children's poem that begins with the phrase, "What you think of me, I will be." Those are powerful words. Adults don't need to say a word for children to get the point. What a teacher thinks of a child will manifest in her body language, facial expressions, and interactions with the child. We must become familiar with the people who are in front of our children because they have the power to build them up or tear them down. Some children have the resolve to push through, while others do not. It's hard to learn from a person who does not believe in you, does not encourage you, and does not challenge you. It's hard to learn if others only see your circumstances (whatever they may be) as a deficit instead of added value. It's hard to learn from someone who thinks learning has a ceiling for some groups. I took the words of my high school counselor with me to college and used them to my advantage. I had something to prove to her and others who had similar thoughts. Every time I found myself in a challenging position, I played those words over and over in my head and I countered them with my mother's words of encouragement, reassurance, comfort, and hope. Just like me, children deserve to be in the room, but we must give them the skills necessary to be successful once in the room. One powerful and much-needed skill is reading.

Many children in the United States of America experienced major interruptions in the learning process while they were learning remotely, and we must work harder (children and educators) to reset our educational practices. Children are very resilient; therefore, pushing the reset button will be new and challenging but not impossible (speaking specifically about third grade down). We can use the pandemic to re-imagine education in our country. As Dr. Gloria Ladson-Billings stated, when we push the reset button, we take everything out and start all over again to get something new. We cannot afford to go back to normal as so many people want. Normal was not good, especially for children of color. Going back to normal will result in more of the same. Rather, we must push the reset button and make new pathways for our children.

In New Jersey, and other states, rather than dwelling on "learning loss" states are focused on "learning acceleration." According to the New Jersey Department of Education, learning acceleration is "an ongoing instructional process by which educators engage in formative practices to improve students' access to and mastery of grade-level standards. The goal of learning acceleration extends beyond recovering the ground lost to COVID-19; it must be viewed as a long-term, comprehensive framework that anchors districts' academic, social, and behavioral interventions to the common purpose of promoting global competitiveness for all students." We cannot spend valuable time trying to recover what children "loss." Rather, we must take this time and this moment in history to look at teaching and learning differently; it will never be the same. We must re-image education. The pandemic has been stressful and challenging but we must push through for our children because they are the future. Negative thoughts beget negative outcomes and positive thoughts beget positive outcomes. What we breathe into our children will have a lasting impact. We can either yield to the "lost years" as some have called the pandemic period and dwell on the skills that children do not have, or we can rise above the fray and get excited about the new skills they have and the "different" learning opportunities that await them. Whatever we do, we cannot allow the pandemic to be another excuse to keep children back. We must work together to raise the bar for all children— and it begins with reading.

Part I:

Laying the Foundation

> "The relative decline of
> American education is untenable
> for our economy, unsustainable for our
> democracy, and unacceptable for
> our children, and we cannot
> afford to let it continue."
> - President Barack Obama

Chapter 1

What's the Problem?

Historically and Statistically

Fourth graders are losing ground in their ability to read proficiently by the end of third grade. In the state of New Jersey, only 27% of third-grade students were proficient in the English Language Arts section of the state test in 2017. The scores were not much better the following two years. In 2018, only 29% of the third-grade students were proficient, and in 2019, only 30% were proficient (New Jersey Department of Education, 2019).

New Jersey is not alone in its early reading woes. According to The National Assessment of Educational Progress (NAEP), only 35% of the fourth graders were proficient in reading in 2019, and in 2015 only 36% were proficient readers (NAEP, 2019). The representative sample included 150,600 fourth graders from 8,300 schools. The NAEP measures literary and informational text to assess students' reading comprehension skills. Students also answered survey questions about their opportunities to learn and their engagement with reading in and outside of school. The reading assessments were administered on computers between January and March 2019. In 2022, students were assessed for the first time since the pandemic. NAEP reported that only 35% of the fourth graders were proficient in reading. Even though these scores represent the pandemic years, the trend remains the same.

Unfortunately, the low percentage rate of proficient readers has been the trend for the last decade. Of the fourth graders who took the NAEP reading test in 2009, only 17% of them were proficient. Nearly one out of every three fourth-grade students in the United States struggles in reading (Rasinki, 2017). White male students are three times more likely to read proficiently in the fourth grade than their African American peers and more than twice as likely than their Hispanic peers, according to data analysis by the Annie E. Casey Foundation's Kids Count Data Center (Casey, 2010). The statistics are even more startling for children of color from low-income families, with just 10% of African American boys and 14% of Hispanic boys reading proficiently, compared to 25% of their white peers. One other interesting fact, across all subjects, is that the United States ranks 25th globally in education. We are the largest, richest, and most powerful country in the world and yet we fail miserably at educating our children. We often say, "the children are our future" but what kind of future will we have as a country if a large percentage of our citizenry can't read?

Stepping away from the hard statistics because I did not want to use just one data point, I convened a group of eighteen educators from preschool through third grade including instructional reading coaches, reading supervisors, and school administrators. They became my focus group that I interviewed for insight regarding reading. My goal was to get first-hand knowledge in real-time from current educators about the state of early reading among Black and Brown children. The individuals interviewed were from small to large school districts with a student body made up of almost all African Americans and Latinx students. However, there were three educators from districts that serve predominantly white students. When asked about the NAEP data and the New Jersey English Language Arts (ELA) data on reading, most of the participants agreed with the data and shared personal accounts of struggling readers in the early grades, providing credence to the data presented on reading.

I also relied on my personal experiences with the subject matter. My dissertation topic was on reading and after thoroughly researching the subject, I found consistency with the statistics presented by NAEP and the New Jersey state assessment data reports. Additionally, My Brother's Keeper Alliance, created by Former President Barack Obama, realized that there is an issue with early reading. The organization has been out front with the message of increasing reading proficiency rates and closing the achievement gap, which is among the most persistent educational challenges we face today. I am not a proponent of using standardized tests alone to measure the academic success of students. I used data on two standardized tests to provide context for the serious nature of the problems that impact early reading in our public schools. In full disclosure, there is a large body of research that categorizes standardized tests as unfair, subjective, and culturally unresponsive to children of color (Au, 2016). Further, education activists Hagopian & Network for Public Education (2015) and other, more progressive civil rights organizations found that high-stakes testing was harmful to children of color specifically, and public education generally (Brown, 2015). According to Au (2016), testing has negatively affected the education of children of color in terms of curriculum and pedagogy, high school exit exams, and dropout rates. Not only are standardized assessments changing how teachers instruct students, but they also impact what content is taught. Tested subjects such as math and reading receive greater emphasis in instructional time, while the arts, social studies, and sciences are neglected (Rose, 2014). In an effort to increase test scores, children of color are more likely to receive skill-and-drill teaching through rote memorization (Kohn, 2000; Zhao, 2018). A scripted and narrowed curriculum in urban districts limits authentic learning and makes it more difficult for teachers to respond to the individual classroom and student needs (Milner, 2013).

The increased use of tests is part of the corporate strategy that has been used all over the world for quite some time; however, we must understand that standardized testing fulfills corporate agendas, not child agendas. Therefore, it is important to scrutinize tests to understand the developers and the content they include. If children do not have the experience and background knowledge to access the content on standardized tests, it will be a challenge for them to perform well. While there is some hesitancy in standardized tests, the fact still remains, many children of color are not proficient readers by third grade and unfortunately, this has been the case for decades.

Practically Speaking

On a personal note, understanding why children do not read proficiently by the end of third grade is important to me because I struggled to read, and I did not like school because of it. My mother had my brother and me when she was very young. She dropped out of school to take care of us and she did a fabulous job. However, she worked a lot and could not help us with our homework, and did not have time to read stories to us. My mother, like so many other parents, relied on the public school system to educate her children. She believed that her job was to ensure that we were in school every day and to provide shelter, food, clothes, and other basic necessities. My mother believed that the educators in the school system knew best and never challenged anyone. She raised my brother and me to listen and learn and never question the teachers. The earliest memory that I have of my reading struggles dates back to before third grade. I did not like school because I had trouble reading. The one activity that would create anxiety for me was reading out loud. The teacher would tell us to take out our reading books and each child had to read a section out loud. My strategy was to try to predict my turn and practice the words before it was my turn to read. I spent so much time practicing that I missed the entire story and when it was time to recall what happened in the story, I could not answer the questions because I did not hear the story.

I was engaged in practicing my section so that I would not be embarrassed when it was my time to read out loud. I practiced hard because if I made one mistake my peers would laugh at me and that frightened me more than listening for comprehension. I also remember being assigned a reading book based on my reading level (I can't remember the exact grade). Because I was not reading at grade level, I would leave my book at home or in my locker. I did not want anyone to see my book because they would immediately know the grade level I was on based on the title of the book. The title of the books and assigned grade levels were common knowledge to the student body.

I also remember being pulled out of classes that I liked (physical education, art, music, etc.) to receive extra support in reading, which added to my frustrations. It was common practice back then to pull low-performing students from non-academic courses for "extra help" (Robinson et al., 2018). My mother thought that the extra help was the best thing in the world and signed off on it. Again, her goal for me was to get a "good" education, by any means necessary, even if it meant attending summer school. I remember attending summer school a few times in the early grades and I did not like it at all because summer school was only for those who were struggling. Summer school was not the coolest thing to do but did my mother care? Nope. My mother took education seriously and did what the teachers recommended; therefore, despite it being lame, she hauled me off to summer school anyway and of course, I was highly embarrassed. In retrospect, I am thankful that she did.

Back to third grade. During the summer before entering fourth grade, my third-grade teacher asked me if I could come by her classroom during the summer to help her get her classroom together for the next year. I did not think anything about it and said yes. I liked her and wanted to help her. On day one of the "help," I noticed three other students in the classroom with me. As we helped our teacher, we were having a great time and we learned so much about each other as she encouraged us to talk openly and freely about ourselves and what we liked.

"Kids don't learn from people they don't like."
Rita Pierson

After about a week, we were asked if we wanted to join her book club. Of course, we said yes because we were having the time of our lives with the coolest teacher in the school. We did not know it then, but it was during the "book club" meetings that we learned strategies to help us with our reading issues. We read books that we were interested in and for once, reading was fun. To my surprise, that same teacher (who was my third-grade teacher) was now my fourth-grade teacher. Needless to say, it was my best year ever. I was excited to go to school, I was reading better and there was no more reading out loud! By fifth grade, I was reading above grade level and never looked back. My teacher was my superhero, and she changed my life forever. I do not know what my life would be like if I was not asked to be a part of that "book club."

"Every child deserves a champion – an adult who will never give up on them, who understands the power of connection, and insists that they become the best that they can possibly be." Rita Pierson

My story is not unlike others; however, I had a champion who took time with me, saw where I struggled, and provided support. Unfortunately, this is not the case for so many Black and Brown children. Children who do not read proficiently by third grade are four times more likely to leave high school without a diploma than proficient readers. Children living in poverty or who have lived in poverty are three times more likely to drop out or fail to graduate on time than their more affluent peers (Casey, 2010). This underscores the need for our children to read proficiently by the end of third grade and for our nation to take a deep look at our educational system in the early years. Everyone is afforded an education, but not everyone has a quality educational experience. Quality education is supposed to be the "great equalizer."

The problem is, who defines quality, and what does it look like? Does it look different for Black and Brown children than White children? Why do we have such disparities within public schools? The data on reading is abysmal and frustrating because there are so many excellent educators in front of our children every day and so many children working hard to excel. I have always been a skeptic of standardized tests and would caution everyone to always take the results with a grain of salt. However, my professional experience, research on early reading, and the experience of current educators absolutely agree that we have a major problem with early reading with Black and Brown children.

What Does It Mean to be Educated?

Ravitch (2016) stated that education is essential to developing human potential and ensuring our society remains prosperous and improving reading scores is crucial to this work. Education means a little more for me. It is an ongoing process that shapes, molds, and guides a person from birth and continues throughout one's life. Education is teaching and learning and the acquisition of knowledge, skills, values, beliefs, and habits that direct individuals toward their role in society. Some say it is the transmission of cultural norms and traditions that contributes to the advancement of society and humanity by assisting individuals with understanding their rights and roles as a citizen. I believe that education is also formal and informal and based on an individual's lived experiences. In this respect, education is all that we experience and may come from multiple sources such as teachers, family, community members, books, social media, or peers. The United Nations stated that "education shall be directed to the full development of the human personality and to the strengthening of respect for human rights and fundamental freedoms." Ultimately, education is about creating an informed society and a more perfect union. Unfortunately, the aforementioned characteristics regarding education are not shared by everyone. In fact, history shows us that people of color were not worthy of an education, let alone a quality one.

Alfie Kohn published an article in the Principal Leadership and gave a different meaning of education. Kohn stated that education is about problems, projects, and questions rather than facts, skills, and disciplines. Kohn maintained that knowledge is acquired in context and for a purpose. The emphasis is not only on depth and breadth but also on discovering ideas rather than on covering a prescribed curriculum. No matter the definition of education, it is not just a formal piece of paper gained from high school or a university. Education is on-the-job training, and it encompasses all our life experiences. The meaning of education matters because it influences the perspectives of educators and impacts how children learn and what they learn.

The Journey Towards Literacy

The segregation of schools led to unequal access to resources, facilities, and qualified teachers for African American children (Gilliam 2014 & Gershenson & Dee 2017). In addition, many schools heavily attended by Black students were underfunded and lacked basic amenities such as textbooks, laboratory equipment, and even indoor plumbing. This resulted in a stark disparity in educational outcomes between black and white children. Despite the landmark Brown v. Board of Education Supreme Court decision in 1954, which declared segregation in public schools to be unconstitutional, the integration of schools was a slow and often violent process. Many schools remained segregated for years after the decision, and even when schools were integrated, black students often faced discrimination and hostility from their white peers and teachers. Today, while some progress has been made in improving educational opportunities for African Americans, there are still significant disparities in access to quality education. African American students are more likely to attend underfunded schools, have less access to advanced coursework, and are more likely to be disciplined and suspended than their white peers. These inequities have long-term consequences, including lower graduation rates and limited opportunities for higher education and career advancement.

As schools are facing these issues with equality, I ask myself, how far have we come from Jonathan Kozol's book *Savage Inequalities* where he described major differences between public schools serving students of color in urban settings and their suburban peers? We know from the Coleman Report of 1966 that children perform better in smaller schools, in smaller class sizes, with a rigorous curriculum, and qualified teachers. Yet many of our Black and Brown children are in educational spaces contrary to what the Coleman Report spells out. Why do our children continue to face such disparities? Is it because the American educational system was not built for equality for all?

In the book *Self-Taught African American Education in Slavery and Freedom* by Heather Andrea Williams, she described how the desire for education among enslaved people was strong, even in the face of severe punishment for attempting to learn. Some enslaved people were able to secretly learn to read and write, often with the help of sympathetic white allies or through their own resourcefulness. Once they acquired these skills, they often shared them with others, spreading knowledge and literacy throughout their communities. This sharing of knowledge was a powerful act of resistance against the dehumanizing system of slavery. By learning to read and write, enslaved people were able to communicate with each other and with those outside of their communities, sharing information, organizing for collective action, and asserting their humanity and dignity in the face of oppression.

After the Civil War and the end of slavery, African Americans continued to face barriers to education, including segregation and underfunding of schools. However, the spirit of community and collective action that was forged during slavery continued to inspire African Americans to fight for their right to education and to create institutions that would support their intellectual and cultural development. Today, the legacy of African American resistance to slavery and segregation lives on in the ongoing struggle for educational equality and justice. By recognizing and celebrating the resilience and determination of those who came before us, we can continue to push for a more just and equitable society for everyone.

Reading Williams' book gave me a sense of pride and rejuvenated my purpose on this earth. The struggle for education was a collective effort and a key part of the fight for freedom and equality. The determination of enslaved people to learn, despite the risks and obstacles they faced, is a testament to the human spirit and to the power of education to transform lives and communities. The establishment of schoolhouses and the emergence of black educators were major milestones in the ongoing struggle for educational equity and justice. These institutions and individuals served as beacons of hope and opportunity for African Americans, helping to break down barriers to education and to uplift entire communities. And the legacy of this struggle continues today, as we work to ensure that all individuals have access to quality education and the resources they need to thrive. By honoring the sacrifices and contributions of our ancestors and continuing to fight for educational equity and justice, we can build a better, more inclusive society for all.

This story was not shared to put one group of people down and raise another; it was added to tell the story of what it took for African American people to learn to read. It was to shed light on the importance of literacy as an instrument of resistance and liberation and to remind us of how our ancestors were determined to gain some control over their lives. They did not wait on anyone, they taught themselves and built schools to educate others. Although anti-literacy laws are well known, sometimes visiting the past helps to appreciate the present. We must be reminded of the long, painful, and arduous journey our ancestors had to endure for us to have the educational opportunities that exist today. Perhaps learning from the past will inspire us to have that same zeal, passion, drive, and determination to change the dismal early reading narrative and ensure children meet the critical reading benchmarks.

Understanding the journey toward literacy makes me wonder what happened to that passion, that zeal, and that sense of commitment to one another for the benefit of the whole. Learning to read during the anti-literacy era was so important that people risked their lives to learn how to read and to teach others to read. Our ancestors knew the liberating power that came with reading. Taking a stroll through history helps us focus and remember the struggles that our ancestors endured for the right to read. They did not wait for others to do it for them; rather they used their resources and did it for themselves. We must draw on their strength and their resolve and roll up our sleeves and pull our bootstraps up and do what is right for children. Our children are bright, intelligent, creative, and beautiful. They only need opportunities, experiences, and at least one champion in their corner and they will show the world their awesomeness.

When we ignore or place band-aids on the real academic issues children face, we are essentially ignoring them. Children were born with greatness. It is up to the adults in their environment and the village that surrounds them to help them walk into their greatness, hone their skills, and unlock their potential. The village has the power to help or hinder. The same strength and power that our ancestors had during anti-literacy laws; we possess today. We have not exercised our power collectively to make lasting changes to move children forward academically. Consequently, many children have been left behind.

There are no laws prohibiting us from reading today yet according to the NAEP report, a large majority of our African American fourth graders cannot read proficiently in the United States. In response to this long-standing problem, legislative initiatives have allocated unprecedented amounts of money to education for staffing, nutrition, transportation, and other operational costs (Lipman, 2013) yet the academic achievement gap continues to grow wider and wider for many African American students. We already know that money alone cannot solve the deep-rooted problems that exist in education because the problems do not rest in education alone. We must consider a complete overhaul or a hard reset of the operating systems in this country; education is just one of those systems. Other systems include but are not limited to criminal justice, health and human services, and housing and urban development.

Additionally, we cannot forget about the economic system and the distribution of wealth, particularly when we have members in our society working a full-time job (40 hours or more per week) only to bring home wages that are below the poverty line. These systems, directly or indirectly, have an impact on the quality of life and the educational experiences that children receive. As previously mentioned, this book is not about reading per se, rather it is about how the established systems in the United States converge, creating an ecosystem for children that has major implications for their lives and their school experiences. In other words, a child's ecosystem dictates how prepared he or she will be before entering kindergarten. If we want our children to read proficiently by third grade, the operating systems that surround children must be revamped. The educational system cannot bear the burden alone as many factors influence children before they enter public schools.

Fast forward: We do not have anti-literacy laws on the books today but there are many children of color living in high-poverty communities across the United States that are severely underperforming academically as if anti-literacy laws were still in existence. Research has consistently shown that there are multiple factors that contribute to the achievement gap for children of color, including low staff morale, negative teacher perceptions, and a lack of cultural connections and affirmations in classrooms (Douglas & Peck, 2013; Evans, 2015; Harper & Davis, 2012; Ladson-Billings, 2001). It's important to recognize that these issues are systemic and cannot be attributed solely to the actions or motivations of individual teachers or students.

Community-school partnerships can be a powerful tool for addressing these challenges and promoting academic success (Epstein, 2013). The black church is one example of a community organization that has long played a critical role in supporting the education and well-being of African American students. By partnering with schools and educators, churches and other community organizations can provide a range of resources and support services that can help to bridge the achievement gap and promote positive outcomes for students. It's worth noting that community-school partnerships can be mutually beneficial, as they can help schools to build stronger connections with families and communities, and can provide valuable learning opportunities for students outside of the classroom. By working together in this way, we can create more inclusive and supportive learning environments that help all students to succeed.

The Black Church

African American students need more than just instructional support to reach academic goals; they need moral support, affirmations from caring adults, and they need hope. The Black church has a rich, powerful, and culturally significant history in the United States (Stuckey, 2013) and has been deemed "the most important institution that has ever existed in the black community" (Joseph, 2015). The Black church can play a critical role in promoting academic success among African American students. By forming partnerships with local schools and community organizations, the Black church can provide tutoring, mentoring, and other supportive services that enhance student learning and achievement (Joseph, 2015). Moreover, the Black church can serve as a cultural anchor for African American students, providing them with a sense of identity, purpose, and belonging that is often lacking in mainstream educational settings (Khalifa et al., 2013; Logan, 2018). By working together with schools and community partners, the Black church can help to create a more inclusive and equitable education system that promotes academic excellence and social justice for all students.

Social learning theory helps explain why the black church may be a positive organization to assist in closing the achievement gap. Social learning theory, proposed by Albert Bandura, posits that learning occurs in social contexts, meaning people learn new information and behaviors by watching other people. Specifically, vicarious learning is a way of learning that allows individuals to learn from the experience of others rather than direct, hands-on instruction (Bandura, 1977). Social learning theory emphasizes the importance of observing, modeling, and imitating the behaviors, attitudes, and emotional reactions of others. The theory considers how both environmental and cognitive factors interact to influence human learning and behavior. Full disclosure, social learning theory is not a full explanation for all behavior.

Important to social learning theory is self-efficacy. Bandura defined self-efficacy as "people's beliefs about their capabilities to produce designated levels of performance that exercise influence over events that affect their lives" (Bandura, 1994 p. 71). Simply put, self-efficacy is a person's belief in their ability to succeed in a particular situation. Self-efficacy encompasses a person's attitudes, abilities, and cognitive skills, according to Bandura. Belief in our own ability to succeed plays a role in how we think, how we act, and how we feel about our place in the world. Self-efficacy skills are critical for academic success and are enhanced through positive role models, consistent encouragement from others, persistence, and a positive outlook. The experiences that children are exposed to in the black church, consciously or unconsciously, aid in building self-efficacy skills in children in ways that may not occur in schools.

When African American students receive guidance from black church members and leaders who have encountered and successfully navigated similar challenging life experiences, the premise is for them to believe that they can succeed as well (McIntosh & Curry, 2020). When students see that others had similar challenges and were able to rise above those challenges, it builds self-efficacy skills. Children can see themselves in a successful light and begin to believe in their abilities. We know that positive role models can be used to encourage desirable behaviors. The church is one of the best places, not to exclude other organizations, to help students reflect on and change negative behaviors. According to McLeod (2016), students pay attention to people they respect, people who genuinely care about them, people they can relate to, and people they believe in. When students positively identify with a role model, they are more likely to imitate the behaviors they have observed in that role model. Positive behaviors will persist if the people around students respond favorably toward the behavior or if students observe positive consequences of another person's behavior (McLeod, 2016).

In the McIntosh and Curry study, observational learning was successful in the Black church because by providing positive role models and reinforcing academic achievement, the Black church can help build students' self-efficacy and motivation to succeed in school. The reinforcement and motivation components are especially important because they can help students overcome obstacles and persist in their academic pursuits. Overall, social learning theory provides a useful framework for understanding how the Black church can serve as a valuable resource in closing the achievement gap for children of color.

Practically Speaking

Any organization can accomplish what has been outlined here regarding the Black church. For example, boys' and girls' clubs, sororities, fraternities, and other organizations do a lot for students and have made a significant difference in their lives. For example, my husband has an organization that was created because he and other like-minded men saw a need in the community. They rolled up their sleeves and began to work with young students throughout our town. They encouraged more men to join them to reach more students. The distinguished men in this organization were committed, involved, steadfast, and immovable. They built solid relationships with young people, and some became surrogate fathers to them. The organization reached countless young people and helped change the trajectory of their lives. Many have graduated from high school and college.

The relationships that were established will last a life time. For example, there was one incident that I will always remember. My husband went to the school for one youngster who was giving teachers the business. The young man was doing his thing in class but when he turned around one particular day, my husband was standing right there...busted! He did not believe that another person could care about him that was not blood related. These are the relationships and partnerships that our schools need. I highlighted the Black church because it has always been the trusted organization in African American communities, the beacon of hope, a refuge, and a sanctuary for so many. We need our Black churches to take their rightful place in our communities and be the light of hope that it once was.

I remember the church where our sons spent the better part of their formative years. They learned how to take care of their elders because they watched church leaders. They learned how to care for others because they participated in making food baskets at the church during Thanksgiving for those in need. They were not afraid to speak in public because they had numerous opportunities to do so as they performed in plays, recited poems and scriptures, and played instruments.

Children did their best because they knew they were going to be held accountable and in full transparency, they were going to received accolades afterwards too. They exercised their rights and voiced their opinions outside of the church because social justice was discussed in church and modeled for them. The children were the center of the church back then and the expectations were high, not only from parents but from everyone in the church. The church helped to instill morals, values, and discipline in children (it was everyone's role, not just the parents).

Everyone believed in the potential of children and encouraged them to dream big. Children were exposed to students receiving scholarships, going off to college, and coming back home to share their experiences. Children tried their best in school because they knew that the pastor would call their names in front of the congregation and give them money for every "A" they received. They were excited to bring in their report cards. There were also times when children did not do well, but the parents still brought the report cards to church and the pastor would review them and have a sidebar conversation with the children.

I am not in favor of providing external rewards for grades, but the gesture was kind, and it excited and motivated the children. In this case, the external reward became a catalyst for children to become internally motivated to do well in school. The church was the village for so many. The children were exposed to a lot, they experienced a lot, and they had many opportunities afforded to them. The idea here is that children would take their "church experiences" and transfer them to school. However, we have children in our schools without "church experiences" or anything similar and many of them struggle, especially when the culture of the school staff is different from their own.

"No significant learning occurs
without a significant relationship." James Comer

Practical Application

What can you do?

1. Meet with your child's teacher and find out what type of questions to ask your child after they read a story. Depending on the development level of the child, the teacher may provide more critical thinking questions other than just "Who, What, Where, When, How, and Why."

2. Establish a reading routine at home that includes both reading to your child and discussing the story.

3. Visit your local library with your children to get them excited about books. Search for picture books, silly books, books that have simple rhyming, and informative books.

4. Model reading as much as possible. Children want to be like the important adults in their lives. Let them see you reading often and express how much you love to read.

5. After reading a story, create a simple and fun activity to go along with it to help build children's interest in reading. For example, read the book, Stone Soup or Alphabet Soup and then engage the children in making soup.

6. Create simple books with children. Decide who will be the author and illustrator. List and follow the steps for publishing a book. Once the book is finished, let the children "read" it to others or record the children reading the story and share the audio with others. Consider hosting a book event for children to talk about their books and invite guests to participate.

7. Purchase books and donate them to local barber shops, doctor's offices, urgent care centers, or any place where children and families may need to wait to be served.

Chapter 2

Reading by Third Grade

Why it Matters?

Children in kindergarten through second grade are busy learning foundational skills and preparing for the very exciting third-grade year. However, third grade is not just an ordinary year. Rather, it is the year where the foundational skills in reading (i.e., decoding words using their knowledge of letter and sound recognition) come together for children to read smoothly. Third grade is an important year in the educational journey of children because it marks the period when children transition from "learning to read to reading to learn."

The expectation is that proficient readers will have the skills to master the more complex content found in the fourth-grade curriculum. Children are no longer reading simple books, but fact-filled informational texts that are more challenging. Third grade is known as the pivotal year for reading and if children miss the opportunity to read proficiently, they may be left behind their peers and could struggle academically for the remainder of their school days. Researchers found that many children who fail to read proficiently by the third grade end up slipping in the later grades and often drop out of school before earning a high school diploma. Once children fall behind, the gap widens making it very challenging to catch up. Trying to catch up is difficult, but not impossible because children must not only master the skills from the year before, but they must also master the skills in the current grade. In reality, they must master two years of skills in one year.

The importance of reading proficiently by third grade cannot be overstated. According to national reading assessment data, two-thirds of fourth graders in the United States are not proficient readers. The statistics are more disturbing for children from low-income homes as approximately four out of five children missed this critical reading milestone. Ralph Smith, managing director of the Campaign for Grade-Level Reading says children of color are disproportionately represented among those who miss the critical reading milestone and among those who drop out.

Why is third grade so critical? In the lower grades (third grade down) children learn foundational skills. In the upper grades (fourth grade up), children build on foundational skills and learn more advanced skills. In other words, children progress from learning and practicing basic skills to mastering them, and then they move on to develop more complex skills. Additionally, reading skills are necessary for almost all content areas, and if children cannot read well, they will have a hard time in almost every major content area.

Reading skills lay the foundation for future academic success. These skills help children understand what they are learning in the upper grades. Missing the critical reading milestone not only leads to struggles cognitively but socially and emotionally as well. Many children who struggle to read may also develop anxiety, stress, and low self-esteem, which typically leads to an avoidance of reading. As struggling children move onto the fourth grade, the academic gap continues to grow. School assignments begin to change and require more background knowledge and familiarity with academic and domain-specific words. Content classes like science and math rely on written analysis, and struggling readers begin to fall behind in these subjects because more than 85 percent of the curriculum requires reading proficiency. Children who are not proficient readers will have difficulty comprehending curriculum materials written for their grade level, which will affect their ability to keep pace with their on-level peers in school and could possibly limit their future career choices. Meeting increased educational demands as children move from grade to grade is increasingly difficult for children who struggle with reading. Reading is the major foundational skill for school-based learning and is strongly related to future academic opportunities and success. As children fall further and further behind, year after year, a vicious cycle begins as children become more disengaged, and drop out of school before completing high school.

Keith Stanovich calls this cycle the "Matthew Effect" after the Bible verse found in the Gospel of Matthew. It states: *"For whosoever hath, to him shall be given, and he shall have more abundance: but whosoever hath not, from him shall be taken away even that he hath."* In other words, the academically rich will get richer and the poor will get poorer, as small differences in academic abilities grow into large ones (Stanovich, 1986). Further, the content areas that rely on reading skills are also inhibited from further development. The longer this cycle is allowed to continue, the more widespread the deficits will become. Reading impacts everything. However, there is a silver lining with the Matthew Effect; it can be turned around with well-timed interventions.

Spotting and acknowledging reading difficulties early offer children a chance to break the underperforming reading cycle and gain access to the help they need. Without significant intervention, children who begin school with weaker early literacy skills do not catch up with children who begin school with stronger skills (Burchinal et al., 2002; Juel, 1988). Most parents and some educators believe children who start behind will catch up within a year or two, but that is not the reality. Rather, children who are one-to-three years behind typically make a year's worth of growth each year, just like other children. The bad news is that they are still one-to-three years behind their grade level.

Researchers stress that closing a learning gap once a child begins school is costly and difficult because the child needs to achieve their typical year of academic growth plus another year of growth to catch up by even a single level (Lesnick et al., 2010). Academic, emotional, and social issues are real for children who struggle to read (Adler, 2001). It is important to address the achievement gap early on to prevent negative outcomes. This can be done by providing early interventions and resources to help struggling students. It is also crucial to address the root causes of the achievement gap, such as systemic racism, poverty, and unequal access to educational resources.

Achievement Gap

Before any further discussions about the impact of reading, the term 'achievement gap' must be defined for context. According to the McKinsey Report (2009), there are four achievement gaps that are referred to the most throughout the United States although there are more. The achievement gaps include: (1) racial; (2) international; (3) income achievement, and (4) opportunity gaps.

The racial gap between African American, Latinx, and White students, is of particular importance when discussing the impact of reading. This gap refers to the persistent disparity in academic performance between students of different racial and ethnic backgrounds, with African American and Latinx students consistently scoring lower than their White peers on standardized tests and other academic measures. This gap is often attributed to systemic issues such as unequal access to high-quality education, poverty, and racial discrimination. The racial achievement gap is a significant concern because it has long-term consequences for students, including limited opportunities for higher education and lower lifetime earnings. It is crucial to address this gap to ensure that all students, regardless of their race or ethnicity, have equal access to opportunities and resources to succeed academically.

The international achievement gap is between the United States and other countries. In this respect, the United States is significantly behind other advanced nations in educational performance and the gap widens the longer children remain in school. As the one-time leaders in education, the United States ranks 18th out of 24 industrialized nations and there is a substantial gap between the United States' top students and the top students in other countries.

The income achievement gap among students is significant. African American and Latinx families who have lower levels of education and income are more likely to live in low-income neighborhoods, where 20-40% of the residents fall under the poverty line making it harder to afford childcare, preschool, and other early education opportunities that provide experiences for children to develop socioemotional and academic capabilities. Students eligible for free or reduced lunch are approximately two years behind their wealthier peers of the same age. This gap is problematic because it begins early and can persist over the lifetime of the child.

The opportunity gap is not discussed as much as the other three, but it is equally important. The opportunity gap refers to the arbitrary circumstances in which children are born, such as their race, ethnicity, zip code, and socioeconomic status that determine their opportunities in life. These gaps disproportionately impact underrepresented students, most specifically, students of color and students living in poverty. Unequal and inadequate opportunities, if left untouched, will continue to negatively impact students and their communities. It is not the innate ability of children that contributes to achievement gaps, but the opportunities to learn. Achievement gaps exist at every level of the American educational system and one contributing factor is the inability to read proficiently.

The Impact of Reading

Learning to read accurately, and fluidly, with good comprehension, and stamina are the necessary elements for school success. Reading is a multifaceted process that involves word recognition, comprehension, fluency, and motivation. Some define reading as making meaning from print that requires children to identify and understand the words in print. Regardless of the many definitions of reading, the goal of reading is to understand and gain meaning.

Practically Speaking

When I was a student teacher, I had a child who broke the code and was able to decode the words written in her reading book. However, she could not answer any questions about the story. We knew that she had issues with comprehending among other things. My cooperating teacher and I created an intervention plan for the child with assistance of the reading coach. The plan included a reading routine at home. We felt good about the plan and were ready to share it with her parents. We knew that a good plan involved bridging home and school. Because I was a student teacher and needed the experience, my cooperating teacher allowed me to schedule the meeting, and prepare the handouts and the talking points that would be used in the meeting with the parents. I was nervous, but I was confident that the parents would be on-board and receptive to the reading interventions that we planned.

I began the meeting by thanking the parents for agreeing to meet and for their commitment to their daughter's education. So far, so good. I proceeded and discussed the child's reading scores and specific skills that the child needed assistance with. I continued, but I noticed the mother becoming more and more frustrated and agitated. The next sentence that I said sent the mother over the edge. I said, "The reading intervention plan that we designed will help move your child toward becoming a fluent and proficient reader." The mother let me have it. She told me in so many words that I clearly needed to go back to school because I didn't know what I was doing and didn't know a reader from a nonreader. She pretty much dismissed me and turned toward my cooperating teacher. The mother insisted that her child could read and that she read to her grandparents and everyone in their home all the time. The mother dismissed everyone and walked out of the meeting.

The next day, my cooperating teacher and I met with the principal to explain what happened because the mother called and was livid with us as she verbally expressed her displeasure. We explained the little girl's reading scores, the reading issues, and the intervention plan. The principal was on board with the plan and supported what we were trying to accomplish. The problem was trying to help the parents understand the purpose and process of reading. When the parents met with us the second time (with the principal in attendance), the daughter was present. The mother had her daughter "read" the book she brought from home. The child proceeded to decode the words and the mother asked why her daughter would need intervention when she just "read" five pages and did not skip a word. The principal asked the little girl three basic questions about the book, and she could not answer any of the questions. The mother took over and asked her own questions, and the child could not answer her either. We explained to the parents that while reading involves decoding of words, it also involves comprehension. We explained that her daughter could say the words but could not obtain meaning from the words; therefore, she was not reading. Unfortunately, scenarios like this happen all the time because not everyone understands the reading process or the goal of reading. Reading is more than being able to read words aloud. Reading is about understanding what is read.

Reading helps build vocabulary and prior knowledge. It improves vocabulary knowledge because the language of written text exposes language users to new words, which increases the depth of word understanding (Huettig & Pickering, 2019). However, prior knowledge is a contributor to reading comprehension and vocabulary development. Prior knowledge has two dimensions: (1) academic knowledge, which refers to how much a reader knows about a topic; and (2) general knowledge, which refers to how much a reader knows about a subject in general (Patterson et al., 2018). The amount of prior knowledge that a reader brings when reading a text, impacts reading comprehension. Prior knowledge aids in the readers' ability to extract explicit and implicit information from a text and integrate that information to gain meaning (Kaeffer et al., 2015). Proficient readers rely on relevant prior knowledge and experiences and relate what they already know to what the text says. Reading is not only good for building vocabulary and prior knowledge, but it is also extremely important for building empathy skills.

Building Empathy and Stamina

One benefit of reading that is rarely discussed is the development of empathy. The Merriam-Webster dictionary defines empathy as "the feeling that you understand and share another person's experiences and emotions" or "the ability to share someone else's feelings." Empathy can also be defined as taking the perspectives of others so that we may be careful and not easily judge other people's behaviors or feelings. How are reading and empathy related? Reading about different characters and situations can help readers develop empathy by allowing them to see the world from different perspectives and gain a deeper understanding of the experiences and emotions of others. Through reading, children learn about different cultures, beliefs, and experiences, which can help them become more accepting and understanding of others (Rasoal et al., 2011). It is important to develop empathy skills in children as young as possible, which can be done through education, families, and communities. Children's empathy skills should be developed and nurtured by a variety of approaches including stories, modeling, role-playing, games, and natural experiences. Young children learn how to empathize from adults and peers around them as they adopt the behaviors and expressions of those individuals. The bottom line, the more children read, the more they will be able to relate to others and be encouraged to be kind and considerate of other people's feelings. As children read stories about other people's lives, it helps them develop the skills to understand the world through another person's perspective. There will be more on empathy in chapter eight.

After children build their reading foundational skills, they must build their reading stamina. Reading stamina refers to a child's ability to focus and read independently for extended periods of time without being distracted or without distracting others, and it ideally grows over time. Having stamina for something means being able to stick with a task for a period of time. This type of stamina, or endurance, builds strength. For example, a runner needs stamina or endurance to run long and will practice consistently over time to build up to running a long race like three miles. Similarly, readers need to practice reading consistently over time with varying lengths of books to build reading stamina. Reading stamina is not a natural process, it does not automatically happen, rather children must practice every day to improve their endurance. When children have good reading stamina, it means they can experiment with more challenging and longer texts in books. Good reading stamina helps young readers build reading confidence, reading fluency, reading comprehension, spelling, and reading vocabulary.

Reading stamina leads to a reading habit. Dictionary.com defines a habit as a settled, regular tendency, or practice. A habit such as silent reading does not occur in a single grade. Rather, it is formed over an extended period of time from grade to grade. How children start out is incredibly important. If they do not receive the kind of support that develops solid silent reading habits by the time they are in third grade, reading proficiently may be challenging. Sadly, many struggling readers engage in reading three times less often than their peers, which is unfortunate because reading fires up the imagination and stimulates and strengthens memory skills. Children who do not have the foundational skills for reading in first grade almost invariably will struggle to read in fourth grade, making it difficult to transition from learning to read to reading to learn in most subject areas. Failure to read proficiently by the end of third grade does not reflect children's intelligence, but rather their opportunities to learn about the world. Two key content areas that reading impacts the most are science and math.

Reading Comprehension and Science

Reading comprehension is the ability to extract meaning from written text and it is significant in science instruction. There is a growing body of evidence that shows medium to high correlations between reading and high academic achievement in science courses (August et al., 2009; Cromley et al., 2010). Many of the skills that are critical for growing strong readers and writers are also core skills in the study of science and math. For example, predicting, understanding cause and effect, understanding sequence, acquiring a rich vocabulary, building background knowledge, and developing the ability to read and write informational text (Michalsky, 2013). Reading skills are essential to understanding many scientific concepts. Unfortunately, even students who make a strong start in literacy in the early elementary grades often do not develop the skills they need to tackle science and other informational texts in the later elementary years. Students need special help to rise to the challenge of reading to learn science. They need not only general literacy but disciplinary literacy skills specific to reading and producing texts in science.

Reading skills are crucial for understanding scientific concepts and for producing texts in science. Scientists and engineers spend a significant amount of time reading and producing texts, and literacy is essential for effective communication and collaboration within the scientific community (McFarlane, 2013; Cervetti et at., 2009). In the science classroom, reading is used frequently as a learning activity for laboratory-related procedures and problem-solving activities, which helps students become engaged in science and interested in scientific phenomena and processes (Rojas et al., 2019). By developing their reading skills, students can improve their understanding of scientific concepts and processes, as well as their ability to communicate and collaborate effectively within the scientific community.

Many children find science texts difficult to read and comprehend for a variety of reasons (Román & Busch, 2015). Science texts often require readers to have prior knowledge of scientific concepts and terminology, which can be a significant barrier for students who struggle to read (Fang & Wei, 2010). Students may struggle with specialized language and unfamiliar vocabulary in science texts, which can impede their understanding of scientific concepts (Fang, 2006). Reading science texts may be difficult for some children because of a lack of prior knowledge and the lack of vocabulary required for the construction of mental representations (MacNamara, 2010). Most scholars agree that prior knowledge, inferential skills, knowledge of reading strategies, and content specific vocabulary are factors that influence the reading comprehension process (Cromley et al., 2010). Moreover, prior knowledge and inference skills seem to play a critical role in the reading comprehension of expository science texts (Hall, 2016). In addition to unfamiliar content, comprehending science texts requires readers to create in their minds a coherent representation, or a model that contains a highly technical and academic vocabulary making reading comprehension in science challenging for struggling readers (Diakidoy et al., 2003; Hall, 2016).

Consequently, when readers arrive at a valid interpretation of a science text, they need to infer how the various pieces of scientific information logically relate to each other and how to garner understanding between the text and prior scientific knowledge they may or may not have learned (Graesser et al., 2002). In this respect, science is a context that requires children to read with a specific purpose in mind (e.g., hypothesize or identify cause-effect relations) using expository texts, which requires science-specific reading comprehension skills (Fang, 2008; Halliday & Martin, 1993; Lemke, 1990). Text comprehension plays a crucial role in the acquisition, construction, and sharing of knowledge.

To learn science concepts, reading comprehension is essential. Learning how to read expository textbooks in science classes requires teachers to have specific and explicit support to help children face the challenges of reading scientific textbooks (Patterson et al., 2018). One may conclude that an effective teacher of science understands the complex and dynamic relationship between reading proficiency and science texts and uses different approaches to foster reading comprehension for science learning.

Reading Comprehension and Math

Across development, the relationship between mathematics and reading scores is strong as early as preschool and kindergarten (McClelland et al., 2007) and remains so through elementary school (Hecht et al., 2001). Mathematics and reading are two fundamental domains children must master for long-term academic and career success. Yet, many children who struggle in math, usually struggle in reading as well. The two are interrelated in that success in math is dependent on one's success in reading. Further, the skills in both are interwoven in ways that are not typically discussed.

For example, according to Purpura et al. (2013), there are three primary early numeracy phases: informal numeracy skills (e.g., counting and comparison without formal numerals), numeral knowledge (e.g., understanding numeral names and their quantities), and formal numeracy (e.g., adding and subtracting using numerals). Likewise, Whitehurst and Lonigan (1998) posited that there are three primary early reading components: oral language (e.g., vocabulary and comprehension), print knowledge (e.g., knowledge of letter names and sounds), and phonological processing (e.g., blending and segmenting sounds). Of the three early reading components, oral language ability is the most consistently related to mathematics skills, particularly during the informal numeracy phase, or adding and subtracting (Lefevre et al., 2010; Purpura et al., 2011). Language skills enable children to represent and understand quantities (Miura & Okamoto, 2003). Children's print knowledge skills have been linked to early mathematics development, particularly in the numeral knowledge phase or the understanding of numeral names and quantities (Austin, et al., 2011; Purpura & Napoli, 2015).

Similarly, numeral knowledge is a necessary bridge between informal and formal numeracy skills (Purpura et al., 2013). Essentially, both mathematics and reading rely on understanding a symbolic code, whether composed of numbers or letters. Beyond recognizing and understanding the function and organization of the symbolic codes of mathematics and reading, more advanced early mathematics skills such as formal numeracy appear to be linked with children's phonological processing skills (Fuchs et al., 2010). Phonological processing skills (i.e., combining and separating sounds to make new words) relate to the acquisition of later reading skills (Fowler, 1991), as well as the number–word sequence (i.e., counting) and computation skills (i.e., adding and subtracting).

Going back to language, Simmons and Singleton (2007) stated that proficiency in the language in which mathematics is taught is considered a prerequisite for mathematics achievement. Understanding the functions and nature of print can logically be connected to early mathematics skills because many aspects of informal and formal mathematics rely on printed numbers or symbols. Additionally, much of the application of mathematical knowledge to basic computational and comparative skills are inherently dependent on children's understanding of language (Fuchs et al., 2008). For example, language skills are important for understanding the concepts of "more" and "less" as well as understanding that some mathematical words can mean the same thing and can often be used interchangeably (e.g., plus, and, add, together). The language of mathematics is not easy because many of the terms used inside the math content area are used outside of the math content area; therefore, it must be explicitly emphasized and taught in the classroom.

Such as in science, words matter. Bohlmann and Pretorius (2002) found three main categories of words: high-frequency words, academic words, and technical words. High-frequency words are those that occur in our everyday conversations and are considered basic words. Academic words refer to words that are found in academic courses. These are words that occur across discipline boundaries and seldom occur in everyday conversations and are categorized as low-frequency words. Technical words are discipline-related words that occur with high frequency in a specific discipline and reflect the "tools of the trade" within that discipline, but outside of the discipline are seldom used. Examples of technical terms in mathematics include integers, logarithm, operation, square root, exponents, etc.

Research has shown that in learning contexts, knowledge of low-frequency words is associated with academic success. Students with smaller vocabularies typically know a higher percentage of high-frequency words, (Corson 1983; Cooper, 1996) which occur predominantly in oral contexts. Students who do little reading in English have little exposure to low-frequency words and may have trouble unlocking meaning in the various content areas in school.

Math textbooks play an important role in math instruction because they influence how many students learn and apply mathematical concepts. The reading of math texts requires close attention to detail as parts of the texts tend to be procedural in that they provide instructions and explanations on how to carry out a task or how to develop conceptual knowledge (Drose, 2019). Mathematics texts are also hierarchical and cumulative, in the sense that understanding each statement or proposition is necessary for understanding subsequent statements. If a particular step in a method, procedure, or argument is misunderstood or overlooked, there could be major consequences for overall comprehension.

Reading mathematics texts requires the integration of all the information in the text. A mathematics reader needs to interact with the text, be alert, and be attentive when seeking understanding, such as the case with graphics. Graphics refers to tables, graphs, schemas, and other visual aids that occur in texts to represent and complement verbal information. Graphic information forms an integral part of math texts. According to Drose (2019), a crucial part of math reading comprehension involves the ability to understand information represented in visual forms and then relate that information to the text to develop reasoning skills. Reasoning in mathematics is considered an essential practice and a core element. Reasoning helps to facilitate students' meaning-making in mathematics and to make the learning visible for students as well as for teachers (Segerby, 2014). Lithner (2008) defines reasoning as the line of thought that is adopted to produce assertions and claims when trying to solve tasks. Baxter et al. (2005) and Cobb (2002) found that reasoning can potentially contribute to visualizing important aspects of specific mathematical content. The demands placed on the students' reasoning competence are high because the language of mathematics is a very specific language, which is often expressed in various ways such as illustrations, words, and symbols. Thus, special demands are placed on the students' reading skills. However, by allowing students to argue and explain their thinking, the comprehension of mathematical content is supported (Boaler & Staples, 2008). Ball and Bass (2003) gave three important explanations for the importance of reasoning in mathematics. First, mathematics is meaningless without reasoning; second, reasoning is considered a fundamental competence because simply memorizing and learning procedures and main ideas are not sufficient to apply to another context. Third, reasoning is crucial for reconstructing knowledge.

There is no doubt a robust relationship between reading ability and academic performance in mathematics. Reading ability does not, of course, guarantee performance in math, but research suggests that poor reading ability functions as a barrier to effective math performance. Less skilled readers have a reading comprehension level of 50% or less, which effectively means that half of what they read is incomprehensible (Segerby, 2014).

Practically Speaking

When I was in third grade, math class created agita for me because I struggled with reading. I would pray for a snowstorm, a blizzard, a fire drill, or anything that would cancel class. If there were no disasters, I simply raised my hand for a bathroom break and I stretched the break as long as possible just to eat up class time. Of course, the teacher caught on and stopped my perfect plan. I enjoyed math when there were numbers only involved and simple computation. The lessons that I despised the most were those infamous word problems. They created such a headache for me.

For example, Train A leaves Chicago heading towards Toledo, Ohio traveling at 70 miles per hour. At the same time, Train B leaves Toledo, heading to Chicago traveling at 60 miles per hour. The distance between the two cities is 260 miles, when do the two trains meet? As a young child, I didn't care about the trains, when they were going to meet, when they were going to leave, or anyone on the trains. I could not understand why math had to involve words. All I wanted to do was add, subtract, multiply, and divide numbers (whole numbers of course, without the words). The mixing of the words and numbers made me sick to my stomach.

During quiz or test time, I just skipped over those monsters and took the "L." I carefully but intentionally calculated the remaining points on the test while excluding the word problems. I realized that I could still do well on the test as long as I answered the non-word problem equations correctly. That was my plan. I may laugh and joke about it now, but the real issue was that my inability to read well, at the time, interfered with my ability to connect with math concepts and skills optimally. I stopped trying to figure out how to solve word problems and skipped over them.

My lackluster reading skills created a barrier for me and I could not access certain parts of the math curriculum. Consequently, instead of me learning how to solve the problems, I gave up and created excuses and plans for me not to engage. This happens to so many of our young students. Reading proficiently matters.

Historical Context for Social Promotion, Ability Grouping, and Retention

So often children who struggled to read in third-grade move on to fourth grade where they fall into a slump because they must shift from learning to read to reading to learn. This is the time when children use what they have learned and all their experiences to make meaning out of what they read. This leap can be daunting and overwhelming for some children. While the more skilled readers are amassing knowledge and learning new words from context, lesser skilled readers may begin to avoid reading out of frustration. In fourth grade, school assignments become increasingly challenging as they require background knowledge and familiarity with "book words" (i.e., literary, abstract, and technical terms). Similarly, classes in science, social studies, history, and math rely more and more on textual analysis, pushing struggling readers behind in those subjects as well. This is the time that children begin to fall further and further behind their peers and the gap in achievement is noticeable.

Due to the tremendous impact of failing to read proficiently by third grade, some states have instituted mandatory retention bills (i.e., Arizona, Florida, Indiana, and Oklahoma). Other states are considering similar bills (i.e., Colorado, Iowa, New Mexico, and Tennessee). However, many education researchers found that holding children back is not the answer. Rather we must understand and deal with the issues that prohibit readers from gaining the skills needed to become proficient. It is within this context, that I challenge the current educational system that has allowed so many children, particularly Black and Brown children, to proceed through the educational system without sufficient reading skills. The answer to early reading struggles for many is to punish the children by holding them back or pushing them along to the next grade because they may have behavior challenges that a teacher may not want to "deal" with for another year.

However, young children who are struggling in school did not get there by themselves, they had help. We have all heard teachers make comments about children time and time again: "She did not act like that in my class," "He knew his stuff when he was in my class, I had no problems," or "Something must be going on at home because he was not like that in my class."

It's funny that we all take pride and proudly exclaim our part when a child is successful, but when a child is unsuccessful and struggling, we are nowhere to be found and some of us may not admit to even knowing the child. If we take credit for the good, we must own up to the bad as well. It takes a village to educate a child. We are all responsible—all of us (caregivers, teachers, school administrators, parents, communities, pediatricians, legislators, curriculum/program developers, colleges/universities, professors, etc.).

Grade Retention

Understanding social promotion, ability grouping, and retention will provide context for how the three initiatives have failed children over the years. Grade retention is the practice of requiring a student to repeat a particular grade when he or she does not meet the academic standards of that grade level. Roughly 10% of American students are retained at least once between kindergarten and eighth grade, with the incidence of retention concentrated among children from low-income families and traditionally disadvantaged children of color (Planty et al., 2009). Advocates of grade retention argue that this is done to help the student learn and sharpen skills in organization, management, studying, literacy, and other academic areas.

Meanwhile, critics warn that retained students may be harmed by stigmatization, reduced expectations for their academic performance on the part of teachers and parents, and the challenges of adjusting to a new peer group. In fact, research suggests that retained students achieve at lower levels, complete fewer years of school, and have worse social-emotional outcomes than similar students who are promoted (Ozek, 2015 & Schwerdy et al., 2017). Additionally, researchers found short-term gains regarding retention with little to no long-term improvement from grade retention and significant harmful effects on students.

In a study of the Florida Retention Policy, researchers found that third-grade retention improved student achievement in the short run, but the initial benefits faded out over time (Schwerdy et al., 2017). The Florida Retention Policy was one of the first that I read that required schools to develop a progress monitoring plan (PMP) for each struggling reader. The plan invites parents to participate in the development of the plan which describes the specific reading difficulties as well as the intensive teaching practices that will be used to help children catch up in reading. The PMP stays in place until the reading deficiency is remediated. According to Florida law, a third grader who scores a level 1 in reading on the state test must be retained in third grade to give the child more time and intensive instruction to catch up in reading. The law further states that substantial reading deficiencies must be addressed before children can move on to the fourth grade. The child who is retained will receive "effective teaching strategies and methods, a high performing teacher, participation in summer reading camps, at least 90 minutes of reading instruction each day (either one on one or in small groups), special books and computer software, frequent progress monitoring, tutoring or mentoring, transition, and after-school instruction."

Additionally, parents will be offered parent workshops and a tutor or mentor that has specialized reading training. At face value, the intensive supports are awesome and what research says is best for children. My point is this, why wait until the child has failed in third grade to offer research-based, developmentally appropriate methods and strategies? Why not provide a PMP for every child beginning in kindergarten and continuing through third grade? Why not offer best practices from the beginning rather than after the child has failed? Why not make PMP available for all students and not just those who are struggling? After all, if the strategies are good enough for struggling readers, I would think that they are good enough for those who are just learning to read as well. Just imagine that if all children from kindergarten through third grade had access to the methods and strategies outlined in the PMP, there may not be a need for retention. I totally understand that some children may require additional support and some students will learn to read regardless of the type of instruction received. I believe that if everyone had access to quality instruction, personalized learning, and other supports outlined in the PMP, it would catch struggling readers early and may reduce the need to retain significantly.

Also, in the Florida Retention Law, if a child has already been retained once in third grade and scores below the required reading mark again, the school must provide an intensive acceleration class that focuses on increasing the child's reading level by at least two grade levels in one school year. I have been in education for a long time and there aren't too many children who are retained in one grade and manage to advance two grade levels the following year. In Florida, if children are retained for a second time, they will be placed in a classroom that has a lower teacher-student ratio than other third-grade classrooms, a higher performing teacher, reading instruction for most of the day, research-based reading instruction, language and vocabulary instructional programs, frequent monitoring of student progress, and the opportunity to master the fourth-grade standards in other subjects.

Again, all great strategies, but why is it offered to only struggling students when they have failed, why not provide intensive support to everyone before failing? I just wonder what would happen if all students in kindergarten through third grade (the grades where they are learning to read) had access to everything struggling students had, would there be a need to retain? For students who are struggling, why not continue to employ best practices and intensive instruction while exposing them to grade-level material in the process? Being proactive instead of reactive could prove beneficial to children and to the school budget.

Primary-grade retention may continue to impact students long after the fact via stigma, student effort and motivation, and other behavioral processes (Andrew, 2014). Studies show grade retention in primary schools leaves lasting scars on students' educational careers and lowers the odds of completing high school. Economic theory predicts that retention policies influence the effort, expectations, and practices of students and their teachers (Babcock & Bedard, 2011). Further, retaining underperforming students may discourage them, destroy their confidence, delay exposure to the next year's curriculum, and may leave them further behind (Thompson & Cunningham 2000). Research has demonstrated that retention provides little academic advantages to students, and the little that it provides fades over a two-to-three-year period. The most notable academic deficit for retaining children is in reading. Retention does not have a positive impact on self-esteem or school adjustment, and it is associated with significant increases in behavior problems.

There are several explanations for why grade retention failed in the past. Historically, retention meant repeating all the work that was done the previous year without regard to children's strengths or their areas for growth, it was punitive and failure to pass grade level work fell on the children. Essentially, we gave children the same work, probably with the same teacher and we expected different results. Another reason that retention did not work in the past was that there was a failure to address the issues associated with retention. The assumption was that by repeating a grade, children will remember the content, pass the grade, and move on to the next grade. The problem was that the issues that caused the child to be retained in the first place had not been identified. The child simply memorized the work and never learned or mastered the work.

The third reason why retention did not work in the past was that the mental health and the social and emotional development of the children were not considered. There was typically no plan to monitor the mental status of children and the impact that retention may have on academic performance. Old retention plans did not have effective intervention plans that included social and cognitive competence. Retention plans did not include culturally relevant instructional strategies, highly effective teachers, smaller class sizes, reduced teacher-child ratios, systematic assessment strategies, ongoing monitoring, developmentally appropriate mental health programs, or extended day and year enrichment programs to intentionally focus on the underdeveloped skills in ways that were different than what children were exposed to during the school year.

Social Promotion

Social promotion is the practice of promoting children to the next grade despite them failing to meet grade level coursework objectives in order to keep them with their same-age peers. The original goals of social promotion, which are currently used in some districts today, were to nurture children's self-esteem and to keep same-age peers together. In the 1960s, concerns about retention and the social, emotional, and cognitive development of at-risk children led many educators, politicians, and parents to pause retention practices and allowed children to advance to the next grade with their peers regardless of their academic performance. Social promotion gained prominence because of the emotional weight that retention caused many children. Also, influential families latched on to social promotion and they began to use their influence and power to pressure school personnel into passing their children. Educators were in favor of social promotion as well because having children repeat grades was costly. Social promotion was encouraged based on research that demonstrated negative effects on children's self-esteem when they were retained. Proponents of retention claim that the social promotion of underperforming children teaches them that effort and achievement are unimportant, forces teachers to deal with a much wider range of student preparedness, and denies students a second chance to learn what they missed. Additionally, social promotion may lead communities into believing that graduates are prepared for college and the workplace because they "graduated."

Eventually, social promotion became unpopular because it moved children along from grade to grade unprepared. Consequently, students graduated from high school basically illiterate. Researchers also found that teachers promote children because of challenging behaviors. Like retention, social promotion alone without addressing the deficient skills is unproductive and ineffective. If children begin to see passing grades as an entitlement rather than a reward or an outcome of working hard, the value of education diminishes. Social promotion has led to children expecting something for nothing, public perception of weakening of standards, and parents suing for educational malpractice because children were not prepared for upper-level learning (Owings & Kaplan, 2001). Contrary to what some may believe, social promotion does not help students graduate high school either on time or at all (Lynch, 2014). Grade retention and social promotion have a negative effect on all areas of student achievement including reading, math, language, and social and emotional adjustment (Jimerson et al., 2005).

Ability Grouping

Ability grouping was the third remedial initiative created to help students achieve academically. Achievement tests were used to place children in three ability groups: high group, average group, and low group. According to ability grouping advocates, low-performing children could pass to the next grade, but they would have lower demands placed on them and lower requirements so that they may concentrate on mastering grade-level work. Curriculum and instruction were modified to fit the children's ability levels. As can be expected, eventually, this practice led to the separation of children by social class where many children living in poverty were placed in the low group. In ability grouping, children in the lower group moved through the school system with a consistently substandard education offered to them. These children were socially promoted, exposed to a watered-down curriculum, fewer demands from them to produce, and lowered expectations from teachers. This practice was supposed to improve children's academic achievement. Ability grouping morphed into "ability schools" which is the same concept as ability grouping but on a larger scale. Instead of groups of children being exposed to an inferior education, we have schools and school districts that serve predominantly children of color who are exposed to prolonged inadequate, inefficient, and ineffective educational experiences.

Cost of Retaining and Promoting Students

There are associated costs related to the lack of academic achievement. The various stakeholders in education, including students, teachers, education policy makers, parents, and employers are all undermined by the pass or fail mentality of the educational system. Lynch (2014) found that when failure means that a student is either retained or promoted without the necessary mastery of skills and knowledge deemed age-appropriate, all stakeholders pay a price. The cost to the individual child is great and could impact the child for a lifetime. The damage to the child's self-concept and self-esteem is of particular importance. As children develop a sense of self and a sense of their own identity, any disruption during this period can potentially cause long-term, and in some cases, permanent damage. Fanguy and Mathis (2012) found that children who are retained or socially promoted are often teased and bullied by their peers and this disruption in the psychosocial development of children can disrupt proper development.

As teasing and bullying increase, some children tend to become more aggressive and begin to take their frustrations out on themselves or others in retaliation to the bullying and teasing. Additionally, children may become disconnected because of retention and social promotion policies. They may disconnect from themselves, from education, peers, teachers, their families, and from the community at large (Lynch 2014). Sadly, researchers have found that Black and Brown children from low-income families are more likely to be retained than their white peers (Jimerson, 2001). Additionally, African American males from low-income families, with low educational attainment, and little school involvement were overly represented in retention data (NASP, 2003).

The overt and unaddressed disparities in our educational system have overwhelmed our urban schools for far too long. However, more alarming is the ever-growing racial, social, and economic discriminatory practices that are hidden in systems like education that continue to perpetuate the miseducation of many Black and Brown children. For example, in 1954 the Supreme Court decision *Brown v. Board of Education stated that* separating children in public schools based on race was unconstitutional, which essentially abolished legalized segregation based on race. Fast forward today, many of our urban school districts are predominantly made up of Black and Brown children, with more than half of the children receiving free or reduced lunch. This is not legalized segregation, but segregation, nonetheless. Many of these schools have high-stakes testing, and strong retention and social promotion policies. Many have over-representation of males in special education, unequal funding, lower expectations of teachers and children, higher truancy, higher delinquency, and higher teacher-child ratios. Additionally, many of the schools are old and dilapidated with many inadequate facilities. Regarding teaching and learning, many urban schools have watered down and inaccurate curricula content. They also have inadequate course selections, less access to Advanced Placement (AP) courses, limited STEM (Science, Technology, Engineering, and Math) or gifted and talented opportunities. Urban schools also typically have less extracurricular activities and less access to current technological advances. While the schools for many Black and Brown children may be substandard and inferior, the children are not.

Public education by design is supposed to provide knowledge and a skillset to the population it serves. In other words, the children who are educated in our public schools will eventually wind up in the workforce. However, large bodies of inadequately educated children have an enormous cost to the labor force, the economy, and social service agencies. Retained or socially promoted children have a higher dropout rate, are less likely to pursue higher education opportunities or technical schools, will earn less money than their peers over time, and may end up relying on social services. Also, to compete in a 21st century global economy, our students must be prepared academically, socially, and emotionally. The lack of academic achievement not only impacts children, but families, the educational system, the economy, and society as well.

For decades, the U.S. school system has tried to use either retention, social promotion, or ability grouping to close the proverbial achievement gap and as the research has shown, nothing worked. The research on the short-term and long-term effects on children who are retained or socially promoted is devastating, but clear. However, knowing the research is one thing, creating legislation, and designing school policies that will make a difference is another. We must use the results from the research to find better ways to support our struggling students. Finding viable solutions other than retention and socially promoting children is a challenge and it will take all stakeholders to find alternate options for children. However, if we can send rich civilians to the edge of outer space for approximately 15 minutes at a cost of $250,000 to $500,000 a seat, surely, we can find a viable solution to ensure that children are proficient readers. Perhaps if we were as committed and vested in our young children, we would get a better return for the dollars spent in terms of advances in science, medicine, technology, and global warming. If we continue to do nothing, we are robbing children of possibilities and the world of great potential.

Even with the abundance of research on retention, several states and school districts have policies requiring the retainment of children who do not demonstrate reading proficiency by the end of third grade. In some states, children as young as five years old can be retained. Fundamentally, I am not opposed to providing children the necessary support they need to thrive. However, I am opposed to some of the practices that are used to "support" children who are underperforming academically, specifically children from kindergarten to third grade. The current system places the blame of academic failure squarely on children, when in fact, it should be placed on their ecosystem. When children underperform in school, they are the only ones who are penalized. I say penalized because in the eyes of children this young, they see grade retention as punishment.

For example, they do not get to move on to the next grade with their peers, they may be treated "differently" in school, they may be teased and bullied by their peers and talked about by teachers, negatively labeled, denied recess and specials to do "extra work", and may need to attend summer school and/or before and after school programs for additional support. At home, some children are also penalized with a wide range of punishment options for underperforming in school. The way children are treated (directly or indirectly, intentionally, or unintentionally) impacts their self-esteem and self-image and could have long-term negative consequences.

When we retain children, we tend to look at the child as the problem. We blame their underperformance on their environment, skin color, home life, parents, lack of parents, language spoken, attitude, or zip code instead of examining the entire system that has surrounded children for the first eight years of their lives. When a child is retained, everyone must take some of the blame and do better. Children this age are not responsible for toxic environments, stressors that may be in their lives and the adverse effects that may develop. Children do not make their own meals, wake up on their own to prepare for school, wash, and iron their clothes, get to school on time, create a home routine, check their own homework, read to themselves, reduce screen time, or put themselves to bed on time. Children do not attend parent/teacher conferences to discuss their strengths and opportunities for growth and ensure that they are receiving a quality education. Creating an environment conducive for learning and growing requires many of the items previously mentioned. Therefore, the child's ecosystem which includes parents must take some responsibility when children are retained.

Additionally, we must look at the schools, the teachers, the curriculum, assessment practices, lesson planning, instructional strategies, interventions, student work, teacher observations, teachers' strengths, and areas for improvement because everything we do has an impact on the developing child. For example, when the teacher and child dynamic is toxic, what do we do about it? We typically do nothing, which impacts the child. As Dr. Rita Pierson stated, children will not learn from people they do not like. Children as young as three years old have an internal radar that goes off when they sense that a teacher does not like them. The teacher and child dynamic does not need to be toxic to be ineffective. There are times when teachers cannot connect with a child because of personalities, instructional delivery, inexperience in a subject area, inexperience at a particular grade level, or the lack of understanding of the curriculum or progression of skills. Another important factor that may surface, particularly in urban schools, is culture. Teachers may have difficulties connecting with children who are different from themselves. Some children struggle to learn when they perceive that their culture is not respected, reflected, valued, appreciated, or acknowledged. It does not matter if the perception is right or wrong, it is what the child believes that can potentially impact learning. Teachers who have a different cultural background than the children may not have the experience, ability, time, or the patience to learn about all the children in their classroom and to ensure inclusive practices. In addition, teachers may feel inadequate and uncomfortable when broaching the subject of culture. Some teachers do not understand the full definition of culture and become defensive and angry as they equate culture to prejudice, racism, bigotry, or discrimination. Being culturally responsive in classrooms takes a lot of work, advanced planning, and many contacts with families, which is why, unfortunately, some teachers just sprinkle a little culture here and there for compliance. It will take more than a sprinkle to build the type of relationships with children that will support learning. We must learn to be uncomfortable with culture now to be comfortable later.

Practically Speaking

One of my sons struggled with math in the early grades. He had a relatively inexperienced teacher who was totally honest with us and stated that math was not her best subject. When our son began to struggle in math, we became nervous, but he worked hard and passed the class. The next year, he was assigned the same teacher because that teacher moved up a grade. My husband and I contemplated whether to ask for another teacher but, in the end, we left him in her class. Our son struggled in math to the point that we had to seek a tutoring service for him. We ended up paying thousands of dollars to improve his math skills when all we had to do was request another teacher. The teacher was wonderful but inexperienced in the profession, lacked the skill set to teach math effectively, and the strategies she used did not work with our son. Sometimes, the teacher-child relationship is like oil and water and will never mix. When there is a disconnect between teacher and child, we may need to examine it before it impedes the growth of the child.

Before retaining a child, I wonder how often we examine non-educational factors that could impede the development of children. For example, are there any health issues, social and emotional factors to consider, changes in the home, or any other toxins or stressors that need to be considered? If extenuating circumstances do exist, they must be acknowledged, addressed, and placed in the remedial action plan for the child; otherwise, interventions may prove unsuccessful. I also wonder about the type of remediation that occurs before children reach third grade. Typically, there are early signs that a child is struggling before he/she enters third grade. Too many times, grade retention is the first resort instead of the last.

Additionally, when a child is retained, he/she is placed typically in the same class, with the same curriculum, same assessment practices, same expectations, same home life, same struggles, and same instructional practices, but we expect different results. Is it the expectation that since children had the content the year before, they should be familiar with the content the second time around and therefore, get a passing grade? If that is the case, then are we placing more emphasis on memorizing rather than critical thinking? Memorizing a skill or concept does not always mean the child has learned or mastered the skill or concept. We must rethink retention and its benefits as a remedial practice and place more emphasis on early prevention that could include, identifying struggling readers early, providing targeted intensive intervention, one-on-one tutoring, changing teachers, changing instructional strategies and methods, implementing culturally responsive teaching, reduced class sizes, and engaging parents, and school social workers. In a policy brief in 2012, Martin West, an assistant professor at the Harvard Graduate School of Education and deputy director of Harvard's Program on Education Policy and Governance, discussed in detail how retaining students in the early grades is self-defeating. He stated, "Policies encouraging the retention of students who have not acquired basic reading skills by third grade are no substitute for the development of a comprehensive strategy to reduce the number of struggling readers." Before we seek to retain a child, we must provide all the support necessary beforehand beginning at the first sign of struggle. In this way, we become proactive instead of reactive. If children do not learn the way we teach, we must teach the way they learn.

Poor Reading Skills and the Impact
on Children and Society

Reading is a skill by which children use books, computers, and other forms of media to gain information in all content areas such as math, science, and social studies. The ability to read and write are essential for academic success and full participation in a technological society. Yet, seventy four percent of struggling third graders still struggle in ninth grade, which makes it hard to graduate from high school. The dropout rates are twice as high for African American and Latinx students as they are for White students. Those who manage to graduate from high school may find their dreams of pursuing higher education a hard hill to climb. A hard reality to accept is that children who struggle with reading now may grow up to be adults who struggle to read. According to the National Center for Education Statistics (NCES), 19% of adults in the United States between the ages of 16-65 scored at level 1 or below on the six-level Program for the International Assessment of Adult Competencies (PIAAC). Similarly, 33% scored at level two. Using the same assessment in the same year, 36% of African Americans and 31% of Latinx respondents scored at level 1 or below in literacy versus 12% of white respondents. PIAAC, better known as a Survey of Adult Skills, measures adults' proficiency in processing skills, literacy, numeracy, and problem solving. Researchers gather information and data on how adults use their skills at home, at work, and in the wider community.

In 2019, NCES reported 21% of American Adults are illiterate or functionally illiterate. According to the United States Department of Education, 54% of adults in the United States have prose literacy below the sixth-grade level. The American Library Association defined prose literacy as the knowledge and skills needed to search, comprehend, and use continuous texts (e.g., editorials, news stories, brochures, and instructional materials). Research has shown that adults who struggle to read have difficulties holding a job, may have prolonged periods of unemployment (because they are unqualified for many jobs), may have a lower salary (on average $23,000 per year as opposed to $48,000 for their peers who attended college), require public assistance, are less informed about current events, less likely to participate in democracy, and have a higher rate of trouble with the law (Austin et al., 2017; Casey, 2010; National Assessment of Educational Progress, 2019).

Data also link children of color to several risk factors associated with weaker reading skills. For example, African American babies born with low birth weights nearly double that of white babies. Low birth weight is often associated with early developmental delays. African American boys and girls are two to three times more likely to be chronically absent in the early grades, which can erode early literacy gains. Also, and unfortunately, struggling readers are overwhelmingly identified as having a learning disability and assigned to special education.

The future is bleak for third graders who cannot read on grade level as they are on track to become our nation's lowest income group, least skilled, and systems dependent citizens. Reading is a prerequisite for most adult employment, continued personal achievement, and for a continued democracy. While it is a cultural belief that prison planners use third grade reading scores to predict prison sizes, there is, in fact, a strong connection between low literacy skills and our country's exploding incarceration rates. According to a special report, *Early Warning*, from the Annie E. Casey Foundation (2010), there are compelling statistics that underscore this connection:

- 85% of all juveniles who interface with the juvenile court system are functionally low literate.
- Juvenile incarceration reduces the probability of high school completion and increases the probability of incarceration later in life.
- High school dropouts are 3.5 times more likely than high school graduates to be arrested in their lifetime.
- 60% of adolescents who abuse drugs also have a reading problem.
- High school dropouts are 63% more likely to be incarcerated than their peers with four-year college degrees.
- Mississippi has the second highest incarceration rate in the nation. The average adult inmate reads on a sixth-grade level. Half of the state's inmates never finished high school.
- According to the National Adult Literacy Survey, 70% of all incarcerated adults cannot read at a 4th grade level, meaning they lack the reading skills to navigate many everyday tasks or hold down anything but lower paying jobs.

Correctional and judicial professionals have long recognized a connection between poor literacy skills, school dropout rates, and crime. According to Ralph Smith, Managing Director of The Campaign for Grade-Level Reading, children who miss the reading proficiency mark may have significant and long-term consequences for children, the communities they live in, and the nation as a whole. Smith states that if the reading problem is left unchecked, it will undermine efforts to end intergenerational poverty, close the achievement gap, and reduce high school dropout rates. The cost of an illiterate society is great. If we as a nation do not get children on track to reading proficiently, the United States will lose an essential proportion of its human capital to poverty. The United States economy is less rich in skills than it was decades ago. The result is that United States workers are on average, less able to develop, master, and adapt to new technologies and methods. Communities with low-achieving local schools produce clusters of Americans that are unable to participate in the greater American economy due to a concentration of low skills, high unemployment, or high incarceration rates. Fluent readers are necessary for the types of jobs that are needed to compete in a 21st century global economy. If a child does not meet the reading proficiency mark, it does not mean the end of the world for that child. Children are resilient and with the right intervention methods, improvement in performance and outcomes can happen. However, to do so, children need a champion who believes in them, and they need a systemic approach to tackling the learning issues. The schools cannot close this gap alone. Rather it will take an entire village to develop proficient readers by third grade.

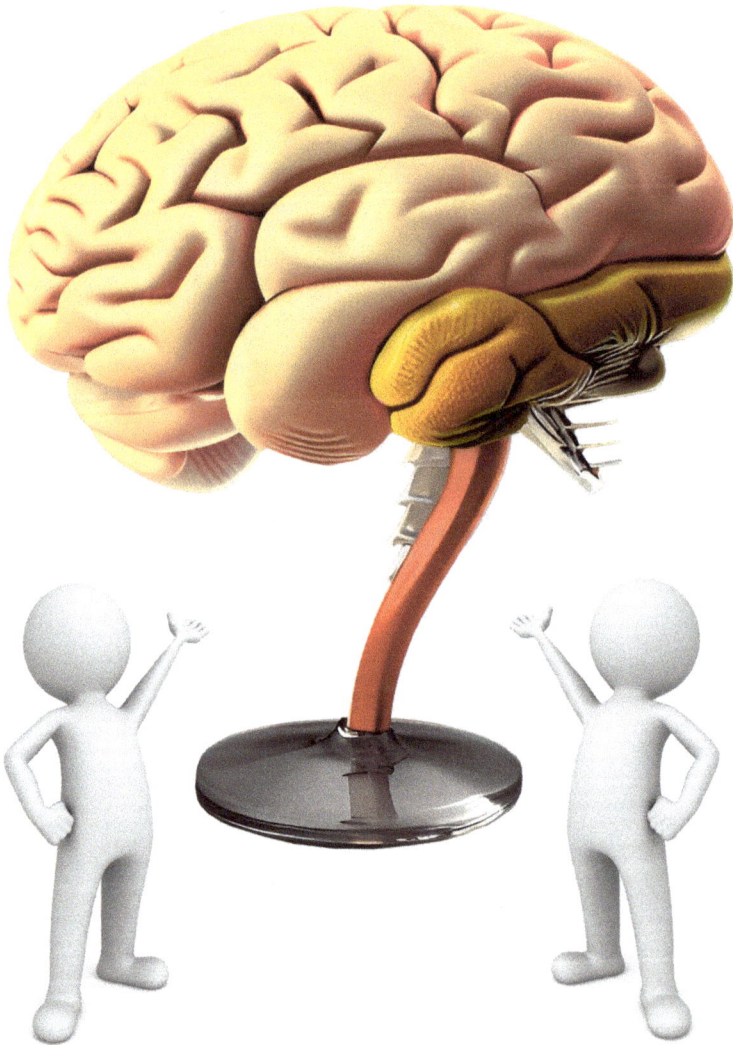

Chapter 3

In The Beginning

Architecture of the Brain

Do events that happen early in a child's life determine the architecture of the brain? To understand the processes of reading, we must start at the beginning with the developing brain. Preparing children for school begins while the child is in the womb. I am not a neurologist but initially, I wanted to become a cognitive psychologist due to my fascination with the brain. I was intrigued by how people learn, solve problems, and make decisions. Over the course of twenty-five years, I learned a lot about the developing brain as it relates to education.

Because all learning involves the brain, the more we understand how the brain works, the better we can structure educational practices to align with the functions of the brain. Being in education for so long, I have learned that anyone responsible for children eight years old and under must have background knowledge about the brain. Knowledge about the brain grounds us, keeps us focused on our purpose in the lives of children, and helps us understand how important our role is in shaping a child's brain. What happens early in a child's life impacts the architecture of the brain.

According to the National Center for Education Statistics, not all children start school with the same language and literacy skills. Research shows, some children enter kindergarten at grade level, others enter one or two years behind, and still others will enter with skills one-to-two years above grade level. To understand why, we must first look at the fetal brain.

What a child knows and how he or she behaves are products of both genetic makeup and the child's experiences before entering school (Willerman 1979; Plomin 1990). Fetal brain development starts before pregnancy may be realized. The brain begins to form early in the first trimester and continues after birth. During pregnancy, fetal brain development is responsible for certain important actions like breathing, kicking, and heartbeats. Therefore, nicotine, alcohol, caffeine, and other illicit drugs are harmful to the mother as well as the unborn baby. Ingesting drugs during pregnancy, as well as constant exposure to stressful life events, natural disasters, and maternal anxiety and depression may increase the chances of birth defects, premature births, underweight babies, and stillborn births. Specifically, exposure to alcohol in utero is associated with various impairments including cognitive, executive functioning, memory, language, visual-spatial ability, motor function, attentiveness, activity levels, and behavioral including adaptive dysfunction (Mattson et al., 2011). Prenatal nicotine exposure is a risk factor for several neuro-biological conditions such as attention deficit hyperactivity disorder (ADHD), learning disabilities, and substance abuse (Eicher et al., 2013).

Additionally, prenatal nicotine exposure influences phonology, reading fluency, reading comprehension, and reading accuracy, which are all foundational to the development of reading and language skills in children (Eicher et al., 2013).

Toxins are extremely harmful because they produce observable changes in the architecture of the brain. Lanphear (2015) discussed the impact on toxins and the developing brain. He discovered that because a child's brain develops over time, it is vulnerable to many environmental toxins. The previously mentioned toxins as well as mercury, air borne pollutants, and pesticides are extremely harmful to a child's brain. Brain cells and the many different types of neurons have a distinct growth phase. The shape and form of cells and neurons may change when exposed to different toxins which can alter the developing brain. Lanphear found that even low-level exposure to environmental toxins can result in substantial diseases and disabilities which may lead to cognitive deficits in young children.

Additionally, a healthy diet is extremely important for the developing fetus. Eating fresh fruits and vegetables, less processed food, and reduced fats and sugars can contribute to a healthy baby and reduce unhealthy risk factors for both the mother and the unborn child. One of the risk factors associated with a poor diet is obesity for the child in the first years of life. Food insecurities, lack of fresh fruit and vegetables in some neighborhoods, and the expense factor associated with eating healthy, unfortunately are issues for low-income families. In a country as rich and powerful as the United States, why is it so expensive to eat healthy, especially when we know the benefits of healthy eating for young children and families? For example, a healthy salad costs double the amount of a Happy Meal. Healthy diets and eating habits at the beginning of a child's life may carry over into the later years and significantly reduce future health issues, challenges, and related costs.

Also harmful to young children is lead. According to the Center for Disease Control and Prevention (CDC) lead is still a major problem for young children. The CDC points out that about half a million children a year, nationwide, between the ages of one and five, test positive for lead in their blood. Lead poisoning happens when too much lead gets into the body through the skin, or when a person breathes it, eats it, or drinks something contaminated by it. Pregnant mothers may transmit lead to their unborn child, which may cause premature births and low birth weight babies. Additionally, lead in the body can hurt the brain, kidneys, and other organs. Lead is toxic to everyone, but children younger than six years old are at the greatest risk. Their bodies absorb lead easier than older children and adults because they crawl and put their hands and other things in their mouths more frequently. The National Center for Environmental Health states that exposure to lead can seriously harm a child's health and cause adverse effects such as: damage to the brain and nervous system, slowed growth and development, learning and behavior problems, and hearing and speech problems. These effects may lead to developmental issues, decreased ability to pay attention, and underperformance in school.

Early experiences provide a window as to why some children enter preschool and kindergarten with large developmental disparities. Children's neurological development in early life is a continuous process, and it builds on material learned before, which supports the premise that educational inequalities occur long before children enter kindergarten (Hippel et al., 2018), What happens early in a child's life matters.

Brain Development

Most brain cells are produced between the fourth and seventh month of gestation (Jensen, 2005). According to Cypel (2013), 90 billion new neurons form in the brain while the baby is in utero. When a baby is born, the brain is premature and has an abundance of cells but with very few connections between them (Music, 2017). In fact, at birth, the brain already has almost all the neurons it will ever have. In the first year of life, the brain doubles in size, by age three, it has reached 80% of its adult volume, and by age five, 90% (The Urban Child Institute, 2015). Amazingly, newborn babies have all the brain cells (neurons) they will need for the rest of their lives—yet it is the connections between those cells that really make the brain work. Brain connections enable us to move, think, communicate and do just about everything. The first three years of life are a time of rapid cognitive, linguistic, social, emotional, and motor development.

The Working Brain

Although the brain is quite complex and intricate, parents and teachers should have a basic working knowledge of the brain to ensure that a child's environment is appropriate for sufficient brain development. A very simplistic overview begins with two kinds of brain cells: neurons and glia. The majority of the brain cells (90%) are glia, but the neurons (the other 10%) are the most understood. Glia are non-neuronal brain cells that are involved in the support of neuronal processes such as producing myelin or the removal of debris like dead brain cells (Tierney & Nelson, 2009). Neurons are the primary functional units of the nervous system and play a critical role in transmitting electrical and chemical signals within the body. Neurons are responsible for receiving and carrying signals or messages from the brain to the rest of the body. These signals help to coordinate many different functions, including movement, sensation, and cognition. Neurons have specialized functions, with sensory neurons sending information from the senses to the brain and motor neurons carrying messages away from the brain to control movement. In addition to these specialized functions, neurons work together to form complex networks that enable the brain to carry out more advanced processes, such as memory, learning, and decision-making. These networks are constantly changing and adapting in response to experience and learning, allowing the brain to optimize its functioning over time. Overall, neurons are essential to performing the work of the brain and play a crucial role in enabling us to carry out the many functions necessary for life.

Neurons are important in the developing brain. For example, neurons undergo a process of migration and maturation that involves the growth of axons and dendrites, which are essential for forming connections between neurons and establishing functional neural circuits. Once a neuron has migrated to its target destination, it can either develop into a mature neuron or undergo apoptosis, which is a natural process of cell death (Tierney & Nelson, 200). This process helps to eliminate excess or damaged neurons and plays a critical role in shaping the developing brain. Mature neurons have a cell body, axons, and dendrites, which are essential for forming functional connections with other neurons. Axons are the primary structure used by neurons to communicate with other cells, while dendrites receive signals from other cells and help to integrate and process incoming information.

The connections between dendrites and axons occur at specialized structures called synapses, which are the basis for neural communication and essential for brain function. When synapses are stimulated repeatedly, the neural connections become more efficient, leading to the development of permanent pathways in the brain. Overall, the growth and maturation of neurons, including the formation of axons and dendrites and the establishment of synaptic connections, are critical processes that underlie the development of the brain and its ability to carry out complex functions such as learning and memory.

Not all neurons are created equal. There are fast neurons and there are slow neurons. In slow neurons, information moves about one meter per second (as fast as you walk or jog). While in fast neurons, information flows at about 100 meters per second (as fast as a racecar). For example, remember a time when you bumped your knee against the corner of a table. You feel the bump right away, but it may take a minute for the message to reach the brain for you to experience the pain. The sensation of your knee touching the table was sent via fast neurons. The pain that you experienced afterward was sent via slow neurons. This happens because of the myelin sheath, which is a soft white material that forms around the axon.

Myelination is the final process involved in the development of the brain. Myelination plays a crucial role in the speed and efficiency of information that is transmitted in the brain. What does this mean for learning? As children learn new skills, repetition and practice increase the amount of myelination around the axon, which leads to faster and more efficient communication between neurons. This process continues throughout our lives, allowing for ongoing learning and skill development. However, damage to the myelin sheath can lead to neurological problems. For example, poor nutrition is a major culprit in hindering the development of healthy myelin. Therefore, it is important to prioritize a healthy diet and lifestyle to support the ongoing development of myelin and optimize cognitive outcomes. As you may imagine, the limited opportunities for access to nutritional food options in low-income families should be a major concern for everyone especially educators.

During the first years of life, at least one million new neural connections (synapses) are made every second, more than at any other time in life. Additionally, synapses are formed at a faster rate during these years than at any other time (The Urban Child Institute, 2015). In fact, the brain creates many more of them than it needs and by age two or three, the brain has up to twice as many synapses as it will have in adulthood.

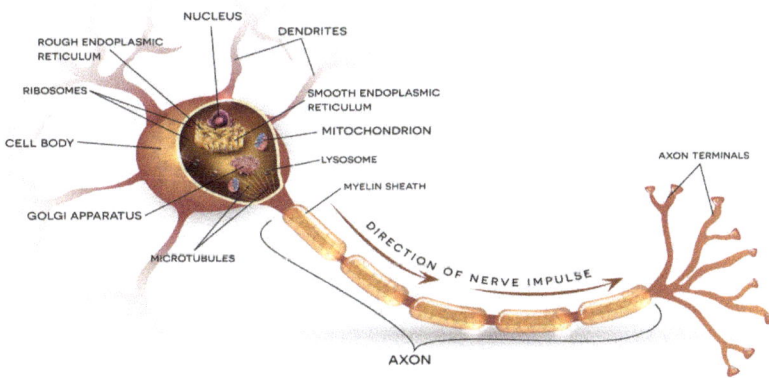

Schematic Drawing of a Neuron

These surplus connections are gradually eliminated throughout childhood and adolescence in a process referred to as 'pruning'. Pruning is a process by which the brain eliminates weaker or unnecessary neural connections to make way for stronger and more efficient connections (The Urban Child Institute, 2015). In other words, it follows the 'use it or lose it" principle where active synapses are strengthened and inactive ones are removed. The strength of synaptic connections changes during learning, based on the amount of stimuli received.

Twenty billion synapses are pruned every day between childhood and early adolescence (Music, 2017). Once a connection is formed it remains wired, but unused cells are pruned although new pathways and wiring can still form later in life. The processes of overproduction of synapses and subsequent synaptic reduction are essential for the flexibility required for the adaptive capabilities of the developing brain (Tierney & Nelson, 2009). Why is this important in education? Synapses play a crucial role in the formation and retrieval of memories. In a healthy brain, there is a balance between the loss of old synapses and the formation of new ones which is essential for learning and memory. Overall, the ability of the brain to continually restructure its network of synapses is critical for learning, memory, and cognitive function in general.

In addition to pruning and myelination, the brain has the ability to reorganize itself by forming new neural connections throughout life. Early researchers believed that the creation of new neurons stopped shortly after birth. Today, it's understood that the brain possesses the remarkable ability to reorganize pathways, create new connections, and, in some cases, even create new neurons; in a concept called neuroplasticity. Neuroplasticity allows the neurons in the brain to compensate for injury and disease and to adjust their activities in response to new situations or to changes in their environment (Voss et al., 2017). The brain is super smart and complex. Neuroplasticity enables children to learn and remember new things and adjust to new experiences. Environmental experiences, such as stimulation, and a person's genetic makeup affect the brain's plasticity. The brain is the most "plastic" during the early years of development. The early years provide the best opportunities for a child's brain to develop the connections needed to be healthy, capable, and successful adults. Connections made in the brain are needed for many important, higher-level abilities like motivation, self-regulation, problem-solving, and communication, which are formed in the early years. However, this is not the case for many young children sitting in classrooms every day.

There is so much more to the brain, but adults working with children eight years and younger only need basic brain knowledge to intentionally shape the brain of a child and provide stimulating learning environments for proper brain development.

Experiences and the Environment

Jack Shonkoff the Director of the Center on the Developing Child at Harvard University equated the developing brain to that of an architect building a house. The brain is built over time and the genetic makeup of an individual provides the blueprint for the brain. However, experiences and environmental factors play a crucial role in shaping how the brain is constructed. Just as a building needs a strong foundation to last a long time, a healthy and supportive environment is needed for the brain to develop optimally. Positive experiences, such as nurturing relationships with caregivers and engaging in stimulating activities, can help to build a strong foundation for the brain (Center on the Developing Child, 2015b). On the other hand, negative experiences, such as exposure to toxic stress or trauma, can lead to a weak foundation and compromise the brain's development (Center on the Developing Child, n.d.-a). The phrase "architecture of the brain" emphasizes the idea that the brain is built through a process of construction, and experiences and environmental factors play a crucial role in shaping this process. By understanding this analogy, we can better appreciate the importance of providing a supportive environment and positive experiences for children to ensure optimal brain development.

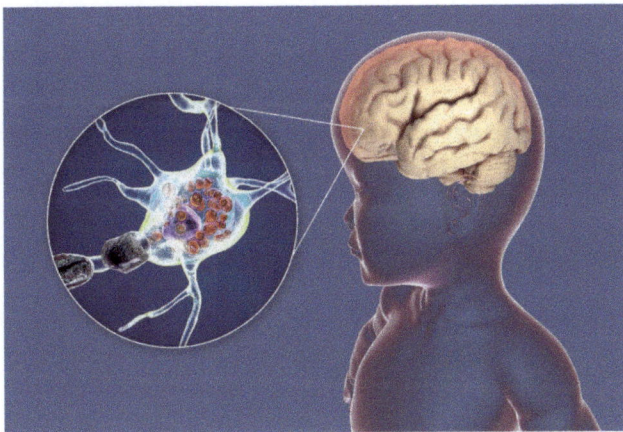

90% of a Child's Brain Development Happens Before Age 5

The brain fine-tunes itself according to the input it receives from the environment. A child's senses provide information about their environment and experiences, and this input stimulates neural activity. This neural activity helps to shape the developing brain, with connections between neurons strengthening or weakening depending on the quality of the input. Overall, it is crucial to provide a nurturing and supportive environment for children during the early years of life to promote healthy brain development and set the foundation for future learning, health, and behavior. It is essential that parents, caregivers, and policymakers recognize the importance of supporting healthy brain development during the early years. This includes providing access to high-quality early childhood education and healthcare, promoting healthy nutrition and safe environments, and ensuring that families have the resources and support they need to provide a nurturing environment for their children.

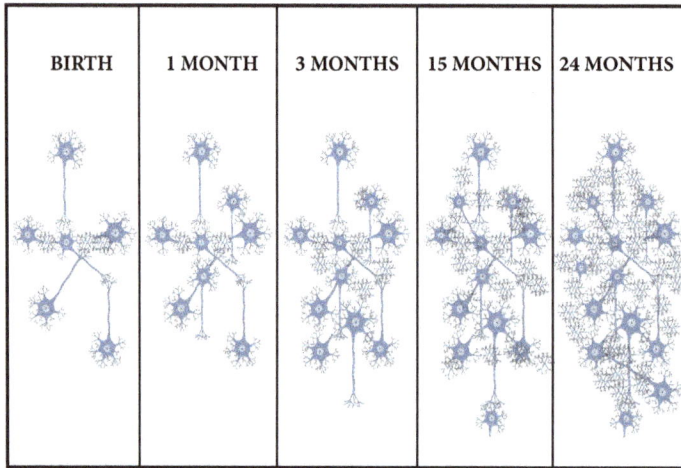

Neuron Connections from Birth. Early Positive Experiences Matter.

Sensitive Periods in Brain Development

There are periods during early brain development where the environment and experiences have the most influence, these periods are called sensitive periods (Center on the Developing Child, 2011b). The term 'sensitive period' is a term developed by the Dutch geneticist Hugo de Vries and later used by the Italian educator Maria Montessori. Sensitive periods are developmental windows of opportunity during which the child can learn specific concepts easier and naturally than at any other time in their lives. From birth until about age six, children learn from their environment without any conscious effort (Montessori, 1966). Children become skilled at numerous activities without formal instruction. They may not even be aware that they are learning. This occurs because it is very easy for children to acquire certain abilities during a specific sensitive period.

However, once a sensitive period has passed, it will be hard for a particular skill or ability to be obtained easily and naturally. At this point, the skill or the ability must be formally taught, and it will take a great deal of effort to learn and will not be as readily acquired by the child as it was during the sensitive period.

A sensitive period is an inner urge that drives a child to make certain developmental milestones (Montessori, 1966). Sensitive periods give a direction to the unconscious powers that children have. Every basic essential human characteristic is established utilizing a sensitive period, like spoken language and movement for example, but not written language because it is not a basic human characteristic. Montessori identified five observable behaviors that characterize sensitive periods that can be seen in children. First, the child will be engaged in a clear activity with a beginning, middle, and end. Second, the activity will be irresistible to the child. Third, the child will return to the activity again and again. Fourth, the child will develop an emotional attachment to the activity. Fifth, the child will appear satisfied when the activity is completed. Sensitive periods are very important in a child's development.

The adults in children's lives must become aware of the sensitive periods, the stages of development, and children's actions to satisfy their needs. When the environment is not properly prepared for sensitive periods, the adult becomes the obstacle that causes frustration to the developing child. Adults must provide the proper environment based on what is needed for each stage of development and help children take advantage of sensitive periods and make the most of them while they last. For example, experiences during sensitive periods play an exceptionally important role in shaping the capacities of the brain for vision, hearing, language, and responses to social cues. Equally important to understand is that the brain does not compartmentalize development. Rather cognitive, emotional, and social capacities are inextricably intertwined meaning learning, behavior, and both physical and mental health are highly interrelated (Birth to Five Policy Alliance, 2011). One domain cannot be targeted without affecting the others. It is incumbent upon everyone who has the opportunity to touch the life of a child to understand their role in shaping the brains of very young children and to understand that a child's brain connections directly reflect the quality of care he or she receives early in life which can last a lifetime.

Due to the rapid growth of the brain in such a short amount of time, it is critical that everyone who is a part of a child's ecosystem seize the moment and capitalize on this time period to ensure proper brain growth from the very beginning because as the brain matures, it becomes harder to change. During the first three years of life, the relationships that children have with adults in their lives are crucial to the developing brain.

Caring and Responsive Relationships

Even though it's better for children to have early positive experiences, the brain always has the potential to change and grow if positive experiences are delayed. It is never too late to give a child positive brain-building experiences (Shonkoff & Phillips 2000). The brain needs a good foundation for all future learning to rest. There are more than 700 new connections formed in the brain every second in the first few years of life and those connections are formed through the interactions of genes and a baby's environment and experiences (Birth to Five Policy Alliance, 2011). Children's relationships with the adults in their lives are the most important influences on their brain development. Loving relationships and interactions with responsive, dependable adults are essential to a child's healthy development. These relationships and interactions begin at home, with parents and family, but also include childcare providers and other members of the community.

The Center on the Developing Child notes that "serve and return" interactions where adults connect with, talk to, and play with babies are crucial during the first few years of a baby's life. Serve and return is where adults respond to a baby and a baby responds back, like a ball in a tennis match. Serve and return games are important for building a child's brain. For example, copycat games build imagination and empathy, naming games build vocabulary and attention, and peek-a-boo games build memory and trust. Responding to a baby's needs early on and consistently also helps to develop the brain. For example, when a baby cries, the adult in his life should respond to the crying by acknowledging that the baby is in distress and may ask out loud, "Are you hungry?", "Let's see", "Is it time for you to eat?", "Is that why you are crying?" Speaking out loud is critical for language development even though the baby cannot speak back.

The adult may continue by saying, "Okay, let's get you something to eat. What are we going to eat today? I see green peas or orange carrots." As the adults prepare the food, they should describe what they are doing and allow the baby to watch and listen. When you describe what you are doing or name objects that the baby sees, you make important language connections in their brain, even before the child can talk or understand your words. For example, when a baby is gazing at his hands, an adult may say, "Yes, those are your hands." The baby is listening to voices, tone, and pitch as well as looking at body movements, and facial expressions. Equally as important, the baby is hearing authentic and meaningful language, which is important in building the baby's vocabulary. The baby is taking in everything that he sees and hears and is responding accordingly. After all, it is a two-way conversation.

The child will not respond with words but will respond by cooing, babbling, or with the movement of legs or arms. We have all seen babies communicate their desires at some point in time. For example, when my sons were babies, I would hold up one toy at a time to see which one they wanted. Immediately, I knew which toy they wanted because their eyes would widen, their cooing became louder, and their legs and arms would begin flailing. The excitement could not be contained. Early experiences and connections are fundamental to the wiring of the brain. I remember hearing older folks say, "Let that baby cry—crying builds their lungs" or "Don't pick up that baby every time she cries, you will spoil her." These types of statements are categorically wrong. The brain is hardwired to seek meaningful connections and if it does not receive them, it causes confusion and stress in the baby. From birth, young children serve up invitations to engage with their parents and other adult caregivers. Each of these little invitations is an opportunity for the caregiver to be responsive to the child's needs. Parents and caregivers who give attention, respond, and interact with the child are literally building the child's brain. It is so important to talk (using real words), sing, read, and play with young children from the day they are born or before, if possible. These activities give children opportunities to explore their physical world, in a safe, stable, and nurturing environment.

On the other hand, parents and caregivers who exhibit an ongoing, diminished level of child-focused attention that fails to support a young child's need for engagement, may have children who fail to thrive. Unfortunately, we live in an era where technology and social media are all-consuming. Adults spend hours per day on social media. Parents who use social media excessively are more likely to be distracted in their everyday parenting and; therefore, less likely to develop a strong attachment to their children. When parents pay more attention to hand-held electronic devices than to their children's safety and developmental needs, the phenomenon is called 'distracted parenting'. Scott (2014) defined distracted parenting as a pattern of behaviors that include hand-held technology use (and overuse), parental neglect of children's basic needs, breakdowns in meaningful and caring parent-child relationships, child endangerment resulting from parental distraction, and inconsistent attention to children's moral, intellectual, and social and emotional development. In other words, distracted parenting is when parents compulsively check social media sites and/or emails and how this habit affects their relationship with their children and their children's overall development. Parental inattention caused by the distraction of portable devices can contribute to developmental delays in speech and cognition, and lead to behavioral issues, such as temper tantrums, severe anxiety, and resistance to discipline.

In a study conducted by researchers at the Boston Medical Center, parents and other caregivers were observed interacting with children while dining at fast-food restaurants. According to the researchers, approximately 85% of the caregivers were consumed with their portable devices (Radesky et al., 2014; Nierenberg, 2014). When a child tried to gain the caregiver's attention, the common reaction of the caregiver was irritation. In one case, a woman physically pushed her son away from her when he took her face in his hands, hoping to divert her attention from a tablet. In this respect, parents are present, but their attention is absent. The problem with the results of this study is that distracted parents communicate to their children that the priority is not them. A child of a distracted parent may be unable to communicate with peers and adults, manage their emotions, appreciate others' perspectives, address basic life problems, or feel a closeness to others.

Psychologist Eileen Kennedy-Moore (2014) suggests that when children try to get the attention of their parents and they are unresponsive or react harshly, it teaches children that relationships are one way. Parent-child bonding begins early on as a newborn gaze into her mother's eyes seeking to learn about the world. Very young children learn about the world largely through face-to-face interactions, vocalizations, and touching. This is how children develop language skills (Alexander, 2014), and distracted parenting may harm the parent-child bond by depriving children of parental interactions and responsiveness. There is nothing inherently wrong with using hand-held devices to engage in social media, texting, or talking. The problem is the overuse of the devices at the expense of children. The brain craves attention from parents and caregivers. When the brain does not get what it needs, children may experience developmental delays, which is another reason why we see disparities in children when they enter school.

Practically Speaking

Similar to what occurred in the study, I remember being in the checkout line at a grocery store behind a woman who was talking on the phone with her child sitting in the cart. I would guess that the child was about two years old and his mother was in her twenties. During the entire time that we were in line, and we were in line for a while, the mother was on the phone engaged in a heated conversation using a few colorful words within earshot of her child. The child had a box of pasta in his hands and was trying to gain his mother's attention. He called out to her, kicked his feet on the back of the cart, and tapped her several times. Finally, the mom turned around abruptly and slapped the child's hand down as he was tapping her to get her attention. Then in a raised voice, she told him that she was on the phone, again using some choice words. The mother turned her back and continued her conversation. Of course, I moved a little closer and engaged in conversation with the little boy. I described and pointed to the pictures, letters, and words that appeared on the box. When I stopped, he clearly wanted more interactions as he pointed to different items on the box for me to name. I continued to engage with him, and he just smiled (of course he pointed to the same thing over and over again). I shared this example not to judge the mother, but to point out the missed opportunities that she had to engage with her son. He was exposed to language and vocabulary at the time, just not the kind that could benefit him academically. I do not know if the exchange or limited interactions between that mom and her son was the exception or the norm, but for so many children, it is the norm, which is a problem for language and vocabulary development.

Parents are busy. They are juggling a lot and may not have the time to give their children the interactions and attention they need to grow and develop. However, developing language and vocabulary skills are free early on, only costing us time. If we do not put in the time in the beginning, it will cost in the end with children struggling to read, becoming disengaged with school, placement in special education, participation in costly intervention programs, heightened frustration, and eventually increased delinquency, truancy, and dropout rates, all of which are costly, either financially or emotionally. To give children the opportunity to be productive contributing members of society, we must put them on the right path early and ensure that they are prepared for academic success.

Attachment

Another aspect of brain development is the ability of a child to form secure attachments from birth. John Bowlby, a British Developmental Psychologist linked early infant separation with the mother and later maladjustments (Cassidy et al., 2013). This eventually led to Bowlby's attachment theory. Attachment is a strong disposition to seek proximity to and contact with a specific figure and to do so in certain situations, like when frightened, tired, or ill (Rosmalen et al., 2016). According to attachment theory, infants need a consistent nurturing relationship with one or more caregivers to develop into healthy individuals (Music, 2017).

Responsive caregiving in the earliest weeks of life leads to reciprocal connections between the brainstem, limbic system structures, and the prefrontal cortex (Leerkes & Zhou, 2018). Attachment theory is about how the earliest caregiving experiences shape the structure and connectivity of the developing brain (Carroll, 2019). A child's brain architecture depends on the establishment of positive relationships. The Center for the Developing Child at Harvard University found that young children experience their world as an environment of relationships, and these relationships affect almost every aspect of their development including intellectual, social, emotional, physical, and behavioral. The quality and stability of children's human relationships in the early years lay the foundation for a wide range of later developmental outcomes that include self-confidence, sound mental health, motivation to learn, achievements in school, the control of aggressive impulses, resolving conflicts in nonviolent ways, knowing the difference between right and wrong, and having the capacity to develop and sustain friendships (McLear et al., 2016).

Mary Ainsworth was an influential researcher who collaborated with John Bowlby and was the first to create a research protocol to define and assess the attachment relationship between children and their mothers. The Strange Situation Protocol (SSP) tests how babies or young children respond to the temporary absence of their mothers. Ainsworth created four attachment types: securely attached, anxiety-ambivalent, avoidant, and disorganized. In a secure attachment, there is a warm and loving bond between parent and child. The child feels loved and cared for and develops the ability to form healthy relationships with others. Children with secure attachments are active and demonstrate confidence in their interactions with others. Anxious-ambivalent children tend to distrust caregivers, and this insecurity often means that they explore their environment with trepidation rather than excitement. They constantly seek approval from their caregivers and continuously observe their surroundings for fear of being abandoned. Children who develop under the avoidant type of attachment have learned to accept that their emotional needs are likely to remain unmet and continue to grow up feeling unloved and insignificant. They often struggle with expressing their feelings and find it hard to understand emotions.

Disorganized attachment is a combination of avoidant and anxious-ambivalent attachment. Children with this type of attachment often display intense anger and rage and may break toys and behave in other volatile ways. The SSP protocol became known as the gold standard for identifying and classifying individual differences in infant attachment (Cassidy et al., 2013). Conversely, parental unavailability or unresponsiveness during early development may contribute to developmental delays and serious psychological issues. If the caregiver is consistently unresponsive and insensitive to the infant's cues, infants lose their secure base of emotional balance and develop early mental health problems, such as aggression, withdrawal, and negative emotions (Lee et al., 2013). Children with attachment issues may suffer from high stress, hostility, attention deficit hyperactivity disorder (ADHD), or reactive attachment disorder (Music, 2017). Insecure attachments in the first few months of life may have harmful effects on children's cognitive, socio-emotional, and behavioral development. Teachers in preschool and elementary schools have children in their classrooms exhibiting the four different attachment types: securely attached, anxiety-ambivalent, avoidant, and disorganized. Forming a secure or insecure attachment early in life is another reason why children may have different experiences when they enter school. Signs of attachment issues may vary depending on each child. Some children may have profound and obvious problems, and some may have very subtle problems. It is important to note that early signs in infants and toddlers often resemble signs and symptoms similar to ADHD and autism (Perry, 2013).

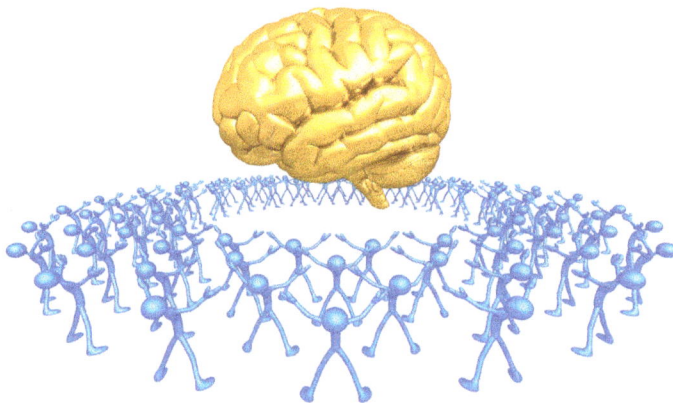

It Takes a Village to Build a Child's Brain.

Signs of attachment issues from the Help Guide

- Infants who do not make eye contact, smile, or reach out to be picked up, or infants who do not coo or make sounds, follow with their eyes, or show interest in interactive games or toys. Additionally, infants who spend a lot of time rocking or comforting themselves may be experiencing attachment issues.

- Developmental delays may surface in fine and gross motor, language, social, and cognitive development.

- Odd eating behaviors are common in children with attachment issues. They may hoard food, hide food, or eat as if there will be no more meals. In addition, they may have failure to thrive, rumination (throwing up food), or swallowing problems.

- Children may exhibit immature and bizarre soothing behaviors. They may bite themselves, bang their heads, rock, or chant. These symptoms will increase during times of distress or threat.

- Children may exhibit a range of emotional problems including depression and anxiety. Since attachment is important for survival, children with attachment issues may seek any type of attachment for their safety.

- Children may model adult behavior, even if it is abusive. They have learned that abusive behavior is the "right" way to interact with others. This may cause problems in their social interactions with adults and other children.

- Aggression is a major issue with children experiencing attachment issues as well as cruelty because these children lack empathy and have poor impulse control. They really do not understand or feel what it is like for others when they do or say something hurtful.

Practical Applications for Parents and Caregivers

- Nurture, hold, rock, cuddle, and engage in gentle physical contact with infants.

- Be responsive, do not ignore cries or needs. Make feeding time special by holding them close and talking to them, and making bath time and diaper changing fun and loving experiences.
- Communicate, even though they cannot talk back. Consistently practice the back-and-forth exchange that occurs in communication. Smile and get excited when babies smile back. Also, self-talk is a good tool to use, which is talking out loud so that the baby knows what you are doing.
- Encourage playtime and let babies explore the world either by holding them and walking around or by allowing enough space for them to crawl around safely.

Strategies for Toddlers

- Give them choices as much as possible.
- Try not to give many "no" responses.
- Encourage and support.
- Allow children to be independent when possible.
- Give hugs and encourage them to test their new skills but be there to support them and encourage them.

Strategies for Preschoolers

- Encourage them to make friends.
- Help them when they need it, but also allow them to be independent.
- Allow them to ask questions, explore, create, test ideas, and inquire about the world.
- Give hugs and positive words of encouragement and affirmations.
- Be consistent, establish rules and logical consequences for breaking the rules, and discipline rather than punishment, there is a difference.

Toxic Stress

According to Dr. Jack Shonkoff, a specialist on brain development from Harvard University, the experiences, genes, age, and environments in which young children live can have powerful effects on every biological system in the body, including the brain, cardiovascular function, immune responsiveness, and metabolic regulation. Unhealthy, stressed-out children are unable to learn effectively. Recurrent hardships and threats in early childhood can lead to the development of chronic diseases later in life, including cardiovascular disease, diabetes, and depression. These health concerns share a common association with elevated inflammation, which can be influenced by adverse experiences in childhood. Therefore, creating positive and nurturing environments for young children and their families are essential for their overall health and well-being, as well as their ability to learn and succeed in life.

Toxic stress is a prolonged or excessive activation of the stress response system that occurs without the buffering effect of supportive relationships. The effects of toxic stress on the developing brain can be long-lasting, leading to difficulties in learning, memory, and self-regulation. Examples of toxic stress include physical or emotional abuse, chronic neglect, caregiver substance abuse or mental illness, poverty, exposure to violence, and/or the accumulated burdens of family economic hardship without adequate adult support. Children who experience toxic stress may struggle with emotional regulation, have difficulty forming and maintaining healthy relationships, and are at higher risk for developing mental health disorders such as anxiety and depression. This kind of prolonged activation of the stress response system can impact the architecture of the brain. The more adverse experiences in childhood, the greater the likelihood of developmental delays and later health problems, including heart disease, diabetes, substance abuse, and depression. If the stress response system remains activated at high levels for long periods of time, it can have a significant wear-and-tear effect on the brain and other biological systems. The importance here is that mobilizing the body's responses to threats diverts energy away from the body's responsibilities to growth and healthy development. As a society, we have a responsibility to create environments that promote healthy development and prevent toxic stress. This includes policies and programs that support families and children, such as access to quality healthcare, safe and affordable housing, and high-quality early childhood education. We can also work to build supportive communities that foster strong relationships between adults and children, which can serve as a buffer against the effects of toxic stress.

The brain and other organs and systems in the body are a team each having specialized capabilities that work together for one common goal. Essentially each system "reads" the environment, prepares to respond, and shares that information with the other systems. How does this relate to reading and education in general? The environments we create and the experiences we provide young children before they turn five have major implications for later academic success. Early experiences are great predictors of early school success.

Children from low-income families may be particularly at risk for poor brain development as their early experiences may be stressful and even traumatic (Berkeley Media Studies Group, 2004). For example, homelessness occurs disproportionately among young children from low-income families which creates lasting effects on children's academic achievement, attendance in school, and stability in their school environment (Fantuzzo et al., 2012). Prolonged poverty and homelessness may have devastating effects on the brain. Genes and experiences help to shape the quality of the brain's architecture and they dictate which circuits and connections are used frequently. The ones that are used the most will become permanent and those that do not will fade away through the pruning process. This is extremely important because without caring adults to provide the experiences that the brain needs, children could be at risk for mental illness, and academic and developmental delays.

A major area of concern for students experiencing homelessness is social and emotional development. Children who are homeless are often disconnected from their social support systems which include family, peers, and neighborhoods. These early disruptions can trigger problems in developing cooperative learning in the classroom which is important for academic and social development. Because the developmental domains are so interrelated, children having problems in the social and emotional domain, often have problems in other developmental domains. Another specific issue related to poverty is vocabulary skills. Dr. Laura Colker is an early childhood author, lecturer, and trainer with over 40 years of experience. She wrote an article on the word gap in 2014 for the National Association for the Advancement of Young Children. Dr. Colker found a significant difference between the vocabulary of children from low-income families and their more affluent peers. One reason for this is that children in families living in prolonged poverty do not have a lot of language stimulation or supportive talk. This is important in that vocabulary development during preschool is related to later reading skills and school success in general.

In addition to academic problems, children experiencing homelessness and living in poverty may be at risk for other problems such as malnutrition, mental illness, hearing and vision impairments, poor housing conditions, unsafe neighborhoods, family stress, fewer learning resources, and the lack of cognitive and linguistic stimulation (Roseberry-McKibbin, 2012). The brain is most flexible early in life to accommodate a wide range of environments and interactions that it may encounter; however, that flexibility will not last forever. We may not have the ability to change all the sources of stress in a child's life, but it is possible to fix some of these issues by providing quality early childcare experiences and preschool programs where staff act as surrogates for children who are experiencing difficulties as a result of the stress. However, it is easier, more effective, and less expensive to build a child's brain right from the beginning.

Resiliency

How does one child experience severe adversity and bounce back into a well-adjusted and relatively healthy adult with a positive outlook on life and a sense of optimism that things will get better while another child who experienced the same adversity ends up psychologically damaged, with a host of mental and physical issues? The answer to these questions may very well rest in what psychologists call resilience. Resilience is the ability to adapt well to adversity, trauma, tragedy, threats, or even significant sources of stress (Pizzolongo & Hunter, 2011). Significant adversity is different from normal every day manageable stress. We know that some stress and challenges are necessary to build resilience. The adversity mentioned in relation to resilience is prolonged and severe adversity. Resilience can transform potentially toxic stress into tolerable stress.

Two key components of resilience that must be present to label someone as resilient are significant adversity and positive adaptation. Resilience is important because it is the human capacity to face, overcome, and be strengthened by or even transformed by the adversities of life. Resilience helps children (and adults) overcome adversity with courage, skills, and faith. A vital and productive society with a prosperous and sustainable future is built on a foundation of healthy children who grow to become contributing members of the economy and the community (National Scientific Council on the Developing Child, 2015). To have strong communities, we must take the health and well-being of our children seriously and help families reduce the risk factors that could jeopardize healthy families and ultimately communities.

Early childhood is an important window for understanding and promoting resilience. Some children develop resilience through natural processes, while others need help. The early years hold great promise for interventions to prevent and reduce risks, boost resources, promote competence, and build a strong foundation for future development. Children can better cope with the negative effects of adversity with the help of protective factors which are conditions in families and communities that, when present, increase the health and well-being of children and families. Protective factors serve as buffers, support, or coping strategies that allow parents to effectively care for their children, even under extreme stress.

Ways to Foster Resilience
- Allow for large portions of the day for children to play. Resilience is all about mastering the environment. Shonkoff, states, "Resilience is building skills and strategies to be able to cope, to deal with your own reactions, and to have some control over what's going on around you, which happens through play." A child's natural ability to play is one of the most important strategies we have developed to build resilience in the face of adversity.
- Teach problem-solving skills. Children tend to bounce back quicker if they can solve their own problems rather than having adults solve them.

They must be given the time to find strategies that work.

- Build empathy. Children can build resilience by becoming more understanding and by seeing other people's perspectives. A good way to promote empathy is by using good children's literature and social stories. Social stories use photographs and descriptive words to guide children through real-life situations. They help children understand expected behaviors, work through interpersonal issues, practice conflict resolution skills, and help understand new perspectives.

- Build secure attachment from infancy. Children need at least one caring adult with whom they can attach to in order to offset the challenges they face each day.

- Help children see "what's next" which simply means to look forward. Using past experiences as lessons for current or future experiences helps children bounce back and become more resilient.

- Create rich environments with plenty of stimulating and positive input, which grows the brain.

- Identify and build on a child's strengths by offering activities that require practice and repetition to improve skills and their sense of accomplishment.

- Provide opportunities for do-overs. Help children realize that mistakes are not fatal but opportunities to grow.

- Support children in conflict resolution. Practice resolving conflicts with children. For example, "There is only one toy truck left and both of you would like to play with it. How do we resolve this problem?

- Build social skills by acknowledging children's efforts. For example, "I liked how you found something else to do when your friend was shouting silly things."

- Help children identify emotions. For example, you may say to a child who may be feeling sad, "It's okay, we all feel sad sometimes… What's making you feel sad?"

- Give choices whenever possible. Children need to feel empowered and sometimes in control. Therefore, you may ask a child if they want an apple or an orange.

- Give appropriate consequences for undesirable behavior. For example, if a child hits, you may say, "Hitting is not okay, so we have to leave the playground now. I know you want to stay but you hurt your friend." The important thing here is to follow through. Do not give idle threats to children.

Practically Speaking

As a parent, I was never informed about the developing brain and how my actions could ultimately shape my children's brains. I was taught in school and read a lot about healthy pregnancies and how to care for a developing fetus, but no one explained that even in utero, babies are learning. I knew they were growing but learning was something that I was not informed about. My pediatrician checked the health status of my babies regularly, provided immunization shots accordingly, and checked for developmental milestones. However, never once did anyone mention anything about the magnitude of brain development, the impact of positive experiences with trusted and caring adults, how to build language skills even though your child can't talk, sensitive periods in the brain for key experiences, the importance of secure attachments, or the impact of toxic stress. I never knew the power I had to shape the brain of my children.

What I know about the brain and early development, I learned in graduate courses or through the hundreds of books and research studies that I read over the years. It would be beneficial for new parents and parents in general to be armed with specific information on growing the brain. Intuitively, many parents provide positive experiences for their growing infant (they may not have any idea about the connections to the brain), but unfortunately, too many parents do not, no fault of their own as babies do not come with an instructional manual.

Understanding the role of early experiences in shaping brain development can be a powerful tool for parents and caregivers. Providing positive experiences, connecting with young children, and providing an enriched and engaging environment are all positive things to do, but understanding why those things are good and connecting them to brain development might incline parents to be more focused and intentional in all they do for their children from the beginning. I am a firm believer in knowing the 'why' behind what I do because it brings a level of understanding which leads to intentional and purposeful actions. So much happens in a child's life before he or she steps into an elementary school classroom and those experiences determine the range of school preparedness for each child. Given the importance of the architecture of the brain and the connection to later learning, medical professionals must become more transparent and intentional with families about brain growth and development. The medical professionals have done a good job discussing the effects of smoking, alcohol, drugs, stress, and proper eating habits on the developing fetus. The campaign for reducing harmful toxins in the body while pregnant benefited children, families, and communities. We have a solid idea of what not to put in the body to protect the developing fetus, but now we must make the case for what parents, caregivers, and teachers must do to support brain development in utero and during the first few years of life. We must position ourselves to put all children, specifically children of color from low-income families, on track for academic and social, and emotional success from the beginning. There must be a sense of urgency in assisting adults with understanding the importance of the first few years of life and the significant role of parents and caregivers. Pediatricians and the health care system are a part of the child's ecosystem and have an indirect role in shaping the child's learning brain. Yes, it takes a village to raise a reader.

A Community Campaign for Growing the Brain
- Offer classes to help parents raise their children from the inside out. There are negative connotations for Lamaze classes and parenting classes for some families from disadvantaged communities, which may prevent them from attending. Some families may not have the funds to attend, some

may not have an interest in attending, and some do not believe that they need a class to teach them how to raise children. By changing the title of the class, adding brain development to the content, and making the class free for all, more families may want to attend. If the course was provided by the pediatrician or OBGYN (virtually or in-person face-to-face), it may encourage more families to attend as well.

- Create webinars, infomercials, and pamphlets that focus on the adults' role in shaping the developing brain. Adults put a lot of faith in their doctors; therefore, if the information is played about growing the brain while they are waiting for appointments, it may generate interest in the subject. Additionally, pediatricians could add growing healthy brains to their wellness checkups for children.

- Medical health professionals could collaborate with family and child community organizations to provide child development seminars that include a unit on the developing brain.

- We must create more undergraduate and graduate courses that focus on the learning brain and school success. When educators have knowledge of the brain and learning, they can ensure that the curriculum, interactions, and environment are supportive.

- Support education reform that invests significant resources in training, recruitment, and retention of childcare professionals responsible for children under five years old. Establish rigorous credentials to ensure sufficient knowledge and skills to teach and nurture with the brain in mind. A child's first five years are too important to leave unattended.

- We need to change our views of childcare professionals and respect them for the significant services they provide for the youngest and most vulnerable learners. We need legislation aimed at ensuring quality in childcare programs, especially in low-income communities.

- Expand the health curriculum in schools to include healthy brain development while the fetus is in utero and for the first five years of life.

"Even though 90% of a child's brain development occurs before age five, the brain is not immediately designed to read. We must teach it to read. The environments we create for our children and everything that they experience creates a resume. That resume will dictate going forward whether reading will be a challenge or not. Developing specific skills early on will help develop the reading brain and lay the foundation for more advanced reading skills to come."

- Dr. Jacquelyn Bobien-Blanton

Chapter 4

Language Development

Say What?

Language development is an amazing, natural, innate process that babies are born knowing how to do. Research tells us that a baby can respond to sounds 10 weeks before birth by learning the mother's voice and the sound pattern of the language she speaks prenatally (Hans & Hans, 2014). Astonishingly, babies are born with the capacity to hear and distinguish all the sounds in all the languages in the world. What an amazing ability!

Yet, we often take this ability for granted. One of the first windows of opportunity for language comes early in life. Acquiring language is a product of active, repetitive, and complex learning. During the first five years, stimulation of language development is essential because the brain is developing new nerve cells and making rapid connections between these cells to serve the function of expressive and receptive language. The child's brain is learning and changing more during language development in the first six years of life than during any other cognitive ability he or she is working to acquire. The sensitive period for language is tremendously influenced by parent-child interactions.

The brain is hard-wired to distinguish many sounds in different languages. The sounds a language uses are called 'phonemes', and English has about forty-four of them. Between four- and eight-months-old, infants show a preference for speech patterns that are typical of their own language. In other words, infants learn which phonemes belong to the language they are learning, and which do not. The ability to recognize and produce those sounds is called 'phonemic awareness', which is important for children learning to read. By six months of age, infants are no longer able to recognize sounds that are not heard in their native tongue, making it difficult for them to pick out sounds they have not heard repeated often. The type of experiences that children have early on are critical for the development of language. Lack of stimulation during this time could delay or slow down the progress of language development. Parents and caregivers play critical roles in influencing the cognitive, language, motor, and social and emotional development of children. Advances in technology have afforded us the opportunity to physically see differences in a child's brain that has been appropriately stimulated, versus one that has suffered a lack of stimulation (Gilmore et al., 2018). Connections that are not stimulated by repeated experiences fade away.

Children need repeated, positive experiences for language to develop. Parents and other adults can support children's brain development for language during the sensitive period by providing experiences that allow children to practice emerging skills. Experiences include opportunities for babies to engage in face-to-face interactions, hear the language spoken often, listen to the written word read aloud, and practice associating objects with words. These activities provide free, language-rich experiences for the baby without undue stress or overstimulation. By starting early and working efficiently, children will build a firm foundation in language that will be able to support more enriched and expanded language in the later grades, which is critical for reading proficiency.

Language and the Brain

The brain is divided into two parts, the right and left hemispheres, and then further divided into six lobes. These lobes include one frontal lobe, one occipital lobe, two temporal lobes, and two parietal lobes. The frontal lobe is the site for complex executive functioning behaviors (e.g., reasoning, planning, and problem-solving), and contains an important site for speech production and phonological processing called Broca's area. The occipital lobe is the site of visual perception and processing. The two parietal lobes are for perceiving and integrating sensory and perception information as well as comprehending oral and written language. The two temporal lobes contain sites critical to auditory processing as well as language comprehension in Wernicke's area. Basically, the Broca's region is responsible for speech output or expressive speech and the Wernicke's region is responsible for speech input or receptive speech (University of Arizona, 2011).

Models of language circuitry identify Wernicke's area as a significant point of convergence for receiving and integrating associations from throughout the brain, and this convergence is important for language comprehension and production. For example, how a person sees an object and then names it, suggests that visual images are conveyed to Wernicke's area and then transmitted to Broca's area where speech output is organized and coordinated into motor commands for the major articulators such as the lips, tongue, and teeth (Turnbull & Justice, 2017). As you may imagine, this is significant for reading. In other words, the ability to comprehend written language relies on the same language circuitry that is involved in spoken language production and comprehension. When we read, the visual information from the written text is first processed in the visual areas of the brain and then transmitted to Wernicke's area for language comprehension. The information is then relayed to Broca's area for the organization and coordination of speech output into motor commands. Children's early neurological development is a continuous process that builds on things learned before. It is imperative for parents, caregivers, and teachers to understand how the brain works, and the importance of the environment and adult interactions, in giving children a good early head start. Language is a complex shared system of symbols that has structure, rules, and meaning. Language starts long before children begin formal instruction. Further, later reading success is powerfully affected by the skills children acquire during their early years (NICHD Early Child Care Research Network, 2005). Children's language abilities at any given time play a powerful role in shaping their subsequent reading success. For example, children's language comprehension at three years old is predictive of various language and reading measures at seven years old. Also, preschoolers' language skills are associated with third- and fourth-grade reading comprehension. Further, kindergarten vocabulary is a strong predictor of fourth-grade and seventh-grade reading achievement. Children with stronger early linguistic skills tend to outperform children with underdeveloped early linguistic skills and this gap appears to widen over time (Casey, 2010). In fact, socioeconomic status (SES) disparities in language skills may already be present in infancy. Characteristics of the home environment, including literacy resources and parent-child interactions partially account for disparities in language when children enter preschool and elementary school.

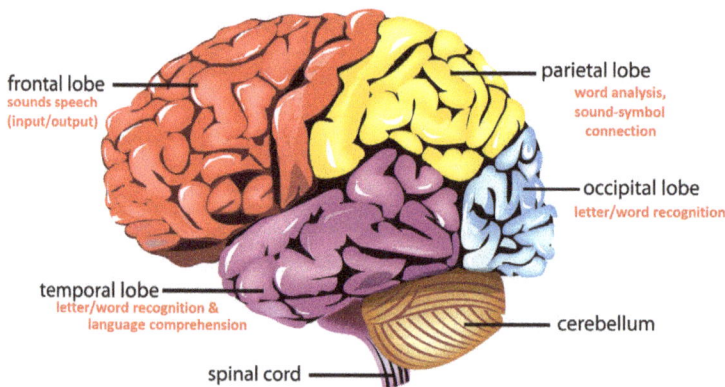

frontal lobe
sounds speech
(input/output)

parietal lobe
word analysis,
sound-symbol
connection

occipital lobe
letter/word recognition

temporal lobe
letter/word recognition &
language comprehension

cerebellum

spinal cord

The Reading Brain

Stages of Language Development

There are three stages of language development that occur in a familiar pattern. As children learn to speak, understand, and communicate, they follow an expected series of milestones as they begin to master their native tongue. However, individual children will progress at their own pace, and interestingly enough, all children, no matter which language their parents speak, learn language the same way.

Stage One - Learning Sounds

- Description - As previously mentioned, infants are born with the ability to hear and distinguish all the sounds in all the languages in the world. During this stage of language development, infants learn which sounds belong to the language they are learning. This stage is critical in the development of language skills and is important for later reading achievement. The best way to promote language development in this stage is for parents to talk to their infants. Babies learn by experiencing and listening to the world around them; therefore, the more language they are exposed to, the better. Additionally, sensory-motor integration is fundamental to school readiness. Infants should have the opportunity to spin, crawl, roll, rock, and tumble. Lyelle Palmer of Winona State University documented significant gains in attention and reading from these stimulating activities. Proper neural pathways are formed when children engage in these sensory-type activities. Who would have ever thought crawling and reading were connected?

- Milestones – At birth, infants can already respond to the rhythm of language and they can recognize stress, pace, and the rise and fall of the pitch. At four months, infants can distinguish between language sounds and other noises (e.g., a spoken word and a clap). At six months old, infants typically begin to babble or coo, which is the first sign that they are learning a language. During this stage of language development, cooing provides vocal practice and entertainment to infants, and aids in the development of motor control over vocalizations. It is important for parents to respond to the coos and babbles, which will encourage and stimulate infants to continue exploring and practicing.

Stage Two – Learning Words

- Description – During this stage of development, children are learning how the sounds in language work together to make meaning. For example, m-ah-m-ee or mommy refers to the person who feeds me. Most of what we say to children at this point is just a stream of sounds. They are not learning words exactly, rather they are learning morphemes, which are the smallest meaningful part of a word. Morphemes are important for phonics in both reading and spelling, as well as in vocabulary and comprehension. The best way to develop language in this stage is to read often to children and have child-centered conversations with them because infants learn best within a social context (Hans & Hans, 2014). Also, another way to encourage communication is to mimic the infant's babbling and cooing and repeat it back to them. Additionally, parents should mirror the infant's facial expressions and describe their actions as well as narrate what is happening around them.

- Milestones – At eight months old, infants recognize groups of sounds and can distinguish when one word ends and when another begins, but they are still learning what these words mean. Infants are likely to comprehend the meaning of words related to their everyday experiences like food and body parts. At twelve months, children can attach meaning to words and once they do that, they can begin to build their vocabulary. At eighteen months, children are practicing communicating and learning how to use the words they are learning. Also, during this stage of language development, children recognize the difference between nouns and verbs.

Stage Three – Learning Sentences

- Description – During this stage of development, children learn how to create sentences and will put words in the correct order. Children also learn the difference between grammatical correctness and meaning. For example, Noam Chomsky the eminent American theoretical linguist, cognitive scientist, and philosopher believed that the basic structures of language are already encoded in the human brain at birth. He created an example to show the difference between grammatical correctness and meaning with this sentence, "Colorless green ideas sleep furiously." According to Chomsky's theory, children will know that although the sentence is grammatically correct, it does not make sense. To promote language development in this stage, adults must model good speech habits by speaking clearly while looking at children, giving them a chance to talk and avoid interrupting them while they are talking and add on to what they say to give them an idea of more complex ways to articulate their ideas and requests. Finally, ask a lot of questions and encourage children to ask questions. Most importantly, keep talking to each other, use varied vocabulary, and pronounce words clearly without leaving off the ending. This is not the time to use slang or the made-up words that our grandparents used as this will be confusing to children once they enter school.

- Milestones – At 24 months old, children understand the basic sentence structure and can use nouns, verbs, and pronouns, for example. They also know the right order of words in a sentence and can create simple sentences like "Me cookie?" meaning "May I have a cookie?" By 30-36 months, approximately 90% of what children say is grammatically correct. The mistakes they make are usually adding 'ed' to irregular verbs to form past tense (i.e. I falled down instead of I fell down). Children have not learned the exceptions to the grammatical rules to form the past tense. By three years old, children continue to expand their vocabulary and develop more complex language.

While children do not pass through these stages at the same pace, most children do progress through all three in typically the same order. One major concern is the quality of language experiences and exposure in each stage of development for children of color from low-income families. Parental income, education, occupation, and the quality of the neighborhood, typically predicts children's cognitive ability and later academic achievement. Socioeconomic status (SES) disparities in cognitive outcomes appear throughout the lifespan and as early as the second year of life. Overall, children from low SES homes tend to experience less linguistic, social, and cognitive stimulation and more stressful events, including abuse and neglect, food insecurity, and environmental toxins. These experiences are likely to have specific effects on distinct brain structures, leading to disparities in neurocognitive skills and achievement (Brito, 2017).

Unfortunately, many children of color from low-income families do not get proper exposure to the amount of language and the quality of language needed in this early stage of development and may lag behind their developing peers when they enter preschool. Specifically, language input for children can be traced back to their home environment and the amount of language exposure. The quality of maternal speech helps to explain the difference in expressive vocabulary growth between children from low SES families and children from high SES families (Brito, 2017). Additionally, children from low SES families encounter less language and engage in fewer complex conversations relative to their more advantaged peers. Parent-child interactions provide context for language exposure and help to shape children's language development.

Tips for Helping Children Learn Language
- Reinforce infant communication through responsive and enthusiastic interactions. Encourage toddlers to use new vocabulary and appreciate their approximations.
- Use infant-directed speech characterized by short, simple sentences spoken in a pitch that is higher than what you would use with older children.
- Repeat words often, point to objects, and focus on nouns and verbs. For example, a mom may say to her infant while looking out the window, "Oh look, Hannah, there's a truck. It's so big. It's red. Where is the truck going?"
- Give infants opportunities to explore and reflect on their discoveries: "Gloria, you found the red ball!"

- Be aware of both verbal and nonverbal communication cues. Respond promptly to infant and toddler needs. Use language to identify and label emotions, and remember to speak with instead of at or to the child. These early exchanges set the stage for future communications.

- Read out loud whether with infants or school-age children and share new words, adventures, and discoveries that good literature and common environmental print offer.

Home Literacy

"Learning starts in infancy, long before formal education begins, and continues throughout life." Magda Gerber

Children typically learn early language and literacy skills at home. In most cases, what children learn before school is influenced by the people in their homes and their communities. Parents are their children's first teachers and as such will shape the environment in which language and literacy skills will develop or not. A home literacy environment refers to literacy-related interactions, resources, shared reading, language, print awareness, and attitudes that children experience at home that promote literacy development (Strickland, 1990). Children engaged in home literacy activities will have a stronger literacy foundation when they enter preschool (Clay, 1989).

Children in a literacy-rich home environment are submersed in rich language and social interactions every day. Consequently, children who are not exposed to rich home literacy environments, lack the needed skills to succeed in a preschool program. The reasons children enter formal school settings with varied foundational literacy skills can be traced back to their home literacy environment. Risk factors that may impede children from experiencing rich home literacy activities include poverty, parents' educational attainment, parents holding multiple jobs, depression, toxic stress, single-parent households, parents' reading habits and how often they read to their children, and the availability of print resources and materials. Home literacy activities influence the development of early literacy skills, which influences reading success.

A rich home literate environment may include formal and informal literacy interactions. Formal literacy interactions refer to activities in which parents directly teach reading or promote print-related skills at home like name writing, and teaching letter names and sounds. Formal literacy interactions are generally associated with "code-based" literacy skills (Hamilton et al., 2016) or automatically associating letters to their respective sounds. Informal literacy interactions include a variety of activities in which parents read to their children or direct their attention to print in the environment, such as advertisements or street names.

Shared book reading is an interactive way of reading books aloud with children that gives them the opportunity to become active participants in the reading session, thus providing a meaningful experience that stimulates learning. The frequency of shared book reading has consistently predicted children's expressive and receptive vocabulary because of the social interactions and the extended conversations that parents and children have while reading and discussing stories. Shared book reading is also linked to print knowledge and comprehension-related skills. Books provide a rich context for language that children may not encounter in everyday speech interactions thus providing learning opportunities that support language and literacy depth. Informal literacy practices are closely associated with the development of broad oral language skills, including vocabulary knowledge, and indirectly linked with later reading comprehension. According to the Literacy Project Foundation, children who are read to at least three times a week are twice as likely to score in the top 25% of reading assessments. Second, the number of books in the home correlates significantly with higher reading scores for children. Third, children's books contain 50% more rare words than primetime television. It is important to read to children early and often.

Furthermore, shared book reading with children helps develop their mental imagery skills. Understanding a story text requires the reader to form a mental representation of that story. Mental imagery is the ability to create images of a story in your "mind's eye" and contributes to successful reading comprehension (Boerma et al., 2016). Kemp's study, published in the journal Pediatrics in

2015, used functional MRI to measure brain activity in 3- to 5-year-old children while they listened to stories. The researchers found that children who had more exposure to reading at home showed greater activity in brain areas involved in mental imagery and narrative comprehension, suggesting that reading to young children can help develop these important cognitive processes. The study also found that the strength of the connection between these brain areas predicted the children's reading skills two years later, suggesting that early reading exposure may help set the stage for later reading success. Overall, the study highlights the importance of early reading experiences for children's cognitive and literacy development.

As children progress in their reading skills and transition from books with pictures to books without pictures, they rely more on mental imagery to understand and remember the story. Research suggests that mental imagery skills are closely linked to reading comprehension (Kemp, 2015), and children who struggle to create mental images while reading may have difficulty understanding the meaning of the text. On the other hand, children who are skilled at creating mental images while reading tend to be more successful readers. Parents and caregivers can support children's mental imagery skills by engaging them in conversations about the books they are reading. Pausing after a few sentences and sharing the mental images you created while reading can help children develop their own mental imagery skills.

Encouraging children to visualize the characters, settings, and events in the story can also help them engage with the text and build their comprehension skills. Less researched and less understood is the impact of indirect parent involvement on early literacy skills. Social learning theorists Albert Bandura suggested that children model behaviors they observe often from key people in their lives; therefore, exposure to parents engaging in literacy activities may be related to an increase in children's participation in literacy behaviors. This was evident in my home.

Practically Speaking

I read a lot, and most times, I read multiple books at a time (seldom do I read one book completely before engaging in another). I have books all over the house, and I always carry a book wherever I go; especially when I have various appointments that require me to sit in waiting rooms. Depending on the book, I will sometimes underline or write in the margins of the book while reading. I never thought that my behaviors were indirectly influencing my son.

One evening, my son (about 3 years old) came running into the living room excited about a story he was reading (picture reading of course), and I was excited that he was going to share the story. He jumped on the couch, opened the book, and was ready to 'read.' When he opened the book, I nearly had a heart attack. I was shocked and surprised to see that he used a red marker and underlined every word in the book (of course they were not even straight lines) and had squiggly marks in the margins. Mind you, it was a library book! In my head, I flipped! He never said a word about the marks in the book (he saw me writing in my books so, in his mind, that was what he was supposed to do). My son just wanted to share the story with me; he was not concerned about the marks, but I was—and on the inside, I was fuming. I knew that he observed me reading from time to time, but I never thought he would actually mimic underlining in storybooks.

I jumped up and went racing to his room to check the other library books and sure enough, he 'underlined' several library books. I was heated; we were looking at a hefty library fine. However, I could not get mad at him because he only did what he saw me do and, in the end, I was happy that he was engaged in the reading process even though we had to pay the library fine. I shared that memory to point out that children are watching, they are always watching even when we think they are not. They are little sponges and will absorb everything, the good, bad, and the ugly. Our son is an avid reader today and yes, he still underlines and writes in his books as well. Sure enough, parents' level of engagement with literacy activities may have an indirect influence on children's interest and participation in literacy behaviors.

"*Childhood is a journey in life and not a race, all the flowers of all the tomorrows are in the seeds of today.*" Puspa Sivan

Practical Application

What can you do?

1. Arrange a meeting with your child's teacher to inquire about how early reading skills are being developed. If not mentioned, discuss the following:

   a.) Experiences with reading aloud sessions.
   b.) Phonological awareness.
   c.) Meaningful environmental prints found around the classroom.
   d.) Letter and sound recognition.
   e.) Meaningful discussions with peers and the adults in the classroom.

2. Give a child the opportunity to build their vocabulary and language skills by asking them to do one or all of the following:

   a.) Have them draw a picture and tell a story associated with that picture.
   b.) Select random photos from a magazine or online and ask the child to make up a story based on that photo.
   c.) Put various objects or items into a basket for children, and then ask them to select one and create a story about it.

3. Build background knowledge and vocabulary throughout early grades with the following.

   a.) Share primary source photos from different events and various locations around the world with your children. Ask them to analyze the photos to practice observational skills. Have them make inferences and predictions. Are they able to write a caption for the photo showing critical thinking skills? If not, help them.
   b.) Consider mentoring a child or sponsoring various experiences for them (i.e., museum, camp, aquarium, zoo, botanical gardens, hiking, beach, planetarium, sporting events, visual and performing arts, etc.).

Chapter 5

Preschool

"The Great Equalizer"

The years from birth to five years old are critical for developing foundational skills. During these years, children develop linguistic, cognitive, social, emotional, and regulatory skills that predict later functioning in many developmental domains (Bakken et al., 2017). The National Institute for Early Education Research confirmed that children who start school before kindergarten are more likely to do well academically and socially throughout their educational careers and are at less risk for reading difficulty than children who do not attend preschool.

Research shows that preschool attendance not only places children on a path for literacy achievement but will also reduce reading intervention costs as more children who attend preschool read above expected first-grade literacy benchmarks compared to children who did not attend preschool (Haslip 2018).

Several factors present a strong rationale for investing in children's learning before age five. First, preschool prepares children academically and socially for elementary school, which is important because many children from disadvantaged communities already have noticeable gaps in these two areas in comparison to children from advantaged communities (Bakken, et. al., 2017). The assumption is that by mastering foundational skills in preschool, children will get more out of the K–12 educational experience. Second, the brain is especially sensitive to environmental enrichment in the years before children enter elementary school. Early experiences in children's homes, communities, childcare settings, and preschool programs interact with children's genetic makeup to shape their brains. The brain grows rapidly during this time and then pruning takes place based on environmental inputs; therefore, the time before children enter elementary school is best for positive stimulus. However, for optimal brain growth, the early environments that children are exposed to, particularly preschool programs must be of high quality.

Investing in preschool benefits all children but particularly children who may be at risk for academic difficulties. Preschool contributes to helping children develop critical school readiness skills needed for long-term academic and personal success (Fuhs et al., 2018). Of the country's 8.1 million preschool-aged children, nearly four million live in or near poverty. Preschool is referred to as the 'great equalizer' for children who may not have experienced a literacy-rich home environment thus placing them at risk for academic challenges when they enter elementary school. Despite the preponderance of research supporting the positive impact of quality preschool programs, it remains out of reach for many low to moderate-income families. The average price of center-based care in the United States accounts for nearly 30% of the median family income, and only 10% of childcare programs are considered high quality (Workman & Ullrich, 2017). According to the Center for American Progress, publicly funded programs such as Head Start, Early Head Start, and state preschool programs are primarily targeted at low-income families, which leaves moderate-income families out. Many moderate-income families have challenges trying to find a quality child care center within budget. Consequently, many settle for lower-quality child care centers, which can be detrimental to the child's overall development.

Limited funding for quality early programs severely hinders access. This lack of access to quality child care centers perpetuates the achievement gap, evidenced by the fact that only 48% of low-income children are ready for kindergarten, compared to 75% of moderate-or high-income children (Workman & Ullrich, 2017). Children from low-income families may have less access to books, fewer shared reading experiences, fewer educational games and toys, fewer literacy activities, and less exposure to out-of-the-home educational experiences like attending zoos and museums. Attending a preschool program staffed by warm, knowledgeable, and responsive adults can help mitigate the impact by offering a safe and predictable learning environment that fosters children's overall development thus creating short- and long-term gains for children.

For example, children enrolled in quality programs are less likely to need special education services during their K-12 years; are less likely to commit juvenile offenses, and are more likely to graduate from high school. In the long term, children are more likely to be employed and less likely to be dependent on government assistance. The positive effects are larger, and more likely to be sustained, when programs are of high quality. Early attendance in preschool matters. Preschool is an inclusive and consistent idea of schooling that links educational leaders, community members, educators, and parents (Manigo & Allison, 2017). In a joint effort to close the achievement gap, these stakeholders play significant roles in increasing parental involvement and engagement, improving school readiness skills, and nourishing social-emotional development in young children. By working together, they strive to ensure a great future for children and build an educational system where failure to read by third grade is nonexistent. While more and more children have access to preschool each year in the United States, the focus must shift from access to quality because the potential of preschool can only be realized if programs are of high quality.

The need for high-quality preschool has never been greater. The experiences and interactions children have in these early years significantly affect brain development and help to establish the foundation for future learning. Increasingly, children are growing up in families where all available adults are working. When it comes to preschool programs, quality is critical. Every day, millions of American families drop off their young children at childcare or preschool. With millions of young children enrolled in childcare or preschool, it is clear that early learning programs, and the people who work in them, have a critical role to play in child development; a role that complements parents. While there are many reasons why parents choose a particular program, there is one thing that is the same: As parents walk away from the classroom in the morning to start their own day, they hope that they have made the right decision and that their child will have a rich and fulfilling day, supported by loving and affectionate caregivers/teachers. Unfortunately, many low-income families often have very few childcare options and limited ways of knowing the quality of care their child is receiving. There is a critical need to better understand the components of high-quality programs to ensure future policies and legislative initiatives adequately support access to quality for all families no matter their income level.

Elements of a High-Quality Preschool Program

(adopted from the Learning Policy Institute Developmentally Appropriate Standards and Curricula)

Developmentally Appropriate Standards and Curricula
- Quality preschool programs are based on early learning standards that address multiple domains of development including cognitive skills, social & emotional, and physical to ensure children are growing holistically in all areas. Standards and curricula must be developmentally appropriate for the age of the children. The National Association for the Education of Young Children (NAEYC) defines developmentally appropriate practice as methods that promote each child's optimal development and learning through a strengths-based, play-based approach

to joyful and engaged learning. Standards and curricula must be aligned from grade to grade in the early grades. Finally, curricula must be implemented to provide fidelity for children to experience the full benefits of attending preschool.

Developmentally Appropriate Child Assessments

- Informal assessments are used to monitor the individual performance and skills of children. It helps to measure progress without any grading criteria. The best examples of informal assessments for young children are observations and children's authentic work. The purpose of informal assessment is to monitor children's progress and identify strengths and opportunities for growth. Assessment practices in quality preschool programs are well-planned, effective, and used to improve instruction and program planning. Teachers observe children throughout the day during the regular daily routine and write anecdotal notes based on what they see and hear in all areas of development over time. Teachers use the information gathered to monitor child progress and to plan lessons that meet the developmental needs of all children.

Knowledgeable Instructional Staff

- Quality preschool programs ensure staff are knowledgeable about how young children learn and develop. Nearly all programs with a track record of success, including the state-run public preschool program in New Jersey require teachers to have a bachelor's degree and a state-endorsed teaching certification with a specialization in early childhood education. Well-prepared teachers have the knowledge and skills to provide engaging interactions and classroom environments that support children's learning. This period of development is too important not to have well-trained, knowledgeable, and skilled teachers. Retaining quality staff is also important, particularly for teachers who are not a part of the public school system. Increasing compensation and requiring certification credentials may reduce turnover, as well as attract quality candidates. We know that the years prior to entry into an elementary school set the foundation for all future learning. Caregivers play a critical role in shaping the brains of children in the early years. They are surrogate parents who provide appropriate and powerful early experiences and interactions that children will carry for the rest of their lives. We ask a lot from caregivers, yet we pay them peanuts. We would never ask a doctor to perform surgery for minimal wages or a lawyer to take on a case for minimal wages, yet we ask caregivers who are responsible for future lawyers and doctors to work for minimal wages. To change the narrative for young learners, caregivers must be compensated for the important work they do.

Developmentally Appropriate Physical Learning Environment & Movement

- According to Epstein and Hohmann (2012), young children need space to use materials, explore, create, solve problems, and to move around in. Children also need space to store their belongings, display their inventions, and to play collaboratively. These spaces must be arranged and equipped to promote active learning. Active learning means giving children space and time to explore materials using their senses either by themselves, with peers, or with adults. "The active learning philosophy holds that learning is a process of engagement with resources and ideas, involves people solving problems and discovering new things, contributes to personal development and social change, occurs sometimes in isolation but more often in collaboration with others, and ignites creativity" (Piscitelli, 2000, p. 40). The learning environment must include engaging and developmentally appropriate materials that are arranged to promote independence and exploration based on children's different stages of development. The indoor environment must have toys that spark the imagination and also allow for exploration and problem-solving opportunities. Learning centers must be clearly defined areas that are arranged for children to have easy access to materials and engage in independent and self-directed learning activities. They should encourage interactions, allow for opportunities for role-playing, and promote literacy skills.

- In addition to the indoor learning environment, children need access to outdoor space where they can move their bodies and engage with the natural world. Children who play outdoors regularly have more active imaginations, lower stress levels, and greater respect for themselves and others (Workman & Ullrich, 2017). At a time when sedentary behaviors are rising among children and youth, any effort to engage them in physical movement is a good thing. Kindergarten and preschool in the U.S. have become more academic, very structured, assessment-driven, and restrictive of children's movement. Children learn by experiencing the world using all their senses and the restriction of movement, or passive learning, impedes the experiential learning process. Movement allows children to connect concepts to action and allows them to learn by trial and error. Movement and activity in young children can help increase memory, perception, language, attention, emotion, and even decision making (Zeng et al., 2017). When language is combined with movement, learning increases by 90%. When children develop gross motor skills such as walking, running, and jumping, they are also developing their cognitive abilities (Carson et al., 2015). Most likely because the cerebellum, which is the main region of the brain responsible for motor skills, is also connected to our visual processing, spatial perception, and cognitive abilities (Cairney et al., 2016). This means that when children use their brains to perform physical movements, they are also exercising and developing many of the same neural pathways that serve cognitive performance and vice versa. Physical movement also causes more oxygen, water, and glucose to travel to the brain, which assists with cognitive activity as well. It is simple, children tend to absorb newly acquired skills better while moving their bodies rather than simply observing.
- It is perfectly acceptable to allow children to move their bodies while they are learning as long as they are safe and do not impede the learning process of others. We hear all the time that children learn differently, yet we provide one way for them to learn and one way for them to show what

they have learned. Differences in the way we learn are called learning styles, which are complex ways for learners to efficiently and effectively perceive, process, store, and recall what they are attempting to learn (James & Blank, 1993). In full disclosure, according to Dr. Polly R. Husmann, a professor of anatomy, cell biology, and physiology at Indiana University School of Medicine, tons of research surfaced that debunks learning styles. However, I firmly believe that there are preferred ways that students and adults, for that matter, understand, remember, and process information. Teachers presenting class material in multiple ways is not a bad thing if it benefits children. Learning preferences are neither good nor bad, they simply exist. As a former teacher, I realize that it is nearly impossible to prepare lessons for each learning style or preference. I also do not believe in placing unnecessary pressure on teachers to present lessons in multiple ways every day and for every lesson. That would be a major challenge for anyone. However, if we know that students are struggling, then we owe it to them to try to help them connect with what we are teaching and make accessing the information easier. Just like adults, some children have a preferred way in which they take in and process information.

- Boys and girls are different, developmentally, biologically (wiring of the brain), and socially; therefore, they behave differently, which in turn, plays an important role in their learning preferences. For boys, in general, their cerebral cortex is dedicated to spatial awareness, and they have less oxytocin and serotonin, which are the hormones that help to bring a sense of calm (Zamosky, 2011). Boys have higher levels of testosterone and dopamine in their blood, which are known to increase impulsive behavior and physical activity (McDougal, 2007). Boys are typically more visually acute, able to think in three dimensions, and more proficient at gross motor skills (Restak, 1979). As you might imagine, gross motor skills, which are more prevalent in boys, are closely aligned to a kinesthetic learning preference. This simply means that children prefer a multi-sensory learning environment for deep learning as they learn through 'doing' (Davis, 1998). A kinesthetic learner is someone who needs to be actively engaged in their learning. They are 'tactile' learners who use movement, testing, trial and error, and a non-traditional learning environment to retain and recall information. Kinesthetic learners do not like sitting still for long periods of time. It's not a wonder that boys are often characterized as unable to sit still in class. Boys of color tend to prefer receiving information kinesthetically and in other ways (Ransaw, 2016). However, they are too often told to sit still, which devalues them as a learner. When we do not provide multiple ways for children to access knowledge and skills, within reason, like standing or manipulating objects while learning, we take away their opportunity to engage in the learning process and make learning unnecessarily harder for them. Additionally, when teachers do not attempt to provide multiple ways for children to learn, it is disrespectful, disingenuous, and leads children to believe that there is only one way to learn. More importantly, children believe that something is wrong with them if they do not learn like everyone else, which can be devastating to their self-esteem.

Indirectly and unconsciously, we can set children up for failure; we are not all the same and we do not all learn the same way. Teachers may find more success with struggling students if they pay attention to learning preferences as much as possible; however, in a classroom of 25 or more children, this is extremely difficult. Therefore, it is important for young children to be competent in all learning preferences including auditory, visual, tactile, and kinesthetic (Cozens, 1999), which is called "style shift", where teachers achieve a balance between teaching strategies and children's unique learning preferences (Ransaw, 2016). This is important because according to Dr. Husmann, the downside of relying on one specific learning preference is that as children get older, they may convince themselves that they can only learn in one way, which can create barriers to their own learning process. I advocate for teachers to use their experience, knowledge about their students, and differentiation of instruction to help students access content. For, example, if a teacher presents information one way, but has a student who is struggling, the teachers should present the information in another way to support the child in helping him/her gain access to the information. In this respect, I advocate shifting to a learning preference when there are students who are struggling to understand and to gain knowledge.

Practically Speaking

We all know children who fidget, wiggle, and squirm. We also know students who are angry, frustrated, irritable, and will shut down with academic pressure. When children do not get enough recreation or active play, they enter schools with underdeveloped bodies for learning. During the pandemic, children did not have many opportunities to move their bodies in ways that they did before the pandemic. I have always stressed that coming out of the pandemic, education will look different. In eleven large urban school districts in North Carolina, things are looking very different for many elementary school students. The districts implemented Brain Body Behavior (B3) for their elementary school students, which combines physical activity with sensory skills and core subjects. In other words, children are physically moving their bodies while using sensory skills including vision, touch, smell, taste, balance, and movement of the head (vestibular), and movement of muscles and joints (proprioception) to learn new material or practice old material in core content areas.

B3 allows children to engage in interactive activities while staying engaged in the lesson. According to one principal in a North Carolina school, B3 "increases a student's ability to engage which also increases their ability to make better cognitive moves and retain information that they're learning." B3 was developed for professionals and educators who work with children daily. B3 works with task cards that include an image and written cues on how to perform the activity. Each card also identifies which sensory system(s) (visual, tactile, proprioceptive, auditory, or vestibular) the activity may help develop when performed consistently. B3 activities are designed to be easily implemented in any classroom, hallway, media center, small tutor room, mobile unit, gymnasium, on a stage, or in a principal's office. Additionally, many of the B3 activities require little to no equipment. In B-3 spaces, one could find taped patterns in hallways, directional stickers along the hallways, wall charts on the walls, and mobility programs to keep children learning throughout the entire school day. Children are paired, which changes every time they enter the B3 lab giving them the opportunity to work with others, practice waiting their turn, and cheer for and encourage someone else. These activities target the whole child by boosting academic performance and social-emotional well-being. According to a North Carolina principal, initially, the children spent one hour in the B3 lab each week; however, teachers are encouraging movement in their lessons every day now. This is an innovative idea to help children move their bodies while they are learning. If we expect different educational outcomes for children, we must look at learning differently.

Ongoing Professional Development, Support, and Collaboration

- Professional development is essential to improvement in education. Through professional development, teachers gain specific, concrete, and practical strategies that directly relate to their instructional practice. When teachers do not get what they need, professional development initiatives typically fail. Guskey (2002) pointed out that one reason why professional development fails is that administrators do not understand how the process of change occurs in teachers. He found three major outcomes for professional development programs including change in the classroom practices of teachers, change in their attitudes and beliefs, and change in the learning outcomes of students. The importance of facilitating change is the sequence in which these outcomes most frequently occur. According to Guskey, significant change in teachers' attitudes and beliefs occurs primarily after they gain evidence of improvement in student learning, not before as so many professional development programs believe. The crucial point that Guskey found is that it is not professional development per se, but the experience of successful implementation that changes teachers' attitudes and beliefs. Teachers believe it works because they have seen it work, and that experience shapes their attitudes and beliefs.

- Hirsh's research highlights the importance of effective and sustained professional development for teachers. According to her findings, sporadic and disjointed professional development can be ineffective and meaningless, whereas continual, collaborative, and on-the-job learning can have a stronger impact on both teachers and students. Hirsh's research also suggests that the duration of professional development is an important factor. Longer-term efforts that involve applications to practice and coaching support are more likely to be successful. This suggests that one-off workshops or trainings may not be sufficient to create lasting changes in teacher practice. In addition, Hirsh found that teachers are more likely to try instructional improvements that have been modeled for them. This suggests that professional development should involve opportunities for teachers to observe and learn from their peers, as well as receive coaching and feedback on their own practice.

- Cooper's research in 2004 suggests that the beliefs and values that teachers hold about teaching before they enter the classroom can have a profound impact on their teaching practices. However, he also notes that well-designed professional development can have a positive impact on teachers regardless of their prior beliefs or values. To effectively implement new strategies, skills, and concepts learned through professional development, teachers must first understand the underlying research and rationale for the new instructional approach. This requires a deep understanding of the theory and principles behind the new approach, as well as the evidence supporting its effectiveness. Observing a model of the new approach in action, with immediate feedback and follow-up support, can also be helpful for teachers to gain confidence and proficiency in the new strategy. However, Cooper notes that the biggest challenge in implementing new approaches is often not learning the new skill, but rather putting it into practice consistently and effectively. Finally, Cooper suggests that teachers may be more likely to change their beliefs about teaching once they see evidence of success with their students. This echoes the findings of Guskey, who found that teachers are more likely to adopt new practices when they see evidence of their effectiveness in improving student learning outcomes.

However, it takes time for teachers to learn a new skill and then implement it to fidelity. If teachers do not see success upfront, they tend to abandon the newfound practice and revert to business as usual before they see growth in children. These two principles present a "catch-22": to internalize a practice and change their beliefs, teachers must see success with their students, but student success is very hard to come by initially, as learning new skills takes several attempts to master. Why is all this important in the learning process and specifically to reading outcomes? When teachers enter their classrooms, they bring with them their culture, values, morals, beliefs, and experiences, whether good or bad. They control what children learn and how they learn, which impacts how children feel about themselves as learners. Student populations are becoming more and more diverse, and teachers need professional development, support, and opportunities to collaborate with peers to ensure instructional practices are culturally responsive, respectful, appropriate, and meet the needs of all children. Teaching is hard work that cannot be accomplished in a silo. If teachers are limited and bound to their own thinking, habits, and practices without the benefit of constructive feedback to improve their practice, we end up with teachers perpetuating the status quo when change is desperately needed to alter the academic trajectory of so many children.

Meaningful Family Engagement
- Family engagement in schools is defined as parents and school personnel working together at all levels to support and improve the learning, development, and health of children. The Global Family Research Project, led by researchers at Harvard University identified relational trust,

mutual respect, and cultural responsiveness as pillars of systemic family engagement. Parents are the experts on their children. Educators and administrators play a major role in shaping family-school partnerships. When schools elevate families as true partners and the experts they are, children benefit significantly. When districts support families through thoughtful, equitable policies and programs, it encourages broader community engagement that can help to enrich student learning and optimize student success. For example, schools that promote family engagement have children with quality work habits, higher grades, faster rates of literacy acquisition, better school attendance, lower rates of delinquency, and higher rates of social competence and academic growth (Cai et al., 1997).

- Quality preschool programs create and sustain family partnerships that are ongoing, built on respect, and promote, accept, and celebrate the cultures of all families. They focus on supporting family well-being, student achievement, and strengthening parent-child relationships. Family engagement opportunities that are successful work because children see the positive connection between home and school. However, despite the benefits, there are many common barriers to parental engagement. These barriers may include busy work schedules for parents, childcare needs, unwelcoming school staff, fears that adults at school will treat their children differently if they raise a concern (especially if they are undocumented), lack of trust, lack of information about involvement opportunities, lack of guidance on how to communicate with the school, bad past experiences, feelings of intimidation, negative perceptions about school and staff, and low feelings of belonging to the school community (Baker et al., 2016).

"Play is often talked about as if it were a relief from serious learning. But for children, play is serious learning. Play is really the work of childhood"
Fred Rogers

Play-Based Learning

A major characteristic of a quality preschool program is play. Play is the tool young children use to explore the mysteries of the physical and social worlds and to understand how the world works (Gopnik, 2012). Through the phenomenon of play, children develop and learn as they participate in activities in every area of the classroom. Play affords children the ability to improve their language, social, physical, math, science, and thinking skills. The development and enhancement of these skills promote their self-esteem (Sussman, 2012). Essentially, play is a tool used to develop skills. As Shonkoff stated, play is the way children learn to master their environment. They learn to try things out and test things, including limits. It's driven by curiosity, and an inborn drive to master the environment.

Emily Cross, a professor in the School of Psychology at the United Kingdom's Bangor University emphasized the importance of active learning for children. Active learning involves engaging the learner in doing, moving, acting, and interacting, which may change the way the brain works and accelerate the learning process. In contrast, passive learning, such as lectures or simply completing classwork and homework, may not stimulate brain activity in the same way and may be less effective for promoting learning. To facilitate active learning, it is important to allow children to use their current knowledge, senses, materials in their environment, and peers to master skills in their own way. This approach is consistent with the views of Piagetian and Vygotskian theories of child development, which emphasize the importance of hands-on exploration and social interaction for learning (Leong & Bodrova, 2012). Play is also an important aspect of learning, as it promotes the development of strong language and vocabulary skills (Toub et al., 2016). Through play, children learn by listening to instructions, stories, or typical conversations between others, which can increase their literacy skills and other areas of academic learning.

Research on play in early learning classrooms emphasizes the important role it has in promoting cognitive, linguistic, and social development in young children. Bergen (2001) found a positive correlation between children's pretend play and their cognitive abilities, as children who engage in pretend play tend to develop receptive and expressive language and mental representation at approximately the same time in their development.

Role-playing and imagination, which are often incorporated into play, can invite complex social interactions such as joint planning, negotiation, problem-solving, and goal seeking. Through these interactions, children learn to think, plan, and use their own skills to interact with others and temper their own behavior. Welsch's (2008) research shows that literature-based play, such as dramatizing stories from children's literature using story-specific props like flannel board pieces, puppets, dolls, and other props, can be a powerful tool for promoting cognitive, linguistic, and social development. This form of play can help build children's vocabulary, comprehension, imagination, and oral skills.

Music's (2017) research highlights the important developmental milestones that children need to reach in order to engage in symbolic play. Symbolic play involves a child's ability to use an object to represent another object, and it is an important indicator of a child's cognitive and linguistic development. The first milestone involves a child's ability to have an action symbolize another action. For example, when a child places himself imaginatively in another role like a doctor or teacher. This type of play involves the child using their imagination to pretend to be someone else and can help develop their social and emotional skills. The second milestone involves a child's ability to have one idea stand for another idea. For instance, when parents or older siblings play with children and scaffold their learning. This type of play involves the child using their imagination to connect concepts and can help develop their language and communication skills. The third milestone involves a child's ability to decontextualize where one object can stand for another. For instance, when a child uses a pot for his drum. This type of play involves the child using their imagination to see beyond the physical attributes of objects and can help develop their problem-solving skills.

The last milestone involves a child's ability to stand outside of reality and just imagine. For example, a little girl pretending to be a mermaid, and her bedroom is the ocean. This type of play involves the child using their imagination to create an entirely new world and can help develop their creativity and critical thinking skills. Overall, symbolic play is an important aspect of a child's cognitive and linguistic development. Through symbolic play, children can develop their abstract thinking skills, which are the foundation for language development. By providing opportunities for symbolic play, parents and educators can help support children's cognitive and linguistic growth.

Most researchers agree that play is fun, flexible, voluntary, and intrinsically motivated; it involves active engagement and often incorporates make-believe (Sutton-Smith, 2001). Free play is an unstructured, voluntary, child-initiated activity that allows children to develop their imagination while exploring and experiencing the world around them. It is spontaneous play that comes effortlessly from children's natural curiosity, love of discovery, and enthusiasm (Music, 2017). It is not the kind of play that is controlled by adults, and it does not include passive play, such as sitting in front of a video game, computer, or television; nor does it include playing with electronic toys (Iannelli, 2021). True free play involves any kind of unstructured activity that encourages children to use their imagination, such as playing with blocks, dolls, and toy cars. Quality preschool programs spend a large portion of the school day engaged in free play. The amount of time in free play or guided play decreases as children get older but must be offered through second grade at least.

Practically Speaking

I remember when my sons were young, they could not watch television during the week and were only allowed to watch for a few hours on the weekend. One son used the time while away from television to create elaborate play themes and turned items found in our home into unimaginable toys. One evening, I called him for dinner, and he came flying down the steps with the most creative superhero costume (I think it was a superhero) that he made himself. He had a regular sun visor on his head turned backward, a belt across his chest (not sure what that represented), a small blanket around his neck for a cape, swimming goggles on his eyes, a sports mouth guard in his mouth, and a metal rod (not sure of the original purpose or where it came from) that he used as a weapon of some sort. Picture that! He looked a mess but he had hours of fun and everything that he used was free and found around the house.

The other son would play choir for hours. He would line up the stuffed animals on the kitchen floor and pretend that he was the choir director. He would sing the lead part and the choir part while directing, unbelievable. He was only three or four years old, but he memorized the songs from church and would perform them at home with his "choir." My husband and I would get in trouble if we walked in front of the choir. It was all good when he had the stuffed animals lined up because we could see the choir, but it was a different story when the choir was invisible! One day, he had his towel (to wipe his face when he began to sweat), pretend piano, and music stand. He was singing and having a good time, again he had both parts, the lead singer, and the choir. Well, my husband crossed in front of his choir and the boy had a whole fit and a major meltdown. I thought something happened to him. I rushed to the kitchen and asked what happened, he said, "daddy stepped on my choir." Of course, my husband said he didn't see the choir, so our son had to show him where the choir was located. Now, some people might have decided to have their child tested at this point, but not me. I was thinking about all the skills this young child was developing like, memory, presentation, recall, language, literacy, imagination, creativity, tone, rhythm, stamina, and resilience; all through play. Children need many similar opportunities to not only develop symbolic play skills but to build their imagination and creativity skills. To be successful and to compete in the 21st century global economy, children need these skills to think outside of the box to effect change.

Guided play maintains the child-directed aspects of free play but adds an additional focus on learning goals through adult scaffolding (Weisberg et al., 2016). It offers an opportunity for exploration in a context specifically designed to foster a learning goal. As such, it features two crucial elements: child agency (the child directs the learning) and gentle adult guidance to ensure that the child progresses toward the learning goal (Iannelli, 2021). Guided play is a successful pedagogical tool for language development. For example, infusing vocabulary instruction into guided play fosters word learning for preschoolers; especially those from disadvantaged backgrounds (Toub et al., 2016). Guided play represents an 'enhanced discovery' approach to learning that increases children's knowledge through immediate meaningful adult feedback (Alfieri et al., 2011).

For example, take two children playing in the block center and engaged in building a structure but it keeps falling and they cannot figure out why. The teacher joins in and gently guides them by asking questions about what they have tried and what they will try next. The teacher may ask the children if they tried a new approach or strategy. She may bring up the issue of sturdy foundations. Children will incorporate the feedback from the teacher as they continue building and figuring out how to keep their structure from falling. Play helps children discover causal relationships through informal experimentation. Light scaffolding, when needed, prevents frustration and enables children to engage in longer periods of playful experimentation, thus increasing their attention span.

Practically Speaking

When our children were very young, we spent a lot of time in the car with them, and it was during those rides that we had the best times. I can remember one son wanting to drive. He found a frisbee and every time it was time to go somewhere, he would run and get his frisbee. His frisbee was his "steering wheel." He would climb in the back seat, put his seat belt on, and just like that, he was in his car ready to go. We couldn't leave the house, even when we were in a rush, without his "steering wheel." To extend and guide his play, I asked many questions to stimulate language and vocabulary development.

For example, I asked about his destination, how he would get there, landmarks he would see, what he would do when he arrived, and who would be at the location. We talked about the traffic signs, whether he would be making a right turn or a left turn, and I also pointed out different landmarks or different types of buildings, homes, and cars. In retrospect, this is the son that has a good sense of direction and is well traveled. Eventually, we made upgrades to our play scenario and incorporated maps. Before navigation systems on our phones and in our cars, we had to use real maps, or we had to print out directions from MapQuest. Of course, my little one, at the time, needed a map as well. Children want to be like the important people in their lives. Therefore, he created his own map with all kinds of colorful squiggly lines that only he knew the significance of.

Now before we began road trips, we had to have the steering wheel (frisbee) and a map. He would put the map in the seat pocket in front of him and we were off. I would always ask him about his map and his travel plans. One time, we arrived at our destination, and I was about to turn the car off, but my little guy yell for me to stop. Of course, I stopped and turned around, thinking something was wrong with him. He was safe, but he had not parked his car (go figure). So, I had to wait for him to park safely before turning off my car and exiting. Talk about restraint, it took everything in me not to laugh because he was so serious. During these times, it wouldn't be unusual to see frisbees and maps in the back seat pockets of our cars. After one son graduated from this type of play, the other one picked up where he left off and improved the "steering wheel." He placed both frisbees together to create a better version and eventually, he retired the frisbee invention and moved up to a "real" steering wheel with a horn, breaks, and buttons for signaling left and right. Talk about taking things to another level! He was the gamer with a need for speed. I'm sure he was pulled over a few times for speeding. When he was younger, he would get upset with me if I didn't tell him ahead of time when I was turning so that he could put on his turn indicator. I could always tell when I failed to tell him when I was turning because I would hear him making screeching sounds while he was turning and speeding at the same time. He would then remind me that I neglected to tell him that I was turning (picture that). There was always an adventure during our car rides, but these play scenarios were enriched with language and vocabulary opportunities that were captured through play.

These great benefits of play are unfortunately vanishing for children who attend schools with high minority and poverty percentages. For many children, recess and play opportunities have been reduced or eliminated and replaced by additional instruction in core content areas (Milteer & Ginsberg, 2011). This is ill-advised as opportunities for play and social and emotional learning enhance school engagement. There are a host of factors that have led to a decrease in play time, including a greater emphasis on academic preparation, working parents with little free time, more electronic screen time, less time spent playing outdoors, limited access to outdoor play spaces, and adults' lack of understanding of the purpose and power of play. As Dr. Peter Gray, Professor of Psychology at Boston College wrote in the *American Journal of Play,* children are designed, by natural selection, to play and wherever they are free to play, they do. However, the last half-century has seen a decline in the opportunities to play. Precisely how fast and how much the opportunity for real free play has declined is difficult to quantify, though historians suggest that the decline has been continuous and great and has led to lasting negative consequences (Iannelli, 2021).

Despite the overwhelming research on play, it is still absent in many early childhood classrooms; especially kindergarten classrooms. Dramatic play centers, block centers, and art easels, to name a few, were discarded long ago in many kindergarten classrooms. Young children are lucky if they get a small break during the school day. Many kindergarten teachers expect more from children than they did in prior years. Now that kindergarten has become more advanced, preschool is seen as prep time for kindergarten and unfortunately, skills that were once taught in kindergarten are now taught and expected in preschool. Currently, we have preschool programs that are highly academic and structured with limited to no time for play. Additionally, in many school districts, kindergarten serves as a gatekeeper, not a welcome mat to elementary school. Children who once used the kindergarten year as a gentle transition into school are in some cases being retained and not permitted to move on to first grade because they have not mastered skills that are not developmentally appropriate for them to master until first or second grade. The pressure that we place on young children is enormous, unhealthy, unnecessary, and may lead to disengagement in school altogether.

Of course, during the preschool and kindergarten years, teachers must teach foundational skills, but it must be done through hands-on experiences and within context for learning to stick. Unfortunately, this type of learning is not likely to become widespread, particularly in underserved communities, which does not align with how young children learn.

In the early years, we must consider memorable learning as opposed to memorized learning. Memorable learning is fun, exciting, enjoyable, relevant, meaningful, and held in children's memories for a long time. Memorized learning is disconnected from children, not relevant to them, repetitive, isolated, and typically not fun to children. Memorable learning will last forever while memorized learning may fade away. Researchers Lipsey et al. (2018) conducted a major evaluation of Tennessee's publicly funded preschool system. They found that children who attended preschool initially exhibited more "school readiness" skills when they entered kindergarten than did their non-preschool-attending peers, but by the time they were in first grade, their attitudes toward school had deteriorated. By second grade, their performance on tests measuring literacy, language, and math skills had dropped significantly compared to their non-preschool attending peers. Researchers posited that overreliance on direct instruction and repetitiveness were likely culprits. Children who are subjected to the same boring tasks year after year have understandably lost their enthusiasm for learning.

It is not so much what children learn in preschool because children can learn quite a lot if the environment and instructional practices are appropriate; rather, it is how they learn that makes the difference. They must engage in free play and guided play to develop holistically. They must have time to learn, grow, and find out who they are as learners and how the world around them works. Children need to be active participants in their growth process and teachers must be able to support them and scaffold learning as needed. Play is not a bad four-letter word; it is a good thing. The Science of Learning is clear, play is a wonderful metaphor for active, engaged, meaningful, and socially interactive learning. It prepares children to become social, caring, thinking, and creative citizens. Child-driven educational methods sometimes referred to as 'playful learning' are the most positive means known to help young children's development (Lillard et al., 2013). If we allow preschool children to experience free and guided play in a developmentally appropriate environment, they will thrive and will become well-rounded individuals with the skills needed to be successful in kindergarten and beyond.

Play is pleasurable, spontaneous, creative, and unpredictable. Whether it is noisy or quiet, messy, orderly, silly, serious, strenuous, or effortless, children find play deeply satisfying, challenging, enjoyable, and rewarding. While it is important to close the achievement gap, schools need to support social and emotional learning and academics at the same time to develop the whole child. We can balance academic achievement and play for our youngest learners. Let the children's laughter remind us of how we used to feel when we were children experiencing genuine playful moments. We must let those feelings propel us to do what is in the best interest of children so that they may enjoy those same feelings when they are older.

As policymakers at the federal, state, and local levels develop strategies to address the childcare crisis, they must simultaneously focus on the importance of quality. To increase access to quality programs for all children, it is critical that all stakeholders fully understand what quality looks like and what structures are needed to support it. Preschool is an important time for significant growth and development as important academic skills like pre-reading develop during this time. However, there are many children who do not experience quality preschool programs. Children who do not attend a quality preschool program may enter kindergarten with less developed skills than those who attend preschool. Positive stimuli received in the initial years have a great impact on the development of skills that are essential for academic success. Children who do not attend a quality preschool program that includes pre-reading skills, lack long-term academic advantages (Ansari, 2018). Skill acquisition is a cumulative process where early learning facilitates subsequent achievement (Heckman, 2008). Exposure to early literacy skills in preschool sets the stage for more advanced literacy skills leading to successful reading experiences in elementary school. Play is not separate from learning in early childhood; it is learning.

Early Literacy Skills in Preschool

The idea of early literacy was introduced by Marie Clay in the 1960s. It developed further in the 1980s to challenge the notion that children were not ready to become literate until they were older and more mature. Since then, early literacy has been recognized as a vital content area in the preschool curriculum with a strong research base supporting its use. Early literacy is everything children should know about reading and writing before they can read or write. These early skills include print awareness, print motivation, vocabulary, narrative skills, and phonological awareness. These important foundational skills are the building blocks for learning to read and write and will establish the foundation for advanced skills in reading and writing in the upper grades. Children who have acquired most of these skills will benefit more from the reading instruction they receive in kindergarten.

Children with deficits in their reading foundational skills tend to have difficulties with reading-related activities and are less likely to ever catch up. Additionally, they are at a higher risk of being classified and placed in special education, less likely to engage in reading-related activities, and less likely to be exposed to content knowledge and vocabulary than their more skillful reading peers (Cunningham & Stanovich, 1997).

Learning to read has long been held as a necessary ingredient for success in school and in life, which is why children are expected to have firm foundational literacy skills in the early grades. Literacy is a complex domain that is made up of many components and stages within the components making it one large developmental continuum. It is important to understand how literacy develops, how the components relate to one another, and what programs or practices promote lasting literacy skills for all children. There isn't one clear path for early literacy development, but rather a series of associated and concurrent experiences that result in the building of knowledge and skills related to the literacy process. Recognizing the stages of development within each component of early literacy is important in providing appropriate learning opportunities and scaffolded support for young children.

A child's success in reading depends on how much is learned about pre-reading at home or in early childhood centers before entering elementary school. Parents, caregivers, and preschool teachers are responsible for providing experiences that promote essential literacy skills. Emerging literacy skills are prerequisite skills that lay the foundation for more complex skills and can be grouped into two categories: constrained and unconstrained. Constrained skills are those that are directly teachable and fixed. For example, the 26 letters of the alphabet, or a set of 20 to 30 common spelling rules. These skills have a ceiling and young children can master them. Within the domain of constrained skills, there are predictive relationships, for example, phonological awareness predicts the ability to decode and spell. Once children master the constrained skills, they can accurately and automatically read many words, and thus successfully comprehend texts written at a second or third-grade level.

Unconstrained skills are particularly important for children's long-term literacy success (that is, success in outcomes measured after third grade). They are strongly predicted by children's socioeconomic status or their parents' educational level. Unconstrained skills are more difficult to teach in the classroom and more difficult to influence through classroom instruction because they are acquired gradually through experience. Unconstrained skills include vocabulary, grammar, discourse skills, and general knowledge of the world or background knowledge. Beyond third grade, children must be able to understand words rarely encountered in spoken language and they must integrate new information encountered in the text with relevant background information for successful comprehension. Vocabulary and background knowledge are unconstrained skills and are crucial to comprehension as the text children encounter become more complex. Knowing what the words mean and having some background knowledge relevant to the text are the strongest predictors of successful comprehension among students who have acquired basic decoding skills. Yet many classrooms in the early grades, particularly those serving children from low-income families, focus predominantly on constrained skills, which are easy to teach and easy to test. Children who do not develop age-appropriate literacy skills by the end of third grade are at high risk of academic failure (Adams, 1990; Mastropieri, 1999). Approximately 40 years of longitudinal research have confirmed that differences between high school dropouts and graduates can be identified as early as the third grade (Casey, 2010). Ensuring that teachers focus on constrained and unconstrained skills in early childhood classrooms must be a priority for reading proficiency.

High quality preschool classrooms expose children regularly to early literacy skills throughout the school day. As mentioned, the early literacy skills critical for reading success include **print awareness**, **print motivation**, **vocabulary**, **narrative skills**, and **phonological awareness**. Together these skills form the foundation for future successful readers.

"Children are made readers on the laps of their parents"
Emilie Buchwald

Print awareness is a child's earliest introduction to literacy. Print awareness is the understanding that written language carries meaning. It is the understanding that print is organized in a particular way. The foundation of all other literacy learning builds upon print awareness. Print awareness is typically divided into two primary categories: alphabet knowledge and concepts of print. Both categories contribute to awareness of how written language is constructed and used. Alphabet knowledge is the ability to recognize and name letters and corresponding sounds, known as the alphabetic principle, which is a strong predictor of later reading success.

Print concepts refer to the ability of children to recognize and distinguish certain features of print and how they work, such as: the layout of the text (front/back of the book), moving from left to right on the page, and differentiating between words and a picture (Strickland & Schickedanz, 2004). Inside and outside of school, children learn concepts about print. For example, they learn about print through reading aloud, talking, environmental print, road signs, or a shopping list. As with alphabet knowledge, concepts of print comprehension follow a basic developmental continuum. One major concept that comes from print awareness is that what is said, can be written, and then can be read.

"One of the greatest gifts adults can give - to their offspring and to their society - is to read to children." Carl Sagan

Print motivation is taking an interest in and enjoying books. A child with print motivation loves being read to, plays with books, and pretends to write. This is an important step towards being ready to read. Print motivation is not something that can be taught directly, but it is a skill that can be developed from birth based on related literacy experiences and routines that children are exposed to early on.

Children who enjoy books are more likely to want to learn to read, and to keep trying even when it is hard. The actions that adults display during shared reading promotes reading comprehension, linguistic expression, and reading models for children (Saracho, 2017). As children show an interest in reading, they may mimic the behaviors that adults display during shared reading experiences, which has been correlated with reading motivation (Holdaway, 2001).

One activity that needs special attention is reading aloud to young children. According to the Literacy Project (2019), reading aloud to young children is the single most effective thing parents can do to help prepare their children to succeed in school. Unfortunately, fewer than half of U.S. children ages five and under are read to every day, placing them at risk for reading delays and school failure. That same report found that 61% of low-income families have very few appropriate children's books in their homes. This limited access to books reduces literacy opportunities for preschoolers. Nationally, about half of the children between birth and five years old (47.8%) are read to every day by their parents or other family members. This reduced one-on-one reading time is significantly higher than children from high-income families.

Reading aloud to children stimulates their imagination and expands their understanding of the world. It helps them develop language and listening skills and prepares them to understand the written word. Reading aloud with children provides them with opportunities to actively engage with the text and allows teachers to scaffold children's understanding of the book's content and features. These experiences help to lay the foundation for later reading skills. According to Betsy Okello of the Notre Dame Center for Literacy Education, the research on the power of reading aloud is extensive and well documented. For example, research has shown that reading aloud improves comprehension (Duke & Pearson, 2009), vocabulary (Massaro, 2017), and fluency (Trelease, 2001).

Dr. Okello posits that reading aloud permits the teacher to model expert, fluent reading of the text, which liberates children from having to decode and allows them to focus on comprehension, acquisition of new vocabulary, and phonemic awareness. According to Massaro (2017), children listening to a read-aloud of a picture book are three times more likely to experience a new word type that is not among the most frequently used words in their everyday language. This is important to understand if we want children to enter school with varying levels of exposure to more complex vocabulary. The kinds of texts that we expose children to help them see what is possible in the world and allow them to develop an endless imagination. Text helps children expand their vision and gives them a sense of who they are and who they can become. It also helps with the development of deeper empathy for others whose experiences may look different from their own.

> *"Reading is important. If you know how to read, then the world opens up to you." Barack Obama*

Vocabulary is simply knowing the names of objects, but it is the most important skill for children to have when learning to read. Having a large vocabulary strengthens children's ability to grasp ideas and think logically. Vocabulary knowledge predicts students' literacy achievement because it contributes significantly to both word identification and reading comprehension skills. A strong academic vocabulary nourishes a student's ability to articulate ideas beyond the immediate context. It increases the ability to articulate a series of events, infer, and think analytically. Children build vocabulary skills through discussing predictions, describing scenes or pictures, and summarizing information in a text. The greater number of words children have, the more they can interpret ideas from others, and express their own ideas. Knowing the vocabulary words associated with a given topic enables children to connect their background knowledge to what they are reading.

By the time children enter school, they should know thousands of words. Unfortunately, many children from low-income families do not have rich vocabulary and often begin elementary school thousands of words behind their higher-income peers. We can build children's vocabulary from birth simply by teaching the names of all the objects in their world as well as by talking with them and by reading to them regularly. Reading is a critical activity for developing vocabulary. Adults must read and reread a variety of books including fiction and nonfiction. Book reading activities build opportunities for children to acquire new vocabulary, extend conversations, play with language, and experience the purpose of print. The number of rare words used in everyday speech is less than the rare words found in children's books. Children who have reading experiences before kindergarten will have more exposure to rare words and will increase their oral language vocabulary significantly (Schaughency et al., 2017). The old phrase, "children should be seen and not heard" is fundamentally incorrect and can hinder literacy development in children. To develop a rich vocabulary, we need to talk with children, and they need to talk back in return. This "serve and return," exchange is critical for vocabulary development. Children's vocabulary at age three is strongly associated with learning to read and reading comprehension at the end of third grade (Hart & Risley, 2003). Other researchers found that Vocabulary at 19 months predicted reading comprehension at age 12 (Suggate et al., 2018).

> *"To learn to read is like a fire; every syllable that*
> *is spelled out is a spark." Victor Hugo*

Narrative skills are one of the early literacy skills that children must have for reading success. Narrative skills require expressive language to help children learn story structure, predict what will happen in a story, understand what they *read*, and build critical thinking skills. Simply put, narrative skills allow children to understand and tell stories. We learn and communicate using stories throughout the day by re-telling events, telling others about ourselves, following and giving directions, reporting, persuading, and describing. Children with underdeveloped narrative skills may exhibit challenges when reading or listening.

For example, they may struggle to grasp key parts of written or oral stories such as the main idea, character development, and implied meaning. Additionally, to answer questions about the text, a child with poor narrative skills may need to go back and read the text several times. When communicating, children with underdeveloped narrative skills jump all over the place, skip important details, go off on tangents, and they tend to go on and on about something. Relationships are also impacted by poor narrative skills. When someone gets stuck trying to communicate, it feels frustrating for both the communicator and the listener. As one might imagine, children from low-income families tend to have underdeveloped narrative skills. The good news is that narrative skills can be taught early in a child's life.

Tips for Building Narrative Skills
- Teach and talk about routines (i.e., bedtime, bath time, mealtime, etc.) in the form of stories. First, I will take off your clothes (beginning), now we are playing with the toys in the bathtub (middle), and now it's time to dry off and put your pajamas on (end).
- Narrate a child's play. If a child is rolling a car on the floor, an adult may say something as simple as: "Where is the car going? Oh, to the store. What will you buy at the store? Oh no, you crashed, but you are okay. Time to head back home to get a band-aid."
- Co-create stories during playtime. If a child is playing with stuffed animals or blocks, create a story together.
- Reminisce with children; they love to hear stories from the past. Tell and retell stories and allow children to tell you the story in their own words.
- Ask questions to elicit more than a yes or no response. For example, "Why do you think the character did that?" "When do you think the character found out?" "What would you do?" "How do you think the character feels in this picture?" "What did you like about this story?" Where do you think the other characters are going?"
- Read often to children as it is one of the best ways to reinforce narrative

skills. Along with asking "wh" questions, include predicting questions as well. For example, "What do you think will happen next?" "Who do you think did it?"

"Teaching them how to read is probably one of the most important duties a civilized society owes to its children." Pamela Snow

Phonological awareness is an umbrella term that encompasses many skills. It is a crucial foundational skill that helps children learn to read. It refers to the ability to detect and manipulate the sound structure of language, such as recognizing and producing rhymes and breaking words into syllables. Research has shown that phonological awareness is a strong predictor of reading success, and children who struggle with phonological awareness are often at risk for reading difficulties. Therefore, it is essential for parents and educators to support the development of phonological awareness in young children, especially during the early years.

Phonological awareness skills typically develop in a specific sequence, starting with the ability to detect and produce rhymes and alliteration, and then progressing to more advanced skills like phoneme segmentation and blending. It's important to note that this sequence may vary for different children, and some children may need more explicit instruction and support to develop phonological awareness skills.

Oral Language Development and Background Knowledge

Equally as important to early literacy development are oral language and background knowledge. Oral language is the system through which we use spoken words to express knowledge, ideas, and feelings, all of which have a strong relationship to reading comprehension. Oral language lays the foundation for the reading and writing skills that children will develop as they progress through school. Having a solid foundation in oral language will help children become successful readers and strong communicators while building their confidence and overall sense of well-being. However, attention to oral language and critical listening skills are often placed on the back burner or left out of early literacy programs. Yet, we wonder why children struggle to become proficient readers. The development of oral language begins during infancy. Most of what children know about language will occur by age five, despite the complexity of oral language learning.

Throughout their school years, children will expand their ability to master speech sounds, use correct grammatical structures, enhance vocabulary, and communicate with a range of people in appropriate ways. Children depend on language for social interaction and communication, demonstration of ability and knowledge, and acquiring new concepts (McGee & Richgels, 2003). A child's familiarity with language and vocabulary is strongly linked to his or her later literacy success. Despite the recognized importance, opportunities for children to develop oral language skills is typically limited in preschool. This may be due to the curriculum, culture and climate of the school or classroom, or instructional decisions made by educators. For example, teachers may primarily ask yes/no questions of children and accept one-word answers when more elaborate responses are required. Another example may be when teachers do not give children ample time to express themselves or give them opportunities to use oral language because classrooms are often rigid, inflexible, nonresponsive to the developmental needs of children, compliant-driven, and controlling. Unfortunately, these types of classrooms are predominantly found in communities where Black and Brown children are the majority. Therefore, children are not able to or allowed to develop their oral language skills to become strong, confident, and successful readers because they do not have enough time to practice these skills.

To help children develop their oral language skills, it is important to understand the skills that make up oral language. Contrary to what most people believe, oral language is not just vocabulary, rather it encompasses five main areas as defined by Turnbull and Justice in their book *Language Development from Theory to Practice.* The five areas include **phonology**, **morphology**, **semantics**, **syntax**, and **pragmatics**; all have an impact on a child's academic success.

Phonology refers to the system of sounds within language that begins in infancy, as children gain the ability to distinguish syllables, words, and phrases. As they grow, children gain an understanding of other aspects of phonological awareness such as rhyme, alliteration, blending, segmenting, and manipulating sounds. Phonological awareness has a tremendous impact on later reading success.

Morphology refers to morphemes, the minimal units of words that have a meaning and cannot be subdivided further. Morphological awareness refers to a child's awareness and ability to manipulate these small units of meaning. Morphological awareness is also related to children's reading success.

Semantics refers to the meaning of words and phrases, including vocabulary knowledge. Vocabulary knowledge can be broken down into two distinct categories: spoken vocabulary, which includes words used informally in conversation, and academic vocabulary, which refers to words used in academic talk or text. Academic vocabulary is a significant contributor to reading ability.

Syntax is referred to as grammar because it is the set of rules that dictate the ways in which words and phrases can be combined into sentences and paragraphs. It is essential to use correct syntax to communicate messages that are meaningful and easy to understand. From an early age, syntax influences the way in which children communicate spoken language.

Finally**, pragmatics** is the social use of language like how to take turns in a conversation, interact in a group, and maintain personal space. Some children who have issues with pragmatics have underdeveloped early literacy skills due to difficulty participating in classroom activities. Oral language is an integration of all these skills; therefore, teachers may focus on targeting oral language as a whole, rather than focusing on each skill separately. By providing rich language experiences, models, and explicit instruction, teachers can support all aspects of oral language development.

Oral language development in children is influenced by a range of factors, including genetic and environmental factors such as socioeconomic status and home learning environment. Research has shown that genetics plays a role in language development, with estimates of heritability ranging from 30% to 60%

depending on the age of the child (Hulme et al., 2020). However, environmental factors such as socioeconomic status and home learning environment also play a significant role in language development. Studies have consistently found that children from low-income families are exposed to fewer words and have less conversational interactions with their parents compared to children from high-income families. This difference in language exposure and parent-child interactions can have a significant impact on a child's oral language development, as well as their overall academic achievement. The home learning environment is another critical factor that can influence a child's language development. Parents who have strong language and literacy skills, provide a rich language environment, and have reading habits that are more likely to support their child's language development. The number of books in the home and the quality of parent-child reading interactions also play a role in promoting language development in you

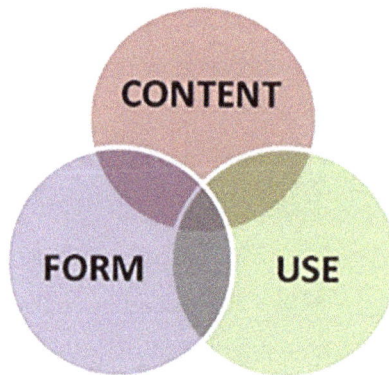

Louis Bloom and Margaret Lahey 1978 Oral Language Circles

Before moving on to background knowledge, we must first briefly discuss **executive function**, which is a key skill for success in school. Executive function is considered an invisible but essential skill. It is a set of mental skills responsible for paying attention, organizing, planning, prioritizing, starting and completing a task, staying focused, understanding different points of view, regulating emotions, and self-monitoring (Castles et al., 2018). We use these skills every day to learn, work, and manage daily life. Executive functioning is described as the "management system of the brain" because the skills involved allow us to set goals, plan, and get things done.

There are three basic components of executive function: inhibition, working memory, and cognitive flexibility. The component that I want to briefly focus on is working memory because of its direct relationship to reading. Working memory is where the brain processes, holds, and manipulates information. It is divided into two types: verbal working memory and non-verbal working memory. Verbal working memory is activated when the brain is processing auditory information. Verbal working memory plays an important role in reading comprehension. For young children, it is essential to the development of decoding skills for reading fluency. Additionally, verbal working memory is needed for remembering instructions, comprehending complex sentences, and remembering what to say when called upon. Non-verbal working memory, also known as visual-spatial memory, occurs when someone visualizes something and holds it in their 'mind's eye.' It is required for keeping one's place in a sentence or paragraph when reading, for mentally manipulating images, and for remembering patterns, images, and sequences of events.

When children struggle with executive function, it is usually verbal working memory. They may find it hard to focus, follow directions, and handle emotions. Children may also have issues with starting and completing schoolwork and tasks. If children are still sounding out words while reading in third grade or above, they are relying heavily on their working memory. This puts a huge burden on the working memory system as it is concentrating on interpreting individual words rather than putting that energy towards comprehension. Children from high-income families typically have better executive functioning skills and better educational outcomes because they are exposed to more learning experiences, opportunities, and resources before they enter kindergarten (Dewitt & Lessing, 2018). Working alongside working memory are the short- and long-term memory categories. Long-term memory is where most of the information you are aware of is stored and is an important part of life, allowing you to grow, progress, and teach others. Information such as childhood memories, the names of the people you know, how to ride a bike, and millions of other things are in your short-term memory. Working memory incorporates information from the long-term memory so that one can apply it to new information to complete a task. The important aspect here is that background knowledge is stored in our long-term memory.

> *"If I have to reduce all educational psychology to just one principle, I would say this: the most important single factor influencing learning is what the learner already knows. Ascertain this and teach him accordingly." Ausubel*

Background knowledge refers to concepts, experiences, information, and text structures that are relevant to a text under study. It is information that is essential to understanding a situation or problem. In other words, background knowledge means we use what we already know to learn new things. Since 1990 and the advent of functional magnetic resonance imaging (fMRI) and other brain-scanning technologies, researchers have been able to see and understand the relationship between what we know already and new information to be learned. For example, Van Kesteren (a neuroscientist) and her colleagues found that there is a particular area of the brain that is activated when people are connecting old and new information called the *medial prefrontal cortex*. They also found that how well learners use this area of the brain is related to the future academic success of the learner. By capitalizing and building on the knowledge that children have, educators have a vehicle for providing grade-level content and meeting the language needs of each student.

Children's background knowledge is retrieved from long-term memory and allows them to have discussions about the new text prior to reading. How does information get into a child's long-term memory? To answer that question, we need to have a basic understanding of how memory works. John Sweller, an educational psychologist, and his colleagues described how working and long-term memory work. The working memory is where we store information for a short period of time while we are processing it and trying to make sense of it. Working memory is extremely limited but an important component of how students learn to read. We can only keep a few items in our working memory at a time, and when the working memory is loaded or overloaded, we need to drop an item before we can take in another item. This has huge implications for teaching. If we try to teach children too much new information at once, in a short period of time, it will not be retained well.

Working memory is different from long-term memory and involves a higher-order cognitive skill that is important for learning and academic success. Working memory is the ability to hold and manipulate information in the mind for short periods, which is necessary for tasks such as problem-solving, language comprehension, and reading. Working memory is associated with the prefrontal cortex, which is a later-maturing, higher-level region of the brain involved in executive function.

On the other hand, long-term memory is a limitless storehouse of knowledge that allows us to retain and recall information over long periods. Long-term memory is essential for learning and includes both explicit (declarative) memory, which is conscious and involves facts and events, and implicit (procedural) memory, which is unconscious and involves skills and habits. When we learn something new, it's important to engage both working memory and long-term memory to ensure that the information is retained and can be accessed later. With practice and repetition, new information can become part of our long-term memory, which frees up working memory for new learning (Morrison & Wlodarczyk, 2009). Overall, both working memory and long-term memory are important for learning and academic success, and developing strategies to enhance both can help children achieve their full potential.

Why is background knowledge so important for reading success? Background knowledge is needed for reading comprehension as the two are interdependent; one is necessary to build the other. Background knowledge is the amount of information or knowledge one has on a particular topic. It is acquired through experiences or the amount of knowledge one retains from reading or listening. Reading a variety of genres of books, listening to multiple media sources, and engaging in conversations on multiple topics increase background knowledge and help children make connections with the text. Making connections is an important reading strategy that encourages readers to share text-to-self connections, text-to-text connections, and text-to-world connections. When students share their connections, through conversation, writing, or illustration, it is a strong indicator of a child's background knowledge. When readers have previous experiences or have gained information about a specific topic or content area, their reading comprehension level is automatically increased. These students can easily analyze and interpret, explain their perspective, infer, and summarize the text. The more information a student has on a topic, the easier it is for the student to read, recall, and understand the text.

Background knowledge plays an integral role in most theories of reading, yet it remains an under-addressed aspect of reading instruction. Background knowledge and vocabulary are the foundational skills that allow us to comprehend what we read. Early life and literacy experiences help build background knowledge in young children. Vocabulary and background knowledge are critical for reading comprehension; however, many children come to school without such early literacy experiences, which severely hinders reading proficiency. The stakes are high. If we do not help all children progress to grade-level proficiency in reading, we put them at risk for a lifetime of reading struggles. Children who do not learn to read well early on will have persistent difficulties in their academic journey. It is critical to address the needs of all readers—especially struggling readers—as soon as possible.

"We must bring back play in the early grades and give children time to engage in play-based learning. Play gives children the opportunity to practice new skills and master current skills in a safe and supportive environment. Besides having fun, play gives children the opportunity to improve their social, physical, math and science, problem solving and critical thinking skills, as well as language development, the development of these skills promote self-esteem, creativity, confidence, and perseverance – all important skills for children to thrive in a 21st century global economy."

- Dr. Jacquelyn Bobien-Blanton

Part II:

Why the Struggle?

"There are many little ways to enlarge your child's world. Love of books is the best of all"
- Jacqueline Kennedy

Chapter 6

Reading Wars

Controversial Reading Instruction

Why is reading instruction so controversial? Why is it so difficult for some children to learn how to read? Why is there so much turmoil and division regarding reading instruction? The answers to these questions are rooted in an educational system built on inequality and an insatiable need for many Americans to possess money, power, and prestige at the expense of Black and Brown children.

For decades, children have been struggling to read and it has been largely left unchallenged, leaving millions of children without effective and sufficient reading skills. The United States churns out more illiterate and barely literate citizens than any other developed country in the world (Kennison, 2005). This chapter will provide insight into the controversies surrounding the reading wars.

The infamous term "reading wars" is a description for the long-running disagreements about the best way to teach children to read. Over the years, educators, politicians, stakeholders, and proponents of phonics instruction and whole language instruction have battled fiercely over reading instruction. This battle turned into a full-scale war that continues today. Reyhner (2020) from Northern Arizona University, stated that proponents of phonics blamed the decline in reading test scores in the United States in 1990 on whole language instruction while the proponents of whole language blamed the drop in scores on students living in poverty. As researchers, educators, and stakeholders continue to argue over the best approach to teaching reading, the argument continues to leave education and young children in a deadlock.

Unbalanced Literacy – History of the Reading Wars

Whole language instruction emphasizes the importance of immersion in meaningful texts and the development of reading comprehension skills. This approach emphasizes the use of authentic literature, whole texts, and real-world reading experiences to help children develop an understanding of how language works (Lemann, 1997). Whole language supporters believe that language should not be broken down into letters and combinations of letters. The essential idea of the whole language approach was that children construct their own knowledge and meaning from experience. Supporters thought phonics lessons were not good for children because they inhibited children from developing a love of reading by making them focus on tedious skills such as breaking words into parts.

In whole language instruction, teachers emphasize the meaning of texts over the sounds of letters. The learning environment has plenty of simple printed text, teachers provide a lot of read aloud opportunities and young children are expected to make a giant associative leap from knowing the alphabet to being able to read whole words. If a word is unfamiliar, it can be skipped, guessed at, or picked up from context. Whole language is considered a "top-down" approach based on a constructivist learning theory where the reader constructs personal meaning from a text based on prior knowledge to interpret the meaning. One good thing about the whole language approach is that it provides students with an environment rich in literacy which exposes them to a varied vocabulary, ideas, and language, which benefits the development of life-long readers. Problems associated with the whole language approach include a lack of structure that has been traditionally supplied by the scope and sequence, lessons and activities, and extensive graded literature found in basal readers. Whole language puts a heavy burden on teachers to develop their own curriculum, which can be difficult for novice teachers. According to Miller (2020), learning to read is not a natural process. The whole language approach to reading instruction is particularly difficult for some children from low-income disadvantaged communities because many do not have the rich vocabulary or solid prior or background knowledge.

As expected, phonics-based reading instruction takes the complete opposite position. Phonics instruction emphasizes the importance of teaching children the sounds and letter combinations of the English language and how to use them to decode words. This approach emphasizes the systematic, explicit teaching of phonics rules and the development of decoding skills. Children learn to read whole words by decoding them from their component phonemes; therefore, sounding out words is a phonics activity rather than whole language. In phonics-based instruction, the teacher introduces a series of spelling rules and teaches students to apply phonetics (how the letter combinations sound out loud) to decode words based on how they are spelled. Phonics attempts to break written language down into small and simple components. Phonics lessons were seen as rote, old-fashioned, and conservative. Opposite of whole language, phonics is considered a "bottom-up" approach where students are first taught the basics (decoding) to build a solid foundation. The advantage of phonics, especially for students who come to schools with large vocabularies, is that once students get the basics down, they can go to the library and read a wide variety of children's literature.

The so-called 'reading wars' have a long history within education and are considered one of the most politicized topics in the field of education. The debate over whole language versus phonics in teaching children to read has been a heated debate dating back to the 1700s. For example, there was a German educator and professor named Friederich Gedike who wrote an essay in 1779 to argue that reading instruction should go from whole words to the parts of these words, or letters. In the 1800s, Horace Mann, the influential educational reformer, and Secretary of Education in Massachusetts railed against teaching children that letters represent sounds. He thought that children would be distracted from comprehending the meaning of what they were reading if they focused too much on letters. He believed children should be taught to read whole words. Incidentally, Mann was not a teacher, but he eventually played a major role in shaping American public education, falling in line with the American tradition of non-educators imposing their ideas about education on educators without a clear understanding of the real-world implications or consequences of their beliefs.

The debate about how to teach reading has plagued the educational system for a long time. Different approaches to reading instruction often have some commonalities but some of the core differences are fatal flaws causing one side to completely dismiss the other. The debates have been ongoing, heated, intense, misleading, confusing, and exhaustive, which have led to distrust, doubt, and cynicism among educators, researchers, and policymakers. The debates between whole language and phonics instruction have been so turbulent and intense that it caused many to select one side and one side only and there was no in-between. Each camp has leaders, large followers, catchphrases, branded items, measures of fidelity, research data, and pledges of allegiance that sometimes blinds people to the pitfalls and possibilities of each.

From the 1700s to the 1800s, the debate over reading instruction continued. In the late 1920s, progressive education became an influential movement as schools began to switch from phonics to whole-language reading instruction. In the1960s the pendulum switched back to phonics after the 1955 best-selling book, *Why Johnny Can't Read* by Rudolf Flesch. The book brought the phonics approach to life, leading to the "back to basic" movement in the 1960s and

1970s. In 1967, the debate was re-ignited with the publication of Chall's classic volume *Learning to Read: The Great Debate*. Chall renamed the two approaches as 'code-based' and 'meaning-based' (Chall, 1967); however, reading instruction was still an either/or between the two approaches thus continuing the great divide. In the 1970s and 1980s, code-based and meaning-based had morphed into new terms like literature-based versus skills-based, implicit versus explicit, holistic versus fragmented, and top-down versus bottom-up. By the 1980s, the pendulum switched back to a decade of whole-language instruction. Such a long history of reading instruction has given today's teachers a wealth of information to reflect on with regards to their instructional practices in reading. From the 1990s to the present day, the two sides of the reading fence had turned into something more complex with each side holding on to its core beliefs so tight that there were no longer debates as to which one was better, rather it had turned into a full, all-out war—thus, creating the term 'reading wars.'

Why such hostility between the two approaches to reading instruction? One reason for the hostility is money. There is a lot of money made in education from textbook adoptions to reading curricula, reading resources and materials, programs, assessments, and professional development. Who profits if there is a sudden truce in the reading war? Money will continue to perpetuate the reading wars regardless of what science and research say. As customary in sales, representatives will do what is necessary to sell a product. For example, according to James Kim, by the 1980s, whole-language theorists had communicated their ideas to decision-makers in state government to change the curriculum and instruction for reading.

One direct path to changing classroom instruction was to work through state legislatures that had centralized control over textbook adoption policies and the authority to shape what goes on in public-school classrooms. Why is this important to reading instruction? In many states, legislatures have the power and the money to dictate the content of instruction, methodologies of instruction, materials, and programs for instruction, the adoption of curricula and assessments, and professional training of teachers. Education is political and it can be messy. The United States has a long history of non-educators making decisions for educational institutions. California is a direct example of how legislative decisions can get in the way of sound educational practices. The following is an account of how the whole-language group "hijacked" the California educational system according to Lemann (1997).

In 1986, the commissioner of education in California pushed California schools to teach the classics of literature and history; therefore, he convened a large meeting of experts and they listened to the whole-language presentation. The presentation called for the dismissal of mindless drills and instill in children a reverence for reading. According to Lemann's account, the commissioner, at the time, thought he was pushing good literature but before he knew what was happening, whole language proponents hijacked what he was trying to do. In 1987, despite the commissioner of education's views, the state of California made a strong commitment to whole-language, in a battle for California's business an English Language Arts framework was created which made possible the victory of whole-language textbooks. This is important because education is big business and if a company wants your business, it will and can do just about anything to gain it, which has significant implications for what we see in textbooks and ultimately what children are exposed to. A large percentage of Black and Brown children attend public schools. Large states like California and Texas control much of what is taught in public schools and unfortunately, the politics in these states dictate what children learn rather than research-based instruction and learning. Back to California, not only did the state drop phonics instruction, but the entire teacher-training system turned completely toward whole-language just like that.

A major challenge to the whole language approach eventually came from fourth-grade reading scores on the National Assessment of Educational Progress (NAEP) report also known as The Nation's Report Card. NAEP was developed in 1969 to measure student achievement nationally in various subject areas. In 1992, the federal government supplied the public and policymakers with comparative information on state performances from the NAEP assessments. In California, 52% of fourth-grade students read below the basic level on the 1992 administration of NAEP. More bad news followed with the release of the

1994 NAEP scores. The average performance of California's fourth graders put the state near the bottom relative to other states, and the decline in scores from 1992 to 1994 was evident among all ethnic and socioeconomic groups. The perceived reading crisis was eventually linked to whole-language practices. Survey data indicated that a larger percentage of California teachers employed whole-language practices than their peers in other states. Since the whole language approach had become the conventional wisdom in reading instruction, any decline (perceived or real) in reading achievement was easily linked to that dominant method of reading instruction.

Due to the fact the reading scores were extremely low in California in the 1990s, it became a political talking point in elections. The consensus was that embracing whole-language was a major mistake. In 1995, legislation was passed without a single dissenting vote in either house. One bill mandated the use of instructional materials to teach reading through phonics. To back the bill, the governor proposed millions of dollars for skilled-based reading instruction. This is an example of what took place in California; however, it happens in far too many states. Take a moment to think about and consider all the children in California and other states who struggled in reading and in other courses during the whole-language only decade. The students did not fail; parts of their ecosystem failed them. The pendulum has been swinging back and forth on both sides of the argument over the proper reading instruction for over 100 years, making the reading wars seem like an inevitable fact of American history. The promise of an equitable and quality education for all students regardless of demographics or individual abilities has been a challenge in the United States. While the reading wars continue to heat up, we find ourselves at an impasse to closing the achievement gap and generations of children who cannot read proficiently.

To add to the reading wars, balanced literacy entered the ring offering a middle ground to the battle between the two reading theories. Balanced literacy was a truce where children would learn the correspondence between sounds and letters of the alphabet, but they would also be exposed to rich literature for meaning and pleasure. According to Fountas and Pinnell (1996), balanced literacy is a philosophical belief that supports the assumption that reading and writing achievement develop through multiple strategies like teacher-directed instruction, modeling, and scaffolding opportunities. At face value, balanced literacy seemed to represent the research provided by the National Reading Panel (NRP) in 2000. In 1997, the United States Congress charged the National Institute of Child Health and Human Development (NICHD), along with the Secretary of Education with the task of appointing a panel of experts to evaluate the various approaches to reading (Miller, 2020). The results were rolled out in the document "Teach Children to Read: An Evidence-Based Assessment of Scientific Research Literature on Reading and its Implications for Reading Instruction."

Building on the recommendations from NRP, the 2001 No Child Left Behind Act (NCLB) included two literacy initiatives: Early Reading First and Reading First, the mission was to enable all students to become successful readers. The NRP found that phonics instruction produces the biggest impact on growth in reading when it begins in kindergarten or first grade before children learn to read independently. The panel further reported that systematic phonics instruction should be integrated into the curriculum to create a more balanced approach to reading instruction. However, interpreting what a balanced approach to reading actually looks like in the classroom is the impetus for the current iteration of the reading wars.

Balanced literacy was supposed to be the answer finally to the reading wars, but as it turns out, it just complicated the wars and added fuel to the fire. After the NRP report, whole language proponents could no longer deny the importance of phonics, but they did not give up their core beliefs that learning to read is a natural process, and of course, they did not give up the reading programs they were selling, after all, education is a big money-making business. Therefore, balanced literacy proponents decided to incorporate phonics into their approach. However, the movement's leaders were fervent advocates of whole language which prompted critics to exclaim that balanced literacy is the same old approach (whole language) with a different label. According to Hanford (2019), the balanced literacy practiced in many classrooms around the country is closely aligned to the whole language approach to reading with a sprinkling of phonics instruction here and there. Although phonics and phonemic awareness are included in daily instruction, it is often not taught explicitly and systematically, which goes against the research on reading conducted by the NRP commission.

Wexler (2019) explained that eventually, balanced literacy became known for two practices: leveled reading and reading comprehension instruction, both very foreign to the whole language approach. Leveled reading became significant in the 1980s when basal readers were tossed out. Leveled reading uses various assessment tools to determine how well children are reading, and then match them to corresponding books. Books were assigned letters of the alphabet corresponding to different reading levels of difficulty. To determine the reading level of children, teachers conduct running records where they listen for the number of mistakes a child makes while reading a passage.

The theory behind leveled readers according to Wexler is that struggling readers will gradually move up the ladder of text complexity until they catch up. The problem with a system like leveled readers and others, according to Wexler, is that they do not reliably predict comprehension. She points out that with the leveled reading system, teachers do not teach students the content and vocabulary they need to access more complex text. Here is the kicker: The *books* are expected to do that, even though students are limited to books that largely consist of words and concepts they already know and understand. The retort from balanced-literacy advocates is that students who work with leveled readers are not just reading, they are practicing the comprehension skills and strategies that will enable them to garner more and more meaning from their leveled texts. Balanced literacy entered the reading wars and took root in many large public school systems in the United States.

This brings us to New York City and Klein, the former New York City school's chancellor. The story is well documented and the subject of the book *The Knowledge Gap: The Hidden Cause of America's Broken Education System and How to Fix It*. In 2003, Klein was set to announce the literacy curriculum for the elementary and middle schools in New York City and asked Calkins to attend. By this time, several hundred affluent schools in New York City public schools had adopted Calkins' balanced literacy approach and many teachers around the world had been trained by her and her team. Calkins did not know what curriculum would be selected for New York City public schools, but she knew that Klein was not a devoted follower of hers. As I stated previously, there is historical context for non-educators and politicians making educational decisions that would impact teachers and students.

Wexler's book points out that Klein had no background in education; he was appointed chancellor by Michael Bloomberg who obtained complete control over the city's schools during his tenure as Mayor. Klein was a lawyer and a successful businessman. Klein was not thrilled with the curricula; therefore, he convened a committee of local education officials to make recommendations for change. Here is how education, politics, and money come together and blur what's best for children. Calkins feared that Klein would select a basal program that incorporated phonics because that's what Bloomberg called for and what the George W. Bush administration provided funds for. Get this, balanced literacy was considered to be at the liberal end of the political spectrum and both Bloomberg and Klein were on the conservative end; therefore, Calkins feared that she would not get the bid for pushing balanced literacy into the school system. During that 2003 press conference, Klein selected Calkins' reading and writing project for New York City Public Schools. Everyone was shocked—including Calkins.

Klein was forced to adopt a supplementary phonics program to avoid losing millions of dollars in federal funds. According to Wexler, years later Klein would say that choosing Calkins's balanced literacy curriculum was the only regret he had about his tenure as chancellor. He concluded that her approach did not pay enough attention to phonics and that it prevented low-come students from acquiring what they needed the most: knowledge. When Calkins' reading and writing project was selected as the curriculum for New York City, Calkins did not have a curriculum to offer. Balanced literacy was not a curriculum it was an approach that relied heavily on training and coaching. It gets better, Calkins was philosophically opposed to mandating a curriculum for reading instruction because she posited that teachers needed the flexibility and autonomy to respond to the needs of individual students. However, principles and beliefs went out the window as money became a motivating factor. Calkins created a curriculum in three weeks! By 2017, her *Unit of Study* series (which many deemed very scripted) was in wide use not just in New York City but across the United States.

Over time, Klein and others grew doubtful of Calkins' curriculum, and in 2008, he rescinded his mandate that all schools use her curriculum. It was uncertain as to whether or not students from low-income families were getting anything of value from the curriculum. Klein became interested in knowledge-building curricula that were supposed to be great for children from less-educated families. As a result, in 2008, $2.4 million dollars from private donors were granted to ten New York City schools to implement a pilot program that extended over a three-year period. The pilot incorporated the principles of systematic phonics instruction, including decodable readers, and covered a range of topics in depth. In 2012, the students in those ten schools scored significantly higher on reading comprehension tests than those in comparison schools. Calkins stated that she had not personally worked with the comparison schools and had no way of knowing if the teachers implemented her curriculum to fidelity.

Afterward, the Department of Education omitted Calkins' program from its list of recommended curricula. However, that was short-lived because as Klein stated, New York City is a balanced-literacy town, and he was right. When Bill de Blasio became mayor after Bloomberg in 2013, he appointed the same person that convinced Klein to adopt balanced literacy years earlier. Just as predicted, within months, the new chancellor arranged for Calkins to hold seminars for hundreds of principals and teachers, and in 2015 she required dozens of the city's lowest-performing elementary and middle schools to implement Calkins' approach. They went back to an approach that did not improve reading scores for many Black and Brown students. As you can imagine, the test score gaps in New York grew and continues to grow according to Wexler. Just a side note, Calkins's Readers and Writers Program at Teachers College received over $10 million in no-bid contracts from the city as noted in the New York Daily News (2014).

New York City is just one example of how politics and money muddy the water in education. Unfortunately, there are many other school districts that experienced and continue to experience something similar. Again, I ask the question, "Is reading proficiency the goal of all students in the United States and do money, power, and influence distort this goal?" The one thing that gets under my skin is that there is no definitive outside proof that Calkin's approach works for all children. Evidence either comes from inside the Calkins's camp or from the fact that it is so popular. Just because something is popular does not mean that it is successful for all students. It is time that we take our heads out of the sand and look at what we are doing to children. Reading curricula and programs like Calkins have been around for at least thirty years and yet, children *still* cannot read. Sad to say but there are many curricula and program developers getting rich off the backs of children. They get rich and children still cannot read. Is reading proficiently the goal for all students? My response is a resounding no because education has become extremely profitable without delivering on promises to educate all children. Money and power are two of the reasons why the reading wars were able to persist for so long.

It gets even better. In opposition to balanced literacy, we have what some have termed structured literacy. This approach to reading, and learning to read, is the umbrella term used by the International Dyslexia Association (IDA) to unify and encompass evidenced-based programs and approaches that are aligned to the Knowledge and Practice Standards (Miller, 2020). IDA defines Knowledge and Practice Standards as "the knowledge and practice skills that all teachers of reading should possess to teach all students to read proficiently" (Cowan, 2016). According to IDA, structured literacy is explicit, systematic teaching that focuses on phonological awareness, word recognition, phonics, decoding, spelling, and syntax at the sentence and paragraph levels. Now, the battle is between balanced literacy and structured literacy. More money is being made on the backs of children. Lorimor-Easley and Reed (2019) argue that those who oppose the structured approach to reading believe that restricting students to phonemes initially, and then to decodable texts, suppresses the development of fluent reading. Those opposed to balanced literacy believe that if children cannot encode and decode naturally, then exposure to unfamiliar text will only lead to practicing compensatory strategies, such as relying on picture cues, while valuable instructional time passes. So, now what?

Lorimor-Easley and Reed (2019) suggested that many young learners would become proficient readers from repeated exposure alone, as suggested by balanced literacy, but there is a population of learners for whom this simply is not enough. Therefore, Lorimor-Easley and Reed suggested that the structured literacy approach is most effective because it avoids making off-the-cuff assumptions about what students are naturally capable of learning implicitly. Through the use of explicit and systematic instruction, students who have mastered the patterns of language will learn quickly and easily, and those who may experience difficulties will get the instruction they need to be successful readers. Balanced and structured literacy approaches to reading were supposed to bring about a truce in the reading wars—but it did not. Controversy keeps the reading wars alive because so many people believe that there can only be one victor or one approach to reading instruction. Remember, education is big business, and it is almost always driven by money. If there is a cease in the wars, one side of the reading instruction camp stands to lose billions of dollars.

Companies are profiting from the reading wars. Meanwhile, children cannot read. Instead of thinking about how much money these companies stand to lose, we must ask what's working for children and what can we improve. Are we providing the best instruction for all children? Whatever method is adopted we must ask, who becomes vulnerable to reading challenges, and how do we support them? The focus must be on the children, *not* the profits made by companies who continue to perpetuate the money-generating reading wars while children still cannot read.

What have we learned from the reading wars? We learned that for decades, we had many children entering fourth-grade reading below proficiency standards. We learned that if we continue current practices, we will continue to fail children. Until we definitively determine and address how best to teach reading, instructional controversies will continue, and children will be left behind in school, and in life. We learned that many teachers are not properly prepared to teach reading. Teachers and administrators who are not trained may not be able to implement best practices in reading instruction. We learned that teachers who are caught up in the reading wars may not have the experience or knowledge to decipher the minutia of the reading wars. For example, there are veteran administrators and teachers who are followers of one side or the other and will not change or alter their views or beliefs no matter what the research suggests or what students need. Teachers are influenced by one method or the other and their beliefs are typically based on how they were taught to read themselves. Other influences include the training that educators receive and the curricula school districts purchase. Unless and until legislators, researchers, and educators come together to determine the best reading method for all students, we will continue to have struggling readers. The one important revelation that surfaced from the reading wars is that weak foundational decoding strategies compromises reading comprehension.

There is a silver lining and hope on the horizon. In May 2022 we learned that Calkins made a major shift in her beliefs about the teaching of reading. She has rewritten her curriculum to include a formal embrace of phonics and the science of reading. After decades of resistance, daily phonics lessons will be implemented from kindergarten to second grade with the whole class. This is major because Calkin's reading programs are the third most widely used core materials to teach reading in the United States. This shift can be a game changer for so many young children who are struggling to read. Can we finally turn the tide and get children the support they need to become proficient readers by third grade? Will we see an end to the reading wars?

Practically Speaking

I turned to my focus group of educators for their insight on the reading wars. They were very familiar with the ongoing reading wars and believed that many students were consequently left behind. One teacher discussed how she was all for the whole language approach when she began teaching almost 20 years ago and thought she was providing good instruction for her students. She said, "I was fond of the whole language approach because I thought it was something good for my population of students, and when it was first introduced, I was attracted to it and I still like parts of it." Another participant stated, "The fact that the whole language approach emphasized real purposes for reading based on the interest of students was the key for me, instead of skilling and drilling." Still another participant stated, "In my district, the whole language approach was the new best thing that we had to implement. When I first entered the teaching profession, it was all I knew."

When I asked what happened to phonics instruction, many of the participants laughed and said it was boring and that they were losing students, "so trying something new was a breath of fresh air." One teacher said she dreaded teaching phonics. I asked about the road to reading proficiency over the years in their individual classrooms with the use of the whole language approach. I found their responses very interesting but not shocking. Every person in the focus group had a story about the whole language approach and student performance in reading. According to the participants, their students still could not read. In fact, one participant said during one of their grade level meetings, she knew that something was wrong because their students were still underperforming in reading even after intensive training of all teachers in the whole language approach, and 90% of the students attended preschool. However, no one attributed the issue to the whole language approach.

One participant stated, "It was so big and everyone was using it— it was the most popular thing going in education." Another participant said, "When the data came out unfavorably that all these students were reading below grade level using this approach, I pointed the blame at the families because surely I was implementing it right." In fact, four of the teachers blamed the families, family dynamics, poverty, student behavior, chronic absenteeism, and lack of parent involvement as part of the reasons why the whole language approach was unsuccessful. I asked about reading proficiency over the years and if there was a connection between reading proficiency and the whole language approach. All the teachers in the group said they knew there was a problem because they were not getting the desired reading results as the instructional approach exclaimed, and most of the teachers in the group had about 10 years of implementation. Many in my focus group did not realize the damage that was done to students because as one participant said, "We were under this whole language cloud." Many districts continued using the same reading approach even though the data seemed to prove that it was ineffective. Therefore, instead of re-evaluating reading instruction, many districts doubled down and continued with the same approach even after several states began to back away from the whole language approach. One participant said, "It wasn't until after decades of low reading scores that our district finally stopped the bleeding and formed a committee to review our options." Most of the teachers in the group are now in districts where intense professional training has occurred or will occur on the science of reading. According to the group, year-long professional development is mandatory for all teachers in the early grades. When I asked about what they learned so far about the science of reading, I was surprised at the flood of emotions that ensued. One participant stated through her tears, "why didn't I learn this in college, it could have made a big difference," in the lives of her students. One of the reading coaches said she did not know how much she didn't know until after she completed the course. Another participant said, "when we know better, we do better." It did not shock me that none of the participants were taught the science of reading in their teacher preparation courses. In most cases, teacher prep courses focus on the components of reading not necessarily on how to teach reading, which could be why first and second grades are so hard to teach. The road map for reading instruction has been so foggy that many teachers can't find their way, which impacts student learning.

The only reading specialists in the group stated that her district wanted to move in a different direction but the budget wouldn't allow them because it was too expensive to change as changing would entail a new reading curriculum, new reading programs, hours of professional development for instructional staff as well as reading materials and supplies. An administrator chimed in to say that the budget drives everything. She said,

"Once you lock into a curriculum, you typically stay put for years because you must complete the training cycle for staff, then you must allow teachers to implement it to fidelity, then you must observe, assess, and then examine student data. This takes years." Several of the teachers agreed with the administrator's sentiments. I am sure that this is the case throughout the country which accounts for decades of underperformance in reading by students. School districts alone cannot move students from where they are to where they need to be without assistance. It takes a village to raise a reader.

Chapter 7

The Science of Reading

It's All About The Brain

"Literacy is the cornerstone of learning, a child who can read is a child who can learn and a child who loves learning is unstoppable." Andy Myers

A central responsibility of schools is to teach students to read. Reading is a fundamental human right that empowers individuals and society. The future success of all students is contingent upon their ability to become proficient readers. According to the National Research Council, we are living in a knowledge economy where the demands for higher literacy skills are ever increasing, creating serious consequences for those who cannot read well.

Students who can read have a place at the table of opportunity, no matter what career path they choose to take. However, reading is not an easy task. On average, it takes two to three years to learn to decode English. It is the toughest alphabetic writing system in the world and students need time and practice to master it. Reading is like a muscle, the more you do it, the better and stronger you become. The good thing about the reading brain is that we can grow it with the right stimuli to produce confident readers. The goal of the United States is to ensure that 95% of its students can read and understand text on a college entry level (Miller, 1988), which is a very lofty goal. However, the current state of affairs regarding reading, leaves me wondering if reading proficiently is the goal for everyone or is it deliberately designed to leave some behind?

The science of reading has allowed us to finally understand how the brain functions during the reading process and it provides a window as to why some children have difficulties reading, while others do not. Based on science, we understand what constitutes best instructional practices. The science of reading is not a new idea; rather, this body of knowledge spans over twenty years. It is not a program but a set of principles that can influence the way we deliver reading instruction to students. The science of reading is a comprehensive body of research that encompasses years of scientific knowledge that spans across many languages and shares the contributions of experts from relevant disciplines such as education, special education, literacy, psychology, and neurology (Ordetx, 2021).

The conclusive, empirically supported research on the science of reading provides us with a deeper understanding of how we learn to read and the skills involved in reading development. This research has helped to demystify the process of learning to read and has provided evidence to support effective reading instruction. Through this research, we know that reading involves a complex set of skills, including phonemic awareness, phonics, fluency, vocabulary, and comprehension. These skills work together to help us understand and make meaning from written language. Based on the research, it is understood that different parts of the brain are responsible for different aspects of reading, and that effective instruction should target these specific areas of the brain.

We know that teaching whole word memorization is limiting and learning phonics empowers students with an exponential effect. For example, if a student memorizes ten words, then he or she can read ten words. However, if the student learns the sounds of ten letters, the child can read: 350 three-sound words, 4,320 four-sound words, and 21,650 five-sound words. The difference in memorizing whole words and learning phonics is major. The research on the science of reading confirmed that there is a right way to teach reading, and that effective reading instruction involves a systematic and explicit approach to teaching phonics, phonemic awareness, and other critical reading skills. This approach is supported by a large body of research and has been shown to be effective in improving reading outcomes for students.

The science of reading was supposed to finally put an end to the reading wars because it brings the elements of both camps, phonics and whole language together. It was supposed to end the wars and arm teachers with instructional practices that would put children on the road to proficient reading. However, after twenty years of valid, reliable, and solid research, we still have many students reading below the proficiency threshold. It is important that we continue to prioritize this research and use it to inform our instructional practices and policies to ensure that all students have the opportunity to become proficient readers. Providing educators with research-based information on reading is a moral obligation.

How the Brain Learns to Read

A lot of what we know about the reading brain comes from Stanislas Dehaene, a cognitive neuroscientist, and author. According to Dehaene, we are living in an era of neuroscientific revolution in the brain where science reveals pertinent information about reading that could change the trajectory of many struggling readers. Advancements in science demonstrated that activity in the brain creates blood flow which can be measured using fMRI scanning. In other words, we can literally see what happens in the brain when someone is reading. Reading is a very complex skill that requires special parts of the brain. From Dehaene's work, we know that everyone was born with the language part of the brain (the speech and meaning parts) which allows us to learn to speak and understand spoken language simply by being around others who are speaking. Additionally, everyone is born with the visual part of the brain as we easily recognize shapes, objects, places, and faces. However, no one is born with the connections between vision and speech, which are the connections that enable reading. Evolution never shaped the brain to read. According to Dehaene, we were not born to read, it is a recent invention. Reading is too recent a skill for it to have become part of the brain's structure from the beginning. Therefore, the human brain adapted specialized regions and networks for language and visual object recognition. When a child receives instruction in reading, these areas are re-purposed for the process of reading and writing. Basically, when learning to read, we must rewire areas of the brain, but the good thing about the brain is that it is flexible enough to handle the task. The brain is very complex and capable of doing amazing things.

Essentially, we must deliberately train the brain to read. How does that happen? The brain is divided into left and right hemispheres. The right hemisphere is associated with visions, depth perception, and spatial navigation. The left hemisphere is where the reading network of the brain is located. The brain undergoes neuronal recycling in order to learn to read. There is not a specific area of the brain that is dedicated solely to reading, so the brain must repurpose existing neural circuitry in order to learn how to read. This process of neuronal recycling is capable of converting the function of a neural circuit to a different purpose, but the original function is not entirely lost. According to Dehaene's research, children initially rely heavily on their brain's visual system to perceive words as pictures or objects, without regard for the letters and sounds that they represent. Children learn to recognize a limited number of words based on the overall visual appearance of the words, often depending on factors such as font, color, and logos that are typically associated with those words (i.e., a stop sign or McDonald's golden arches). This is known as the pictorial stage of reading development. However, the processes that characterize the pictorial stage are insufficient for the development of proficient reading. To become proficient readers in an alphabetic system such as English, children must learn to coordinate additional systems within the brain. This includes developing phonemic awareness, which involves the ability to hear and manipulate individual sounds in words, as well as learning phonics, which involves the relationship between letters and sounds. Overall, the brain's ability to recycle neural circuitry is crucial to the process of learning to read. By coordinating various systems within the brain, children can develop the skills necessary for proficient reading and achieve greater success in reading comprehension and overall academic achievement.

Practically Speaking

A personal example of the pictorial stage of reading is when two of my nephews stayed with my husband and me while their parents were on vacation. We were so excited and wanted to ensure they had a good time. One day, on our way to an event, we rode on a popular route that had many stores and restaurants. It was rich with environmental print. One of my nephews shouted from the back seat of the car, "McDonald's, I want McDonald's." My husband and I quickly looked around, but we didn't see a McDonald's anywhere. My nephew became upset and began to cry because we passed what he thought was McDonald's. I said to myself, "This can't be good." When we circled back around, we realized that what my nephew was fixated on was the golden arches of the Midlantic Bank. He associated the big yellow "M" at Midlantic Bank for McDonald's. We explained that it was not McDonald's, but he was not having any of it; he was hot. We laugh about that incident to this today, and it happened over 30 years ago. Thankfully, we did find a McDonald's, avoided a disaster, and placed a smile on the faces of two happy campers. The point is that my nephew was relying on the visual system in his brain with no regard to letters and sounds. The golden "M" to him clearly represented McDonald's.

Another example was when my son was about three years old sitting in the back seat of my car. I remember parking the car in front of our home and as I was backing up, he shouted with great enthusiasm, "Mommy, I know how to spell license plate." I replied with matched excitement, "Oh really, spell it." He began saying random letters and numbers and said, "See, I told you." At first, I was a little confused but when I turned around and looked at the car in front of me, I realized that my son 'read' the letters and numbers on the license plate of the car that was in front of us. Well, I was just as excited as he was and gave him a high five. No, I did not lose my mind; I just realized that he used the visual side of his brain to recognize an object or the license plate and he assumed that the letters/numbers on the object named the object. He made a tremendous leap in that he recognized that letters made up words and words represented objects. I was over the moon! It may sound silly and insignificant but I was happy because he was exhibiting pre-reading skills. At that moment, he knew that letters of the alphabet, when combined, form words and words have meaning and represent objects. For him, the letters on the license plate stood for something and since it was on the license plate, he logically thought that the letters spelled the words license plate. Amazing at three years old!

My son was happy with his newfound skills. He began to "spell" everything. One evening we were having dinner and of course my son said, "I can spell apple juice", and of course, I encouraged him and asked him to spell it. I knew what was coming, but my husband had no clue. My son spelled apple juice by reciting the letters, "M-O-T-T-S." We high-fived each other and celebrated. My husband gave both of us a side look and walked away. He shook his head and left the kitchen as if to say, I am not even going to touch that one, clearly, something is definitely wrong with both of them. I did not need to correct my son because he did not know letter sounds yet, rather he recognized objects and letters and thought that the letters on the object identified the object. I was just overjoyed that he was well on his way to building a foundation for reading.

Back to the science of reading. Eventually, children will learn to recognize an increasing number of words automatically, freeing the brain from the cognitive overload required for decoding those words letter by letter. This shift is made possible because learning to read literally changes the brain. Neuroscience research revealed four areas in the brain (see Figure 1) that must work together to make reading possible: phonics, oral language, meaning, visual word form area or "letterbox". In the brain of proficient readers, the four areas are connected and work together through neural connections. For nonreaders or developing readers, the connections have not yet been formed.

In the reading brain, phonics (connecting letters with the sounds they represent) triggers oral language (the understanding and production of spoken language) which then triggers meaning (the alignment of spoken and written words with their meanings). During this time, there is rapid brain activity as neurons begin firing in the brain that can be seen using fMRI scans. Next, in response to the unique demands presented by reading acquisition, a specialized area is developed within the brain's visual system, or the letterbox (Cohen, et al., 2002 & Dehaene, et al., 2002). Learning to read transforms some of the visual structures of the brain in order to turn them into a specialized interface between vision and language (Dehaene & Cohen, 2007). The brain's letterbox supports orthographic mapping, which is the process that permanently bonds the speech sounds in a word (phonemes) with the spelling of those sounds (graphemes). The orthographic mapping process is essential to fluent reading, as it allows readers to recognize and process words quickly and efficiently. Once a word has been orthographically mapped, it becomes a sight word, which means it can be recognized and processed automatically without the need for conscious decoding. This frees up cognitive resources for higher-level comprehension tasks, such as understanding the meaning of the text as a whole. The orthographic mapping process makes fluent reading possible.

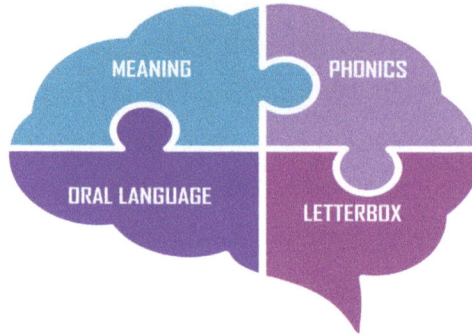

Figure 1: How the Brain Learns to Read

According to Dehaene, another feature of the reading system that is significant that readers must overcome is mirror invariance. The same part of the brain responsible for visual word form or the letterbox is responsible for mirror invariance. The brain recognizes an object like a chair no matter the orientation of the chair, whether flipped left, right, up or down; we still recognize it as a chair. In reading, children need to unlearn this for letter recognition. The alphabet contains pairs of letters such as "p" and "q" or "b" and "d". With mirror invariance, the brain treats these letters as identical. It is no wonder that young children often struggle with the identification of these letters. To read fluently, children must learn to discriminate between these letters perfectly. Mirror invariance is a universal feature of the brain that all children possess and must unlearn. As previously stated, we were not born to read; rather, we must teach the brain to read (Stanovich, 1994).

Frameworks for Reading – Simple View of Reading and Scarborough's Reading Rope

Neuroscience provides information on the reading process within the brain and education research reveals the nature of effective reading instruction. Based on the science of reading and education research, we know that elements from both sides of the reading camps, phonics, and the whole language approach are important for reading development. Reading is a product of decoding and comprehension. It sounds simple but learning to read is much tougher than people think because certain aspects of learning to read are highly unnatural. Good readers are phonemically aware, understand the alphabetic principle, and they apply these skills in a rapid and fluent manner. Good readers also have strong vocabulary and grammatical skills, and they relate reading to their own experiences (Lyons, 1998). Difficulties in any of these areas can impede reading development. Further, learning to read begins way before children enter kindergarten. Children who have stimulating literacy experiences from birth have an edge in vocabulary development, understanding of the goals of reading, and developing an awareness of print and literacy concepts. Conversely, the children who are most at risk for reading failure enter kindergarten and the elementary grades without these early experiences.

In 1997 congress convened the National Reading Panel (NPR) to review reading research. Based on the science of reading, the panel noted that reading instruction must include phonological awareness, phonics, fluency, vocabulary, and reading comprehension. However, many popular approaches to reading instruction are not aligned with the science of reading because they omit systematic teaching of speech sounds. To understand the theoretical underpinnings of the reading process from the viewpoint of educators, we must examine the Simple View of Reading (SVR) and Scarborough's Reading Rope frameworks. Both are aligned with modern neuroscience even though they pre-date much of the research. The SVR (see Figure 2) is one of the most research-supported frameworks for reading and asserts that students need skills in two areas: the first is reading each word in text accurately and fluently and the second is comprehending the meaning of text being read (Hoover & Gough, 1990). The SVR formula, Decoding x Language Comprehension = Reading Comprehension was proposed by Gough and Tunmer in 1986 and serves as a broad reference to the complexity of reading, assessment, and reading instruction requirements. Understanding this formula helps educators by pinpointing where to target reading instruction and serves as a framework for helping students progress in reading based on assessment data and strengths and weaknesses in the decoding and language comprehension components.

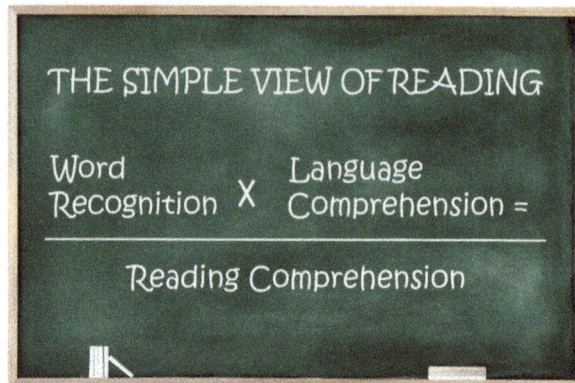

Figure 2: Gough & Tunmer's 1986 Simple View of Reading

According to Gough and Tunmer, word recognition or decoding is the act of reading in its simplest form. It is the ability to match sounds to symbols, segment a word sound by sound, and then blend the sounds to form the word. To read fluently, readers need to break the alphabetic code (sound-symbol correspondence) automatically. Language comprehension is deriving meaning from spoken words when they are part of a sentence. Reading comprehension is deriving meaning from print. Comprehension is complex and involves several higher-level mental processes that include thinking, reasoning, imagining, and interpreting (Baker et al., 2017). When students are unable to decode words, reading comprehension is lost. Students need to decode the words and understand the words and if one of those components is weak, reading comprehension will be negatively impacted.

The simple view of reading demonstrates that reading difficulties fall into three basic types: (1) poor language comprehension where a student has adequate decoding skills but weak language comprehension skills, (2) poor decoding where a student has adequate language comprehension and weak decoding skills, or (3) weaknesses in both areas. For students in the early stages of reading, or those who struggle, reading is particularly difficult and requires careful instruction and intervention. Problem areas must be identified, and instruction and intervention to address these areas must be carefully planned and delivered. Teaching reading aligned with the body of research that comprises the science of reading is critical to positively impacting student outcomes.

To understand the complexities of learning to read, Dr. Hollis Scarborough created the reading rope (see Figure 3), using pipe cleaners to convey how the different "strands" of reading are all interconnected yet independent of one another. The strands also demonstrate the various skills children need to master to become proficient readers. For many students, learning to read is a challenge and the rope model can help educators better understand what it truly takes to create skilled readers. Scarborough's reading rope elaborates on the simple view of reading by identifying component skills within the two domains of word recognition and language comprehension. Christensen posited that foundational word recognition skills are woven together to support increasingly automatic reading while language comprehension skills work together so that reading becomes increasingly strategic. Woven together, these strands become the rope that represents skilled reading. All the components are interconnected and interdependent. If just one strand is weak, it affects the rope (and the reader) as a whole. When all the component parts intertwine, it results in skilled, accurate, fluent reading with strong comprehension.

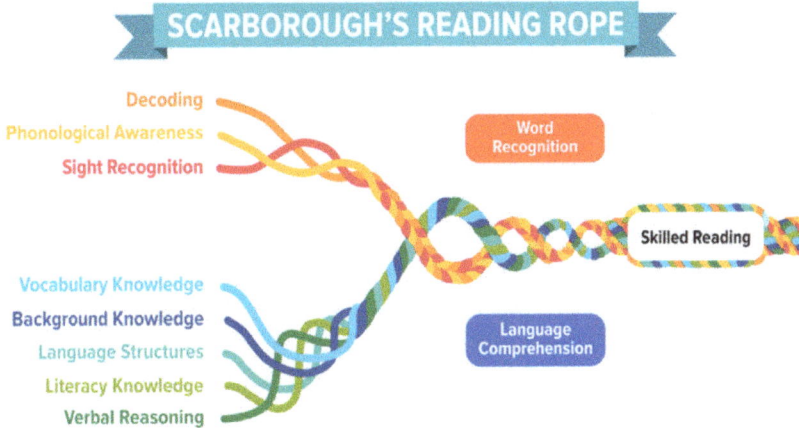

Figure 3: Dr. Hollis Scarborough's Reading Rope

The Reading Rope has two strands. The first strand focuses on word recognition skills, which include phonological awareness, decoding, and sight words. These are the skills we tend to think of most when we talk about teaching children to read. Phonological awareness is the understanding that words are made up of sounds. Children learn to speak without ever needing to see a written word. However, when learning to read, they need to recognize that the sounds they make with their mouths correspond with the words they see on the page. This is a very early skill that sets the stage for what follows. Decoding is what we picture when we see beginning readers sounding out the words letter by letter. It includes phonics, letter blends, silent letters, and more. Children proficient at decoding can sound out all the words they see on a page, even if they do not know what the words mean. Sight word memory is also referred to as our orthographic lexicon, which includes all the words we can read accurately and effortlessly. Literate adults have a sight word memory of about 30,000 to 70,000 words. In third grade, it is estimated that "skilled orthographic mappers" anchor 10-15 new words per day into their sight word memories. Sight word recognition is foundational to fluent reading.

The second strand of the reading rope is for language comprehension. If children do not know what the words mean, they are not reading. Fluent readers understand the text they read as a whole, and they draw meaningful conclusions. The second strand of Scarborough's rope is incredibly key in creating strong readers. The strand includes background knowledge, vocabulary, language structure, verbal reasoning, and literacy knowledge. First, readers rely on background knowledge to attend to and make sense of what they are reading. This is especially important for readers who are still relying heavily on word decoding rather than rapid word recognition. Having knowledge about a variety of subjects, topics, and ideas makes it more likely that students will be able to make sense of what they are reading and add to their body of knowledge. Second, an extensive and rich vocabulary enables readers to make sense of what they are reading. A reader with rich auditory and oral vocabularies will find it easier to read through text that contains words they have not seen in print before. Third, the language structure on the reading rope generally means syntax and semantics. Syntax is the arrangement of words in a phrase or sentence. The English language has patterns and rules for the way words are ordered. It also has some flexibility and variety in acceptable patterns, and even then, speakers and writers are allowed some leeway with these patterns. Semantics is the study of the meanings of words, phrases, and sentences. Knowledge of the meaning of a text is essential to reading. Fourth, verbal reasoning refers to the understanding of when and how words are being figurative and literal. It includes metaphors, analogies, idioms, and figurative language. Fifth, literacy knowledge is the exposure to a wide array of genres and styles, and it includes print concepts. Print concepts refers to how print works and include letters, words, reading left-to-right and top-to-bottom, spaces between written words, letter order, etc. Genres of literature refer to a distinctive type or category of literary composition such as the epic, tragedy, comedy, novel, and short story. A strong curriculum covers fiction, nonfiction, and poetry in all forms. The more types of reading children encounter, the more advanced their literacy knowledge becomes.

Many teachers find Scarborough's Rope useful in two main ways. First, it helps teachers identify where struggling readers may need more help. Once they identify the weak strand, a teacher can adjust or offer enrichment to help that student succeed. Second, teachers can share this model with families to help them understand why their child is struggling or why teachers use various teaching strategies in the classroom. The reading rope is a good tool to reinforce the importance of reading at home, which is essential to building the literacy skills children need in school and throughout their lives. For older struggling students, if they are not comprehending what they are reading, many times teachers jump to the conclusion that language comprehension is the issue. However, it could be that the student never learned to be good at decoding. There could also be the opposite issue. There could be a student who is brilliant at sounding out words but struggles to make sense of the text. This child may need more instruction in vocabulary, verbal reasoning, syntax, and so on. Or there could be a student who struggles in both areas. Assessing the reading needs of students is key in reading instruction for all students but particularly for struggling readers. It must be noted that struggling readers are not just students from high-risk environments; rather, children from more advantaged, literacy-rich environments have trouble learning to read as well (Scarborough & Dobrich, 1994). However, these children are afforded the opportunity to have tutors to help them learn to read. The environment alone does not give a full and complete explanation of reading struggles.

Best Practices in Reading Instruction

The simple view of reading and Scarborough's reading rope frameworks clarify the essential elements that are needed in the reading process. What should be emphasized instructionally is based on brain development and its processing systems. For readers to navigate through text and utilize language comprehension strategies, a level of automaticity in word recognition needs to be secured. When words are recognized instantly, readers can focus their attention on constructing the meaning of text. The images of the simple view of reading and the reading rope give visual images of the process of reading. This does not mean that reading is a simple process. According to the National Reading Panel (NICHD, 2000), the essential components of reading instruction include phonological awareness, phonics, fluency, vocabulary, and reading comprehension. It is important to note that each of these components is highly connected and should not be taught as distinct skills. The simple view of reading, the reading rope, and components of reading instruction provide a good explanation and plan for effective reading instruction. The components of reading instruction are aligned to the simple view of reading and the reading rope frameworks. Phonological awareness, phonics, and fluency comprise word recognition in the simple view of reading and the first strand on the reading rope. Vocabulary and comprehension comprise language comprehension in the simple view of reading and the second strand on the reading rope.

Components of Reading Instruction

According to the National Institutes of Health, more than a third of children in the United States cannot read by the 4th grade. The great news is that this unacceptable rate of failure, which disproportionately harms students of color, can be reduced or eliminated by understanding the cognitive processes early readers need for skilled reading, which include attention, auditory and visual processing, working memory, and more. Additionally, when teachers utilize effective reading instruction that includes **phonological awareness**, **phonics**, **fluency**, **vocabulary**, and **reading comprehension**, the rate of failure can be reduced significantly. Typically, the components are taught together in a comprehensive literacy program.

Phonological awareness and phonemic awareness, are used interchangeably but they are not the same. To understand phonological awareness, we must first understand the difference between phonological awareness & phonemic awareness as too often people use both interchangeably when they are two different skills. Phonological awareness is what enables you to hear the sentence, "My brother plays soccer", and immediately determine that it contains four spoken words. It allows you to quickly identify that 'sat' and 'cat' rhyme, while 'bat' and 'boat' do not. And it enables you to determine that the spoken syllables /pic/ and /nic/ together make the word picnic and that the spoken word parts /spl/ and /ash/ put together to make the word 'splash'. Identifying and manipulating speech at the word, syllable, and onset-rime level are the marks of phonological awareness.

People often think that reading begins with learning to sound out letters. But most young children are preparing to read long before they understand the connection between letters and sounds. In preschool, for example, children are usually exposed to various types of language play, songs, rhymes, and stories in their daily activities. Eventually, children produce rhymes on their own. They also begin to break words apart into syllables or single sounds. Most children pick up phonological awareness naturally. Phonemic awareness, on the other hand, is what enables you to hear and manipulate the smallest units of speech, called phonemes.

It is phonemic awareness when you identify that the word 'cap' has three sounds, /c/ /ă/ /p/, while the word 'split' has five, /s/ /p/ /l/ /ĭ/ /t/. Phonemic awareness allows you to hear the individual sounds in /f/ /r/ /ŏ/ /g/ and know right away that this is the word 'frog'. And it is what tells you that 'stop' without the /s/ is 'top', that adding /s/ to the beginning of 'mash' gives you 'smash', and that changing the /ĭ/ in 'quick' to /ă/ gives you 'quack'. Phonemic awareness is the ability to hear and manipulate units of sound in spoken words, which includes sensitivity to words, rhyme, alliteration, syllables, onset, and rime, and individual sounds. It is about understanding that words are made up of sounds.

Phonological awareness is an umbrella term that involves a group of skills (see Figure 4). One such skill is phonemic awareness, which as previously stated involves tuning into individual sounds in a word, or phonemes. It allows us to break apart a word into its individual sounds and blend single sounds into words. Once children can manage single sounds in words, they are ready for the next step in reading: decoding. Decoding is the process of translating written language into spoken language. It involves recognizing the individual letters and their sounds, and blending them together to form words. It is a critical skill for learning to read and is typically developed in kindergarten and first grade. Phonemic awareness is an essential component of decoding because it enables children to recognize and manipulate the individual sounds in words, which is necessary for accurately sounding out and blending words (Kilpatrick, 2015). Without phonemic awareness, decoding can be a difficult and frustrating process. The goal of decoding is to build words into our sight word memory, and phonemic awareness allows this to happen. Essentially, phonological awareness and phonemic awareness skills are important precursors to reading.

How is it possible that children with a robust oral language experience and frequent early interactions with literacy activities also have difficulties learning to read? The answer may be found in longitudinal research that clearly indicates that deficits in phonemic awareness skills not only predict difficulties in learning to read, but they also have a negative effect on reading acquisition. While phonemic awareness is necessary for adequate reading development, it is not sufficient by itself. Children must also develop phonics concepts and apply those skills fluently in text.

Phonics is a method of teaching reading that focuses on the relationship between the sounds of spoken English and the letters or groups of letters that represent those sounds in written language. Phonics instruction typically begins with familiarizing children with letter-sound relationships. Research has shown that phonics instruction is an effective way to help students learn to read.

Phonological Awareness

| Word Analysis | Rhyming & Alliteration | Syllable Awareness | Phonemic Awareness |

Figure 4: Phonological Awareness

The brain is not naturally wired for reading, so the specialized letterbox area of the brain must be repurposed through neuronal recycling. This process enables the brain to recognize letters and strings of letters and to decode words more easily. Multimodal instruction, which combines visual, auditory, and kinesthetic learning experiences, is often the most effective way to teach phonics to students. By learning the letter name, shape, and sound through a variety of modalities, students are better able to retain the information and apply it when reading and spelling words.

Practically Speaking

As I was preparing to write this book, one of my sons called me and I could not talk to him because I was about to attend a webinar. I told my son that I was preparing for a webinar on phonics and couldn't speak with him for long. He said, "Phonics... Is that the same as the Hooked-on Phonics thing you made us do during our summer breaks?" We laughed and I said, "Yes, it is." When my sons were learning to read, I knew that they were missing the phonics piece and decided to explicitly teach it at home since it was not taught systematically in school. This was over 20 years ago, but I knew then how important it was for reading proficiency.

Multimodal instruction has been shown to help children tremendously with phonics. For example, the pictorial mnemonic strategy is where a letter is associated with an image of a character or object whose name sounds like the actual letter of the alphabet and the character or object forms the letter of the alphabet (see Figure 5). One thing that is not recommended is the teaching of one letter a week approach because it is not a sound strategy, and it would take 52 weeks to get through the alphabet. Rather, students should be introduced to a few letters at a time and as soon as they recognize a few letters and the corresponding sounds like M, S, and A, teachers should begin blending those sounds and make words to extend the continuance and stretch the sound. For example, students could make the words, am, Sam, at, mat, and sat.The English spelling conventions are very complex, but phonics rules are still very helpful in breaking the code. Solity and Vousden (2009) found that if students know 64 of the most common letter-sound correspondences, they would be able to recognize 100 of the most common words in English and would be able to identify 90% of words young readers tend to see in texts. Similarly, Hanna (1966) found that spelling for 20 phonemes is predictable more than 80% of the time. Spelling for 10 phonemes is predictable more than 80% of the time. Spelling for 8 phonemes is predictable more than 78% of the time. For the most part, very few words are truly irregular. Word building or orthographic mapping must be a strong focus of phonics instruction. Orthographic mapping helps students map into their long-term memory the correctly written form of any word so that they can automatically recognize it. Therefore, word family instruction is still recommended because as students build their orthographic mapping skills, they not only lock in letters and sound combinations but groups and patterns of letters with their sounds.

Fluency is defined by Merriam-Webster as capable of moving with ease and grace. Fluency in reading is reasonable and accurate reading at an appropriate rate with suitable prosody (expression) that leads to accurate and deep comprehension and the motivation to read (Hasbrouck & Glaser, 2012). Fluency in reading is essential for building comprehension skills, as it allows readers to focus on understanding the meaning of the text rather than decoding individual words.

Figure 5: Pictorial Mnemonics Examples

Phonological awareness and phonics are important foundational skills for developing fluency, as they help readers recognize and decode words quickly and accurately. Fluency is not just about reading quickly, but also about reading with expression and inflection, which helps to make the reading sound natural and conversational. Fluent readers are able to read aloud smoothly and effortlessly, without stumbling over words or pausing excessively. It is important to teach fluency early in the process of learning to read, as it sets the foundation for comprehension skills. If students spend too much time decoding individual words, they may not have enough cognitive space to focus on understanding the meaning of the text. Sight word recognition is also an important component of fluent reading, as it allows readers to automatically recognize common words without having to decode them each time they encounter them in text. Sight words are words that are automatically recognized. Proficient readers have between 30,000 and 80,000 sight words.

Practically Speaking

The focus group of educators that I interviewed agreed that most of their students suffer from fluency issues. This makes sense in that fluency strongly depends on phonological awareness and phonics. If students are struggling in either of the two areas, they will struggle with fluency. Fluency is the building block for reading comprehension. When students spend a lot of time trying to figure out words, they do not have time to process the meaning of what they read, and they tend to give up on the process altogether. The educators in my focus group realized they do not spend nearly enough time on foundational skills, but according to them, the time is not built into the curriculum or the reading block. One educator said, "Things are just too fast, and our reading block is just too short for all that we must cover, and the sad thing is, the students suffer."

Another educator stated that she sends home additional homework for children to work on foundational skills to compensate for what she cannot do in the classroom. The travesty is that many teachers know what students need to read successfully but their hands are tied because they must follow the guidelines established by school, district, and state. There was one statement from an educator that struck me deeply. This individual resigned from her position as a first-grade teacher of 15 years and became an adjunct professor at the university in the town where she lives. Her story tugged at my heart because she struggled in making her decision to leave public schools and the students that she cherished deeply but she felt that she was doing a disservice to them. She stated that year after year, she would do the same thing (in reading) and get the same results, which became depressing. She further stated, "When you know better, you should do better but when your hands are tied, you can't do better, so I had to make a choice." Her last statement really gave me pause, she said, "If it is not good enough for my biological children, it should not be good enough for anyone." I immediately thought, "How deep is that?" Why should we expect the best for our own children, but provide less than the best for other people's children? I wonder if we taught other people's children the way we expect our own children to be taught, would we have a reading problem in the United States? As a society and an educational institution, we must do better.

Vocabulary and Reading Comprehension are closely related, and both are dependent on background knowledge and a large vocabulary bank. Students who have a broad range of background knowledge and a large vocabulary are better able to understand and engage with a variety of texts. Fluency is an important factor in supporting reading comprehension. When students are able to read fluently, they are able to focus more on understanding the meaning of the text rather than on identifying individual words. This allows them to engage more deeply with the text and to develop their comprehension skills. Background knowledge is another key factor in developing reading comprehension. When students have prior knowledge about a topic, they are better able to understand and make connections with the material they are reading. Purposeful conversations and engaging read-aloud activities can help to activate students' background knowledge and develop their comprehension skills. Comprehension is developed through purposeful conversations and engaging read-aloud activities. Students should practice comprehension strategies before, during, and after reading. For example, before reading a story, teachers must gain an understanding of what students already know about the subject. Teachers should also build background knowledge by providing information about the subject to help students connect with the story.

Another strategy is to find ways for students to connect with the story perhaps by placing themselves in the story. Also, teachers must be sure to provide embedded vocabulary support for unfamiliar or new words. When students learn the meanings of new words, they should learn about the larger ideas and concepts behind those words. A strong vocabulary bank contributes to a large knowledge bank, which supports better reading comprehension. Prior to reading a story, introduce new words with child-friendly definitions, provide activities with the new words to reinforce word meaning, be sure that words are connected to the text, and check for understanding with students. During reading time, teachers must give students the opportunity to pause and think about what's happening in the story, make predictions, and consider the author's choice of language, and character development in the story. After reading a story, students should describe the characters, setting, and plot. Teachers could also provide opportunities for students to compare the text to other stories or make a connection to the story of some kind and answer who, what, when, where, and how questions.

Elements of Effective Instruction

The essential components for reading proficiency have been researched and documented for years. The problem is not what needs to be taught, but how it should be taught. Many empirical studies show that a large portion of students at risk for reading difficulties can develop and maintain "normalized" reading skills when provided with the right intervention" (Kilpatrick, 2015). A convergence of brain science with education science helps to identify the key elements of effective instruction that can bring to fruition the vision of universal literacy. The National Reading Panel (2000) identified five key components of effective reading instruction: explicit, systematic, cumulative, diagnostic, and responsive. Explicit instruction is clear, direct, and provides students with scaffolded support and timely feedback. This helps to ensure that students understand what is being taught and can apply the information to their reading. Systematic instruction is carefully ordered and free of gaps in understanding. Students progress through the material based on mastery, and they receive reinforcement or additional support when needed. Cumulative instruction builds logically on what has been learned previously, with concepts presented from simple to more complex. This ensures that what students learn today prepares them for what they will learn in the future. Diagnostic instruction involves gathering actionable data that can be used by teachers to identify the next steps for each student. This allows teachers to tailor their instruction to meet the needs of individual students and ensure that they are making progress. Responsive instruction requires teachers to adjust their instruction when necessary to meet the needs of their students. This may involve using different teaching strategies or providing additional support or challenge as needed. Effective instruction is essential for students to gain and master essential reading skills. By providing explicit, systematic, cumulative, diagnostic, and responsive instruction, teachers can help students develop the skills they need to become confident and proficient readers.

The Reading Ladder, created by Nancy Young (2017) states that 5% of students learn to read effortlessly, 35% learn to read relatively easy with broad instruction, and 40% to 50% (the bulk of students) learn to read using code-based explicit, systematic, and sequential instruction. For 10% to 15%, learning to read proficiently requires code-based explicit, systematic, and sequential diagnostic instruction with many repetitions. Substantial evidence shows that many students in the first and second grades and beyond will require explicit instruction to develop necessary phoneme awareness, phonics, spelling, and reading comprehension skills (Seidenberg, 2017). But for most students, these skills will not be sufficient. For students having difficulties learning to read, each of the foundational skills must be taught and integrated into textual reading formats to ensure sufficient levels of fluency, automaticity, and understanding. Our brains are much more similar than they are different, and all students need to learn basically the same things to change their non-reading brains into reading brains according to Seidenberg. What students need to learn for reading proficiency does not change.

One of the most consistent findings in all of education research is that students become better readers when they get explicit and systematic phonics instruction. Sadly enough, this is not the case for far too many students, especially children of color. In 1998, the National Research Council wrote, "Demands for higher literacy are ever increasing, creating more grievous consequences for those who fall short." Almost twenty-five years later, this is still true. The problem is that the education world is relying on reading instruction that is based on "outdated assumptions about reading and development that makes learning to read harder than it needs to be, a sure way to leave many children behind (Seidenberg, 2014, p. 240)." The education world is aware of the skills and the type of instruction needed to produce proficient readers. The questions to ask are, if this information is widely known, and why are so many students still unable to read. The answers may be found in the connection of research to practice, or the lack thereof.

Research and Practice

Over the years, a lot of the research on reading was conducted by the National Institute of Child Health and Human Development (NICHD), which is part of the National Institutes of Health, a federal agency that emphasizes basic biomedical science and health-related research. I wondered why a health research organization is interested in reading. I also read a statement by Lyons, one of the leading researchers, who said, "Learning to read is critical to a child's overall health and well-being. If a child does not learn to read in our literacy-driven society, hope for a fulfilling, productive life diminishes. Further, difficulties learning to read are not only an educational problem but a serious public health concern." From Lyons' perspective, it makes sense to equate illiteracy to health and well-being. Being a proficient reader has major implications for a student's entire educational experience and success in life. Some teachers are better prepared at teaching students to read while others are not. Over the past years, the science of reading has compiled information that holds important implications for empowering teachers with the knowledge to help students succeed in reading. The bad news is that many teachers have not been introduced to this information or have dismissed it altogether, which impacts students' ability to read proficiently. The scientific community has achieved a broad consensus on how children learn to read, what causes reading difficulties, the essential components of effective reading instruction, and how to prevent reading difficulties. According to Louisa Moats, an education consultant, and researcher, there are thousands of studies on reading, making it the most studied aspect of human learning.

Dr. Kim Gibbons stated in an article in 2020 that not knowing how to effectively teach reading is not the problem. Rather, the real problem is the gap between science and practice. Even though data show that the science of reading is effective, the information has not yet made its way into many elementary school classrooms. Many educators do not know the science, and in some cases actively resist it. According to Gibbons, the resistance is the result of beliefs about reading that have been deeply held in the educational establishment for decades, even though those beliefs have been proven wrong by scientists over and over again.

Practically Speaking

Not surprisingly, but only three of the educators in my education focus group had knowledge of the science of reading; the rest never heard of it or its application to reading instruction. One teacher shared that her district provided a mandatory reading course about the science of reading for all teachers in grades K-3 over a three-year period. She found the course to be "thoroughly informative, scientific, very heavy but useful, and daunting but doable." She stated, "It will take time to absorb and process the abundance of information from the course, but it is something that we must do, everyone who teaches reading should be required to take the course." The teacher could not believe after teaching for more than ten years and obtaining multiple degrees and certifications in education that she was never exposed to the science of reading. She shared bits and pieces of what she learned in the course with colleagues in other school districts and no one she knew had the training. She stated, "I'm glad my district made this course mandatory because it will benefit our students."

Another teacher in the cohort has been a reading teacher for over twenty years and is a strong supporter of the whole language approach. She stated, "We had whole language, which was supposed to revolutionize education, but it didn't. We also had hooked on phonics; that didn't work either. Now we have balanced literacy, which is a little of this and a little of that. You just don't know what to believe anymore; there are too many changes in education." Many teachers share some of the same thoughts and these same individuals are teaching reading to young students without the proper training to do so. No fault of their own as some teachers do not know that their current practices are not aligned with the science of reading. They simply don't know what they don't know. Meanwhile, we have millions of students who cannot read proficiently. Then we blame it on poverty, language barriers, home life, or behavior; however, research has proven that students from high-income families struggle to read as well.

Gibbons stated that in the most recent report from the National Council on Teacher Quality (2020) only about half of the traditional elementary teacher preparation programs across the country are teaching scientifically based reading instruction to future teachers. Moats believed that support for multi-tiered instruction and preventive intervention depend first and foremost on capable, educated teachers. Unfortunately, many teachers and administrators who could benefit from research to guide reading instructional practices do not yet trust the idea that research can inform their teaching. One reason for this lack of faith is the disagreement about reading development and instruction among education leaders. Most great scientific discoveries have come from a willingness and an ability to be wrong. Researchers and teachers could serve children much better if they had the courage to set aside assumptions when they are not working.

The fundamental purpose of science is to test our beliefs and intuitions and provide us with evidence-based information about the world around us. This is particularly important in the field of education, where teachers and educators must be open and receptive to change when the research data is clear and consistent about effective reading instruction. It is time for the educational world to embrace the fundamental belief that all students can learn to read. This means using evidence-based reading instruction that is proven to be effective, rather than relying on outdated or ineffective methods. If we continue to do what we have been doing, we will continue to see great variability in reading outcomes and further disadvantage the most vulnerable students. By embracing evidence-based reading instruction and remaining open to change, educators can help to ensure that all students have the opportunity to develop strong reading skills and succeed in their academic and personal lives. In medicine, if researchers found new ways to save lives, health care professionals would adopt these methods as quickly as possible, and would change practices, procedures, and systems in a heartbeat. Educational research has found new ways to save young minds by helping them to become proficient readers; it is up to us to promote these new methods throughout the educational system; young students' lives depend on it (Moats, 1999). If the education world took a page from the medical world, we could change the course of so many students.

In a groundbreaking article in 2020, Emily Hanford found that most teachers nationwide are not being taught the science of reading in their teacher preparation programs because many deans and faculty members in colleges of education either do not know the science or dismiss it altogether. As a result, millions of students have been set up to fail. "There are schools and school districts across the United States trying to change reading instruction, but according to Moats, ill-informed, ineffective reading instruction is the norm and the gap between science-based ideas and practices and those most often used in classrooms remains very wide and persistent." In the 2016 issue of the Journal of Childhood & Developmental Disorders it stated that part of the problem rests in schools of education at the college and university levels because faculty have ignored the scientific knowledge that informs reading acquisition; therefore, the prospective teachers at these institutions fail to receive proper training.

In 2016, the National Council on Teacher Quality, a Washington, D.C. based think tank, reviewed the syllabi of teacher preparation programs across the country and found that only 39% of them appeared to teach the components of effective reading instruction. Seidenberg says scientific research has had relatively little impact on what happens in classrooms because science is not highly valued in schools of education. Prospective teachers are not exposed to it or they are led to believe that the science of reading is one of several perspectives. He further stated that in a class on reading, prospective teachers are exposed to a menu in which they have 10 or 12 different approaches to reading instruction, and they are encouraged to pick the one that fits their personal teaching style best. The problem is, teachers are not learning to read, the students are, and we must provide instruction that meets their developmental needs, not instruction that caters to teaching styles or preferences. To change the reading discourse in our schools, we must change the culture of education from one based on beliefs to one based on facts.

In the early 2000s, Butler and colleagues from the Barksdale Reading Institute wanted to know if teacher preparation programs in Mississippi instructed teachers to teach reading in ways backed by science. They engaged in a study of the teacher preparation programs at the state's eight publicly funded universities. They reviewed syllabi and textbooks, surveyed the students in the classes, observed some of the classes, and interviewed the deans and faculty. Butler and colleagues found that teacher candidates in Mississippi were getting an average of 20 minutes of instruction in phonics over their entire two-year teacher preparation program. Butler and her colleagues presented their findings to state education officials and pleaded with them to take action. In 2003, in a rather extraordinary move, the Mississippi Department of Education mandated that every teacher preparation program in Mississippi require two courses in early literacy to cover what was in the National Reading Panel report. It is not uncommon for colleges and universities to resist outside regulation or mandates from state officials, especially when it comes to what is taught in the classroom. Professors and faculty members value academic freedom, which allows them to design and teach their courses as they see fit. However, in the case of Mississippi's mandate for early literacy courses, it was based on the National Reading Panel report, which was based on the science of reading. This means that the mandate was grounded in evidence-based research, and therefore had a strong rationale for being implemented. Despite this, it is not surprising that resistance to the science of reading persists among some faculty members and administrators. Changing long-held beliefs and practices can be challenging, especially when they are deeply ingrained in the culture of an institution. It was extraordinary because even though states have the authority to regulate teacher preparation programs, only a handful of states have specific requirements about what prospective teachers learn about reading.

The Mississippi Department of Education mandated two courses in early literacy for all teacher preparation programs in the state in 2003, based on the science of reading outlined in the National Reading Panel report. However, it was not clear how much impact this had on the practice of teaching reading. In 2015, Mississippi legislators passed the "Literacy-Based Promotion Act," which stated that students who were not reading on grade level by the end of third grade could not be promoted to fourth grade. Millions of dollars were appropriated to provide training in the science of reading for all elementary school teachers in the state. However, Butler and her colleagues found that, despite appearing to teach the components of reading identified by the National Reading Panel report, many teacher preparation programs were not adequately preparing their students. When interviewed, many faculty members admitted they had not actually read the report and did not have a good understanding of the science of reading. As a result, a governor's task force recommended that college instructors receive the same training as elementary school teachers. While participation in the training was not required, a measure was passed to encourage it.

Since 2016, teacher candidates in Mississippi are required to pass a test on reading science. If they do not pass what is known as the Foundations of Reading Test, a license to teach elementary school in Mississippi will not be granted. It is now in the best interest of faculty to teach the science of reading because if they do not, their students will not get jobs. In the Mississippi example, legislators, colleges and university faculty, and public school administrators followed the science and created a system to ensure that all students receive reading instruction based on the science. It takes a village to raise a reader.

Things are Getting Better

In full disclosure, many states are moving in the right direction regarding reading instruction. In an article written by Natalie Wexler in 2022, she provided an update and a summary of early literacy instruction in the state of Tennessee. Tennessee is part of a network of 13 states working to address early literacy under the support of the Council of Chief State School Officers (CCSSO) and so far, Tennessee's efforts have been among the most ambitious. The CCSSO is committed to ensuring that all students have access to the resources and rigor they need at the right moment in their education. The CCSSO ensures that children receive strong, standards-aligned instruction from teachers equipped with high-quality instructional materials aligned to standards with professional development accordingly. It is encouraging to hear about the progress being made in Tennessee with regards to early literacy instruction. The state's use of federal funds to provide evidence-based reading instruction, protocols for assessing decoding difficulties, and remediation for students who need it, as well as professional development for teachers, are all important steps in improving literacy outcomes for students. It is also promising that the state is investing in revamping training for future reading teachers and encouraging families to be more involved in literacy activities at home. The focus on building academic knowledge through literacy curricula that dive deeply into topics in history and science is also an important aspect of ensuring that students are prepared for success in all areas of their education. It will be interesting to see how other states in the CCSSO network are progressing in their efforts to improve early literacy instruction.

Practically Speaking

I continued my conversations about the science of reading with my education focus group. The teachers who had gone through the reading course acknowledged that they felt better about reading instruction and finally felt that they had a "grasp on how to teach and what to teach" for the first time in their careers. One teacher said she learned more about the brain in one year than in her entire lifetime, stating, "Reading is all about the brain." The science of reading is not a curriculum or program; it is a detailed description of how the reading brain works and once teachers have a clear understanding of that process, they are better able to provide the best reading instructional practices to build proficient readers.

According to the focus group, most of their students enter kindergarten with sufficient skills because most had preschool experience. However, something happens during first and second grade when students begin to experience reading fadeout (see chapter 10 for more on reading fadeout). Participants believed that instead of students progressing toward reading proficiency, they began to regress and fall further and further behind as they moved up in grades. I asked what they thought contributed to regression and the group was split. The participants who did not have the science of reading training attributed regression to all things outside of the school building like poverty, absenteeism, low vocabulary skills, English proficiency, and special education.

The participants who had professional development in the science of reading attributed regression to a lack of foundational skills and the lack of alignment practices from grade to grade. One participant said, "We lost our way when we moved away from the basics; if students don't have a foundation in reading, they will begin to regress beginning in first grade as we have seen for so many years and could not put our finger on it." The reading coach stated, "Reading is a cumulative process where lower skills serve as a base for advanced skills." Things are truly getting better. There is hope!

Practical Application

What can you do?

1. Schedule and watch the film The Right to Read to build background knowledge of the current reading concerns (see link below). The documentary is about a community activist who fights to bring the science of reading to his school district. Afterwards, use the study guide for a rich discussion about the film. Based on the information gained from the film and your discussions, create an action plan for reading proficiency in your school community. The plan should include the school, the family, and the community and must be specific, measurable, attainable, realistic, and timed.

    https://www.therighttoreadfilm.org/

2. Watch Sold a Story (see link below) which is a six-part podcast series that exposes the truth about how children were taught to read for decades using a popular approach that was not based on the science or research. As a results, millions of children struggled to read proficiently. After watching the documentary, meet with school leaders to inquire about the approach to reading they are using. If the district's reading approach is not grounded in the science, investigate the reason as to why not.

    https://www.iheart.com/podcast/3-sold-a-story-103249311/

"Reading is not an easy skill to master. However, the science of reading provides us with the tools needed to nurture the reading brain. We do know the skills and the methodology to teach reading. Knowing this information is one thing, but implementing it to fidelity is another. If we want to change the reading narrative, we must turn to the science and embrace it instead of denying and turning away from it.

Reading is a cumulative process; a continuum that begins at birth and extends through third grade. The time is right to do what's right by children."

- Dr. Jacquelyn Bobien-Blanton

Part III:

Normalizing Best Instructional Practices

"Since culture and differences are essential to humanity, they should play a central role in teaching and learning. To ignore them is to assure that the human dignity and learning potential of ethnically, culturally, and racially diverse students are constrained or minimized."
- Geneva Gay (2002)

Chapter 8

Culturally Responsive Teaching

I Am More Than What You See

Culturally relevant teaching (CRT) was made popular by Dr. Gloria Ladson-Billings in the early 1990s. She defined the term as one "that empowers students to maintain cultural integrity, while succeeding academically." Although CRT has been around for over 30 years, the term is still relatively misunderstood and/or not practiced or implemented properly in many schools throughout the United States.

It is important to note that culturally responsive teaching (CRT) is a complex and nuanced concept that has been debated among educators and scholars. While there is no one definitive definition, CRT generally refers to a teaching approach that acknowledges and incorporates the cultural backgrounds and experiences of students into the classroom, curriculum, and teaching strategies. This approach is intended to help students from diverse backgrounds feel more connected to their learning and to improve their academic achievement. However, as noted by Sleeter (2011), the implementation of CRT has been uneven and often ineffective. Some educators may view CRT as simply adding cultural activities or content to the curriculum without fundamentally changing the teaching practices or power dynamics in the classroom. In some cases, CRT may even reinforce negative stereotypes or misunderstandings about certain cultural groups. To truly implement CRT in a meaningful way, educators must engage in ongoing self-reflection, cultural competence training, and collaboration with students and families to create a classroom environment that is truly inclusive and supportive of all learners.

The educational system in the United States has come a long way in its attempts to acknowledge the impact of CRT on student achievement. However, acknowledgement is just one step in improving the learning experiences for all students. We need to improve the implementation of CRT and move past the compliance phase. Currently, many schools believe that they are culturally responsive and to a certain degree they are. Before moving into the tenets of CRT, we will first explore how it is implemented in many public schools today.

According to Sleeter (2011), culturally responsive teaching is practiced by educators in four distinct ways, all of which have positive intentions but poor results. The four ways include **cultural celebrations**, **trivialization**, **essentializing**, and **substituting**.

Cultural celebrations are a common practice among many educators. It is about celebrating the culture and traditions of other groups. However, it separates culture from academic instruction. Some schools have created ethnic clubs and celebratory events, but that is the extent of CRT. This approach leaves out relationship building, communication, and instruction, which are critical in

CRT. It is the substituting of the cultural celebrations for academic learning that is the problem because the cultural celebrations are seen as the endpoint rather than using culture as a tool to teach engaging academic knowledge and skills through the cultural processes and knowledge students bring to school with them. Teachers then miss the opportunity to build relationships, communicate, and provide instruction that is engaging, respectful, relevant, and meaningful to all students. In **trivialization**, teachers often use surveys and checklists to get to know their students but never venture out into the student's community to gain a deeper or personal understanding of the cultural norms within the community. Trivialization aids in getting to know students but fails at using the information to assist in the teaching and learning process.

Essentializing is the practice of categorizing groups of people within a culture, or from other cultures, according to essential qualities. In other words, it is the practice of attributing particular characteristics to everyone identified with a particular category. For example, one might attribute having rhythm to all African Americans. Educators who view CRT from this viewpoint assume a fixed and homogeneous conception of the culture of the minority group and believe that students who are members of that group identify with the same conceptions. Therefore, if teachers understand the essential qualities of the minority group, they do not need input from the students themselves. Teachers have projected onto the students an essentialized view of who they are. Projections and assumptions do not show value or respect for student's racial/ethnic cultures and do not encourage students to be themselves.

When teachers **substitute culture** for addressing the underlying systemic issues that contribute to educational disparities, they are ignoring the larger societal factors that affect their students. These systemic issues include racism, poverty, and other forms of oppression that have historical roots and continue to impact marginalized communities today. Therefore, it is important for teachers to not only incorporate cultural responsiveness in their teaching but also to address systemic inequities that contribute to disparities in educational outcomes for marginalized students. By doing so, they can create a more equitable and just learning environment for all students. Substituting culture is a major problem in many public schools where the instructional staff's culture is different from the student population because instruction could be impacted. Shields et al. (2005) found that teachers' views of minority students in deficit terms, have inevitable negative consequences for their longer-term academic success.

Teachers who view and practice CRT in these four ways have missed opportunities to connect with and learn about their students on a deeper level. These missed opportunities hinder teachers from providing instruction that is equitable, engaging, respectful, relevant, and meaningful to all students. If teachers do not implement CRT to fidelity, as Dr. Billings-Ladson intended, students will continue to be subjected to ineffective teaching and learning practices and the marginalization of Black and Brown children will continue. Culturally responsive teaching is not only essential for children of color, but I would argue that it is essential for all children. When children genuinely learn about, appreciate, and celebrate others who are different from themselves, they are in a good position to recognize stereotypes and injustices when they surface. When members of our society come to terms with the value of diversity, we may be able to finally get over the hurdles that keep us separate and apart. Those hurdles include stereotypes, biases (implicit and explicit), prejudices, discrimination, and racism. CRT is absolutely necessary for educational reform and specifically for motivating students in becoming proficient readers.

Culturally Responsive Teaching in the Early Years

It is important to begin culturally responsive teaching as early as possible in a child's life because experiences in early childhood play a significant role in shaping a child's brain development and future outcomes. Dr. Bruce Perry, a renowned child psychiatrist and neuroscientist, explains that the brain develops sequentially from the bottom up and from the inside out. The basic functions of the brain stem, such as emotions, are processed in the bottom of the brain, while the more complex and rational functions of the cortex are processed in the top of the brain. In essence, for information to reach the top of the brain, it must first pass through the bottom of the brain. In other words, our brain is organized to act and feel before we think. What does this mean? A child's experiences with emotions and feelings during their early years can significantly impact their ability to process and understand complex information later in life. Early exposure to culturally responsive teaching can help children develop positive attitudes and perspectives towards diverse cultures, helping them become more empathetic and accepting of others. Understanding how personal experiences shape brain development is critical for education because it emphasizes the importance of creating supportive learning environments that promote positive experiences for students. The developing brain stores parts of our life experiences, and these experiences help us interpret the world and create a unique worldview.

Why is this important for education? Each of us has a unique worldview that is shaped by our life experiences. Now, if we take that thought into the educational system, we must ask ourselves, who's teaching our children? What are their worldviews? How does their worldview impact teaching and learning for children who are different themselves? A person's worldview will be revealed in all that he or she does. To change our worldview, Dr. Perry believes that we must have positive and consistent experiences over time. In this way, experiences have a chance to move from the bottom part of our brain (the emotional side) to the top part of our brain (the rational side).

Moving back to the classroom and the connection to reading, we know that reading requires motivation and consistency to develop stamina and proficiency. In order for children to be motivated to read often, they must have some connection to the reading material. They must have a reason to read that is meaningful, interesting, and challenging. Unfortunately, many students in low-income public urban schools in the United States are taught by teachers who have a worldview of Black and Brown children that is consistent with negative stereotypes, biases, racial connotations, and the belief that those in the majority (White and middle-class) are superior. This negative worldview is seen in everything that the teacher does in the classroom including instruction, content, materials and supplies, projects, assessments, attitudes, interactions with children and parents, classroom rules, and the overall culture and climate of the classroom. Therefore, CRT is critical for young Black and Brown children.

Children of color who are denied the opportunity to learn about their history in the United States and who are constantly depicted in negative and disparaging ways, develop unhealthy worldviews of themselves and those who do not look like them. As we have learned in previous chapters, children cannot learn from people they don't like or trust. Distorted worldviews impact teaching and learning and it does not get better as children grow up to become teenagers and adults. If the people that make up a child's ecosystem do not help to shape healthy worldviews, we end up with unfortunate events that occurred in 2020.

Taking a closer look at the events that unfolded in the United States in the summer of 2020, I realize that those events did not happen by accident nor can I say that they happened because CRT was missing. However, I can say that the events could have been different if those involved had been exposed to the tenets found in CRT. The following real-life examples of what occurred in the United States during the summer of 2020 and beyond provide real context for why CRT is critically important and needed in our public-school classrooms to bolster learning.

During the summer of 2020, the United States became the epicenter of a racial reckoning as it was forced to reconcile the past and the present. Since the 2016 presidential campaign season, many Americans became emboldened and felt safe to show their true colors regarding racism and all the other "isms" that exist in the United States. We witnessed the resurgence of hate groups in full view, espousing their beliefs for the world to see and hear. We cannot forget the *"unite the right"* rally in Charlottesville, Virginia in 2017. A group of white nationalists holding lit tiki torches marched through the campus of the University of Virginia, as some chanted Nazi-associated phrases while holding up offensive signs. One person rammed his car into a crowd of counter-protesters, killing one person and injuring 19 others. During that same period, we had children unnecessarily separated from their families at United States' borders and some have yet to be reunited. All the dirt that was once done in the dark slowly came to the light and the United States found itself edging ever so close to a full-scale cultural war.

What happened in 2020 was a result of decades of frustration, oppression, racism, social injustice, failed criminal justice reform, and inequities in education, employment, wages, housing, and healthcare. The year 2020 was a perfect storm. We learned just how fragile democracy is and how in a blink of an eye, it could be ripped out from under us. On January 6, 2021, we experienced an insurrection in the United States Capital because of a polarized nation where truths have been so bent out of shape that they have actually broken into tiny pieces. However, it was the death of George Floyd, a Black man from Minneapolis, who was killed by a white police officer that shook Americans from their numbness to racism and police brutality. It was recorded by a bystander and went viral. We witnessed the officer kneeling on the neck of Mr. Floyd for over nine minutes, which resulted in his death. The massive protests that ensued kindled a reckoning over the nation's dark past and inspired many social justice movements not only in the United States but across the world. In the United States, we revived conversations about racism and the entrenched inequities that continue to plague this country. The conversations turned fiery and further divided the country in just about every area imaginable. One thing that was finally made clear to many was that racism never disappeared in the United States despite the passage of federal and state mandates prohibiting racial discrimination. Unfortunately, racism is deeply rooted and passed on from generation to generation.

A short walk through 2020 provides a glimpse of disturbing events that brought the U.S. to a boiling point. If we harken back to the concept of distorted worldviews, we understand why we had sitting U.S. Representatives who blatantly supported political violence, pushed wild conspiracy theories, and made extreme anti-Muslim and anti-Semitic comments, which led to death threats against opposing U.S. Representatives. We had other legislators "like" and "share" social media posts that supported the execution of members of the opposing political party. Another representative was photographed holding a gun alongside images of representatives of the opposing party with a caption that read "going on the offense against these socialists." As we continue our walk, we cannot forget the modern-day lynching of Ahmaud Arbery, a 25-year-old black man who was out jogging midday in a Brunswick, Georgia neighborhood when he was confronted by an armed white father and son pair who took his life for no reason other than an assumption and the color of his skin. We also remember the botched police raid, that took the life of Breonna Taylor who was asleep in her own apartment when officers barged in while executing a search warrant. We cannot forget about the white woman who called the police on a black man who was bird-watching in Central Park and falsely accused him of threatening her and later faced a misdemeanor charge (the incident was recorded and went viral). How about the noose that was found in Bubba Wallace's team garage? Wallace is the only full-time African American driver in NASCAR's top circuit. Who can forget Trayvon Martin, Michael Brown, Tamir Rice, Eric Garner, Freddie Gray, Andre Hill, Daunte Wright, Alton Sterling, Sandra Bland, and Walter Scott?

Practically Speaking

I don't need to look at the news for stories like the ones previously described. One of my sons was confronted by a police officer coming out of a popular pharmacy chain. My son has multiple degrees and is a professional young man. He purchased an item from the store and walked out with a friend that he went to high school with (a white female) both were conscious of taking care of the earth and refused a plastic bag at the time of check out. As both walked out of the store, my son was the only one who was stopped and asked for his receipt. On another occasion, my son was doing his job when a white woman called law enforcement on him because the woman thought he was "up to no good" and was casing the street where she lived. When the police arrived and found out who my son was, they apologized and walked over to explain the situation to the woman who called them. Instead of offering an apology to my son, she slammed her door. Actions speak louder than words.

The slamming of the door is symbolic in that there are still people who feel that Black and Brown people should not have significant roles in society. When we allow fear, hatred, stereotypes, and biases to control our thoughts and actions, we end up with dramatic events such as those that occurred in 2020. A person's thoughts, actions, and ideologies are based on their worldview which has been developing since birth.

As we continue our walk, we turn towards the COVID-19 pandemic, which exposed the deep inequalities in the United States in areas such as education, healthcare, wages, housing, and other benefits. The pandemic also gave rise to inconceivable racist attacks against Asian Americans, and the disproportionate rate of death of so many people of color. As we turn the corner, there was Jacob Blake, a 29-year-old black man who was shot seven times in the back at point-blank range by a white police officer. We witnessed the trial of Kyle Rittenhouse, the white 17-year-old teenager who killed two people and injured one using an AR-15-style semi- automatic rifle that had a 30-round clip during a protest in Kenosha, Wisconsin. The case exposed the biases in the criminal justice system as the events that took place in the courtroom were highly unusual and led to a not guilty verdict. We saw first-hand how a 14-year-old teenage black boy in the lobby of the Arlo SoHo hotel with his father was physically and verbally attacked by a white woman who accused him of stealing her iPhone. However, the woman left the phone in an Uber vehicle, and it was eventually returned to her. To make matters worse, the hotel manager, without any justification, asked to see the teenager's phone to ensure that it was his and not the woman's.

Additionally, we witnessed two young teenagers who were involved in a fist fight in a New Jersey mall when two police officers approached, one officer yanked the white teenager by his clothes and sat him calmly on a bench while the other officer jumped on the black eighth-grade boy who was already on the ground, not resisting arrest and pinned him to the ground and handcuffed him. The other officer left the white teenager (unhandcuffed) sitting on the bench, unattended, and joined the other police officer where she placed her knee in the back of the black boy who was already down with his hands behind his back and still not resisting arrest. All of these events played out in front of impressionable and vulnerable young children. The toxicity of racism is permeating through every part of our lives.

This is the current state that we find ourselves in because of hate, the lack of understanding, empathy, awareness, acceptance, compassion, moral decency, the inability to agree to disagree and move on, and an unwillingness to see the perspectives of others. We have become numb to stupidity, violence, brutality, death threats, lies, racism, oppression, and bullying. Our children are watching and listening, and the sad part is if they hear and see this stuff long enough, it becomes their norm – their worldview. Whether black, blue, brown, or white, we all matter, but it is concerning that Black and Brown lives are cut short at a disproportionately higher rate than others, not to mention the rate at which they are harassed, humiliated, profiled, and mistreated in the process. Distorted worldviews cause people to act and react in irrational ways and because of their previous experiences, their emotions won't move past the base of the brain where emotions live to the top smart part of the brain where rationale lives. Consequently, we experience events like those previously mentioned in our nation.

Whitewashing History – Book Banning

Over the last ten years, we have seen the results of explicit and implicit biases within our nation. Explicit bias is where individuals are aware of their prejudices and attitudes toward certain groups and make overtly racist comments. Real-life examples include recent disparaging, derogatory, and offensive comments made about fellow Muslim-Americans, undocumented individuals, Asian-Americans, African Americans, and Latinos. The comments were made by prominent elected officials and repeated on public television and all-over social media. To try and grapple with this, we must go back to the concept of distorted worldviews. One could only imagine the experiences those individuals were exposed to that would create such distorted worldviews.

On the one hand, we have implicit bias which suggests that bias is present but not plainly expressed or unintentionally expressed. Then there is racism, which is the actual overt set of beliefs about the superiority of one race over others. How do explicit, implicit, and racism impact education and specifically reading. The answer is that it opens the doors to whitewashing, erasing, distorting, or covering up history from the curriculum found in public schools throughout the United States. Additionally, to control the narrative established by the majority in the United States, we have legislators and parents coming together to ban books and censor education. Needless to say, banning books and censoring education have a tremendous impact on a child's motivation to learn. More on implicit and explicit biases in the latter part of this chapter.

Since January 2021, 37 states have introduced bills or taken other steps to restrict or limit how teachers may discuss racism, sexism, and any issues of systemic inequality in their classrooms. Fourteen states have imposed these bans and restrictions either through legislation or other avenues. According to Education Weekly, a popular educational magazine, throughout the 2020 legislative sessions, most of the bills were centered on a list of prohibited "divisive concepts." In September 2020, under an executive order, certain types of diversity training in federal agencies were banned. For example, training sessions could not promote ideas that one race or sex is inherently better than another, or that all people of a certain race have unconscious bias, or that the United States is a fundamentally racist or sexist country. By the way, all have subsequently been placed under the umbrella of critical race theory, which has become the new "monster" in the United States. However, critical race theory is not really taught in K-12 schools in the U.S. but in law schools. The essence of the theory is so far removed from what society has arbitrarily defined it to be. Critical race theory is an academic concept that is more than 40 years old. According to Sawchuk (2021), the core idea is that race is a social construct and that racism is not just merely the product of individual bias or prejudice, but also something embedded in legal systems and policies.

The basic tenets of the theory emerged from a framework for legal analysis in the late 1970s and early 1980s by legal scholars Derrick Bell, Kimberle Crenshaw, Richard Delgado, and others (Cob, 2021). Although many would want us to believe that critical race theory teaches that certain races are better than others or that individuals are inherently racist, the scholars that developed the theory maintain that it does not. Rather, the theory states that racism is part of everyday life, and people, white and nonwhite who do not intend to be racist can nevertheless make choices that fuel racism. The theory further asserts that the emphasis is on outcomes, not merely on individuals' own beliefs and it calls on these outcomes to be examined and rectified. Regarding education, scholars who study critical race theory examine how policies and practices in the educational system contribute to persistent racial inequalities and advocate for ways to change them (Sawchuck, 2021). Critical race theory has become the catch-all phrase of those seeking to censor educational discussions dealing with race or racial justice in U.S. public schools. Because so many have not read, processed, or digested the theory, it became a dirty term and instead of taking the time to read the theory and having an open dialogue about it, we maligned it and attached negative connotations to it to the point that no one really needs to read it, they just assume it's bad. Nowadays, any term or phrase that has the word "race" in it is automatically feared, misunderstood, or totally off-limits for discussion. The word is so negatively charged that mentioning it in any context, evokes anger, bitterness, fear, and rage. How does one word hold so much power?

Legislators in the U.S. have moved to ban books that provide an honest account of this country's history. This disturbing trend makes clear that the ultimate goal is to censor, silence, and suppress Americans' ability to be fully informed or 'woke' about their country and the lived experiences of their fellow citizens. For example, in one district in Tennessee, the *Autobiography of Ruby Bridges* was challenged. The famous story is about a six-year-old braving an angry mob of white parents who were furious that a black child was attending a formerly all-white public school in New Orleans. According to Heather Schwartz in an article written by Brian Lee for the Daily Gazette in 2021, the parents complained that in depicting the white backlash to school desegregation, the book violated the state's new law in sending the message that all white people were bad and oppressed black people. My retort is that it happened, and many people did not want the races to mix in public schools at that time, but things have changed. Just because we do not discuss history, does not mean that it did not happen or that it will go away. Rather, this is a teachable moment to show how brave Ms. Bridges was and to show that not every white person agreed with those who made up the angry mob. Surely, our children can grasp the understanding that not all White people are bad and not all Black people are bad. They can also handle the concept of past and present.

The same group also pushed for books about Rev. Dr. Martin Luther King, Jr., and the March on Washington he led for civil rights in 1963, to be removed from the county school curriculum. The group claims that the facts about this seminal period in U.S. history and the philosophy of this iconic civil rights leader will inflict emotional trauma on students. I wonder, which students will be inflicted with emotional trauma? Do we sacrifice the emotions that one group may have about this pivotal moment in history for the emotional trauma that it may have on another group of students? We, as a country, and as human beings, cannot protect the feelings of one group over the feelings of another group. Wlodkowski and Ginsberg (1995) stated, "Any educational or training system that ignores the history or perspective of its learners or does not attempt to adjust its teaching practices to benefit all its learners is contributing to inequality of opportunity."

Still, in Tennessee, the book *Maus,* which is about the Holocaust, was banned because of curse words and nudity. The book was banned because it was inappropriate for eighth graders. This is an easy one to fix; then we shouldn't read it to eighth graders. There are plenty of books about the Holocaust that are more appropriate for that age group. If we are concerned about profanity and nudity (which we should be), we better check our eighth graders' social media accounts, not to mention the behaviors that are displayed on television of some of our elected officials. Additionally, Toni Morrison's *Beloved*, a Pulitzer Prize-winning novel about American slavery has also been targeted. In Texas, a legislator recently released a list of 850 books that he wanted to ban from school libraries claiming the books "make students feel discomfort" because of their content about race and sexuality. The legislator wanted to examine the books to see if they are being used in public schools and potentially breaking the new laws in Texas. I wonder what students he was referring to. The Katy Independent School District in Texas removed *Class Act* and *New Kid* by Jerry Craft from its school libraries due to their discussion of racism. A parent who objected to the material stated that the books may make "white children feel like oppressors."

We cannot get into the business of passing laws that prioritize the feelings and well-being of one group over another. One group's worth is not more important than another. Additionally, York County, Pennsylvania succeeded in the temporary ban of over 30 books that discussed issues of race. We shouldn't worry about certain book topics that are carefully and thoughtfully discussed in classrooms under the careful guidance of professional educators. The topics in the books mentioned here are not what we should worry about, rather we should be more concerned with what our children are watching on television, and we should be extremely concerned with their open use of social media, which has relatively little to no safeguards for children and almost no censoring or filtering processes to keep them safe. The web is a great big source of information for children that can be retrieved in seconds: the good, bad, and the ugly. The real threat to our children is not the books on the ban lists but television, cable, and social media.

Banning books and censoring what children read and learn about in public schools has a tremendous impact on what children are exposed to. According to Education Week, more than 25 states have introduced legislation that could restrict or ban what students learn and what teachers can teach about our nation's history. Bills introduced in Missouri and Indiana require teachers and schools to make instructional materials available for parents to review. Florida went further to give parents a "private right of action" to sue if they believe their children are being taught critical race theory. According to Texas law, teachers can address controversial current events or issues in class, and if they do, they must share "contending" perspectives without giving deference to one side. For example, teachers cannot say that slavery constitutes the true founding of the U.S. or that slavery and racism are anything but deviations from the nation's founding principles.

Since 2021, there have been 66 gag orders introduced in more than 25 states that significantly restrict how topics such as U.S. history, segregation, and slavery can be taught or even discussed in classrooms. These restrictions largely censor discussions about racism by referring to the subject as divisive and harmful. These types of bills push politics to the forefront of education and have made critical race theory the culprit for such drastic and damaging changes in education. The theory has been used as a weapon and leveled at our ever-so-diverse democracy. We are back to the days when the true, undeniable historical experiences of marginalized groups in the United States are being whitewashed, censored, denied, and glossed over because the truth may make one group of citizens uncomfortable. Yet, we are comfortable with mass shootings, COVID-19, unregulated social media platforms, and current gun laws. We are also comfortable with teachers and students practicing active shooter drills and teachers fighting off intruders armed with AR-15s to protect children, but we don't trust the same teachers with the curriculum or with sensitive topics in books. My retort is that sometimes we must become uncomfortable to become comfortable. America, it's time for a change.

Distorted worldviews, biases, and racism are all embedded within our public schools. The United States is a very polarized country with a lot of people using fear to shape public opinion. There are a lot of angry people who are not listening. They are communicating fear and blocking the strong desire for change. Therefore, more than ever before we need CRT in our public schools. We discussed what CRT is not at great length, but what is CRT?

CRT is an approach that recognizes and responds to the unique cultural and linguistic backgrounds of students in the classroom. CRT requires teachers to develop communication skills that reflect the values and beliefs of their students, to implement student-centered instructional processes, and to choose curricula that are relevant to the cultural and ethnic diversity of their students (Brown, 200; Wlodkowski & Ginsberg, 1995). CRT also involves building close relationships with students, particularly in urban settings where students may experience feelings of alienation and struggle with identity development (Brown, 2001).

While many universities and colleges offer courses and field experiences in urban education, the question remains whether these programs can adequately prepare teachers to respond in culturally responsive ways to the needs of diverse learners. Effective teaching and learning play a critical role in children's educational outcomes, particularly in reading. However, it is important to recognize that education is not simply about acquiring knowledge and skills, but also about developing a sense of identity and belonging in the world.

Culturally responsive teaching can help to create safe and supportive learning environments where students feel valued and respected for their unique backgrounds and experiences. By incorporating diverse perspectives and experiences into the curriculum, CRT can help to broaden students' understanding of the world and promote empathy and understanding among learners. Ultimately, CRT has the potential to change the landscape of education by promoting equity and social justice, and preparing students for success in a diverse and interconnected world.

Education Defined

The definitions of education from Dictionary.com and Merriam-Webster. com focus on the acquisition of knowledge, skills, and personal development through a process of discovery and truth-seeking. Education is seen as a social process of living, rather than just a preparation for future living. Educators are seen as individuals who help to bring out the potential of themselves and others, by engaging in a cooperative and inclusive activity that looks to help us live our lives as well as we can.

According to Kotinsky, education is a deliberate, hopeful, informed, respectful, and wise process that aims to build understanding and enable action. It is grounded in the desire that all individuals may flourish and share in life, and is a cooperative and inclusive activity that helps us to live our lives to the fullest. The definitions highlight the importance of education as a process of personal and social development that involves the acquisition of knowledge, skills, values, and morals. It emphasizes the role of educators in facilitating this process, and the importance of creating inclusive and cooperative learning environments that enable all individuals to flourish.

Learning is indeed both a process and an outcome. As a process, it is ongoing and integral to being and living in the world. It involves actively engaging with information, experiences, and perspectives to develop new knowledge, skills, and understanding. As an outcome, learning leads to a new understanding or appreciation of something, which can be applied to future situations and experiences. At its core, learning is driven by the belief that change for the good is possible. We invite people to engage in the learning process with the hope and expectation that it will lead to positive outcomes and personal growth. Learning requires an open mind and a willingness to seek out knowledge and understanding, even when faced with uncertainty or challenge. As Hooks (2003) suggests, nothing can keep an open mind from seeking after knowledge and finding a way to know. This highlights the importance of curiosity, resilience, and persistence in the learning process. Ultimately, learning is a powerful tool for personal and social transformation, and it is essential for individuals and societies to continue to grow and evolve.

These are very nice definitions of education, but what does it mean to be educated? What makes someone educated? How do you become educated? What is the purpose of education? My responses to these questions do not really matter. What really matters are the responses from our school leaders, teachers, school community, and state education departments. Their responses will ultimately dictate how our children are educated. Their responses matter, as those responses will drive the content of what is being taught, who will teach it, how it will be taught, when it will be taught, and the depth and breadth of what will be taught. The people responsible for educating our children (outside the home) have the power to promote or hinder positive, relevant, and meaningful educational experiences.

It is important to provide context regarding the current situation in this country and begin discussing how to turn the tide through education reform. We must understand how important education is to a strong, healthy, viable, and well-informed citizenry that is inclusive of everyone. How does all this relate to reading specifically? The reading curricula, programs, materials, guides, books, content, instruction, and assessments are all predicated on how educators, legislators, and other stakeholders perceive the learning capabilities of students, particularly students of color.

If perceptions are low because of historic reasons such as poverty, language, disability, home life, zip code, behavior, and skin color, then the educational experiences will be reflective specifically in what is taught and how it is taught. As Emily Styles so eloquently states, "Curriculum needs to function both as a window and as a mirror to reflect and reveal most accurately both the multicultural world and the students themselves."

Education that incorporates both windows and mirrors is essential for helping students develop a well-rounded understanding of the world and their place in it. Windows provide students with the opportunity to see the realities of others and to learn about unfamiliar perspectives and experiences. This can help broaden their knowledge and understanding, as well as increase empathy and compassion for others. Mirrors, on the other hand, allow students to see themselves reflected in what they read and learn. This can help build confidence and self-esteem, and create a sense of belonging and identity. When students see themselves in the reading material, the classroom environment, and the assignments, they become more motivated to read and are more willing to take on challenges. This can lead to increased proficiency and a lifelong love of learning. Reading proficiency is essential for success in the 21st century global economy. Confident readers are more innovative, creative, curious, and knowledgeable. They are also better able to imagine the impossible and think critically. Therefore, it is important for education to prioritize reading and provide opportunities for students to engage with both windows and mirrors in their learning.

Reading opens the doors of opportunities and allows students to learn about themselves, others, and the world. I cannot tell you the places I have gone and the experiences I encountered through reading. I did not grow up with much but I was rich because of what I was exposed to through books. Reading is powerful and it is liberating because it allows you to "know" for yourself. Additionally, reading builds empathy skills and when students are more empathetic, chances are, they will become more accepting, respectful, kind, loving, patient, hopeful, less afraid, and more understanding. Researchers found that people who read a lot of fiction become more empathetic because fiction is a simulation of social experiences, in which people practice and enhance their interpersonal skills (Oatley, 2002). Empathy as mentioned in chapter two is the cognitive and intellectual ability to recognize the emotions of other people and to emotionally respond to other people. Empathy includes sympathy and concern for others.

Researchers Bal and Veltkamp (2013) found that when an individual reads a story, he/she predicts the actions and reactions of the characters, by inferring what they are thinking, feeling, and intending. To do this, the reader often identifies with the characters, takes their perspectives, and becomes emotionally involved in the story causing the reader to sympathize with the characters in the story and experience the events as if it is the reader's own experience. These types of reading experiences provide opportunities for readers to practice being empathetic while gaining a better understanding of the world. People learn about human psychology from fiction and gain knowledge about how to react to other people in social situations. Reading enables us to become better at understanding other people, which is important in eliminating stereotypes. We are so divided as a country and as a people because we do not understand one another and we do not spend enough time with one another. The lack of understanding and time spent causes fear, anxiety, panic, and nervousness toward those who are seemingly different than we are. These feelings cause us to become defensive and push us in the direction of racist and discriminatory behaviors. As humans, we typically fear that which we do not know. We are quick to believe the stereotypes of a group but slow in taking the time to get to know the individuals in the group. I often say it's easy to have negative and ill thoughts about someone or a group you don't know, but it's hard to have those same thoughts after spending time with the group and getting to know the members.

We do not need to censor history or ban books because the content may make one group of people feel bad. On the contrary, the opposite is true, having an open mind and a willing heart builds empathy skills, opens the doors for dialogue about sensitive topics, and bridges gaps that exist between groups of people. I wonder if the concern is about children feeling bad, or the adults? The content in some of the books that are on the ban list is not meant for anyone to feel bad, but it is a time for people to sit down together and discuss the content and acknowledge the events followed by an explanation that is developmentally appropriate for the age of the children. By providing a thoughtful and accurate account of events that happened long ago and connecting it to current events, we help children make sense of history and we help them establish their purpose in the world and their role in making it equitable and just for everyone. Also, when we distort history, we deprive children of knowing how our country originated, how we arrived at this moment in time, and how we move forward. Children are resilient and can handle more than we think they can. They are more understanding and empathetic than some adults and are very capable of processing and understanding sensitive information when presented carefully and appropriately for their age.

Learning about others is an added value and it helps to reduce misconceptions, prejudices, distortion, division, and disrespect. The more students learn about others who are different, the more they begin to understand why some feel as they do, act as they do, and think as they do. Students learn to stand up against injustices and inequalities to make the world a better place for everyone and significantly reduce incidents such as those that occurred in 2020. To live up to the definitions of education, we cannot whitewash history. Students need factual information to build understanding, make informed decisions, and offer differing perspectives while nurturing truth and possibility. Censorship in education will not bring students together, rather it will cause further division. We are so much more when we learn about the history of others.

When we know our history, we learn not to make the same mistakes and to move along our journey differently. Learning about historic events that occurred in the United States is not meant to make anyone feel bad or less than, it is about telling the whole truth, and not just the parts that are deemed more palatable for some. The more we try to bury the past, the harder it is to reconcile and move towards a better future. We must come to terms with how this country was built, accept it, learn from it, and move past it. We cannot move forward if more than half the citizens in the U.S. do not accept and acknowledge what occurred in the past or choose to deliberately censor education rather than having uncomfortable conversations. If we shut down communication and discussions about racism, where it came from, and how it continues to pervade the fabric of our lives, we will continue to experience events and incidents that led to the racial reckoning of 2020. Dr. Perry (2021) discussed changing this narrative in his recent book *What Happened to You?* He suggested that we need to couple cultural sensitivity with real experiences and relationships to change a person's worldview about people who are different. Specifically, he stated "The long-term solution is to minimize the development of implicit bias. We must think about ways to raise our children with more opportunities to be exposed to the magnificence of human diversity earlier in their lives. And we must change the inherently biased elements of so many of our systems."

How do we move forward, if we do not understand what landed us in the current culture and climate? Or is it that racism is beneficial to some people; therefore, discussions to understand it and remediate it, hinders the agenda of those who stand to benefit and profit from it? Covering up or blurring the past will not make it go away. The more we learn about others, the better we become at recognizing stereotypes, racism, bigotry, and hatred. Knowing the plight of others changes our conversations, our interactions, and our thought patterns. There is a quote by an anonymous author that says, "History is not there for you to like or dislike. It is there for you to learn from it. And if it offends you, even better. Because then you are less likely to repeat it. It (history) is not yours to erase or destroy." There is no need to hate others to love ourselves. Likewise, we do not need to be afraid of our history or future, but we must move towards reconciliation for the sake of our children.

This sidebar relates to reading proficiency because it has a direct link to what our children are exposed to in public schools. Learning requires motivation and if children do not see themselves in the books they read or the assignments and projects they must complete, it is hard to become motivated to learn. It is hard to learn when you constantly see negative images of people who look like you. It is hard to learn from someone who does not respect or accept you. It is hard to trust a system that constantly views you as a threat and uneducable; therefore, undeserving of quality education. It is hard to trust a system that does not acknowledge your contributions to history. Try teaching children who already believe that the world thinks they are unteachable. What is the impact of that on them? What goes on in their heads and how do they move and interact in educational spaces? We must work hard to free our children's minds of those negative narratives while they are in our classrooms and push those negative thoughts out the way to provide room and space for meaningful learning to occur. This sidebar paints a clear picture of why we need to change our course of action in this country. What we are doing is not working for a large population of people. We cannot keep doing the same thing year after year and expect different results.

These last few years have been a wake-up call for action. We must find a different approach to bring about change. We must hit the reset button. One way to begin this process of reform is through education. As Maya Angelou stressed, "When we know better, we should do better." Through education reform, we can build a better tomorrow for all citizens. Education is the antidote to ignorance. We can prepare our students to lead the way and build a bridge in a country so divided. Culturally responsive teaching is a well-researched approach that promises to provide access for all students and particularly children of color. It is not an easy thing to do, but it is work worth working for.

It is not human differences that undermine children's development, but rather unfair, hurtful treatment based upon those differences. NAEYC

Cultural Responsiveness

After generations of inadequately serving our culturally and linguistically diverse student population in schools, educators need strategies to best support diverse student populations and create systemic changes in schools. Over the last 10 years, the population of students in the United States from homes that are culturally and linguistically diverse has significantly increased and this trend is likely to continue according to the U.S. Department of Education. The change in student demographics has created cause for concern in the educational world because research has shown that a student's race, ethnicity, cultural background, and other systemic issues significantly influence their achievement (Harry & Klingner, 2006). As the number of students from diverse groups continues to grow, educators are confronted with the necessity to ensure successful educational experiences for every child.

When referring to CRT, I will draw from the work of two researchers Dr. Gloria Ladson-Billings and Geneva Gay (2002) as well as other leading researchers on the topic including Nieto (2000), Moll (1992), and Delpit (2006).

Dr. Ladson-Billings and Gay expanded on the definition of CRT. Culturally responsive teaching is using the cultural knowledge, prior experiences, frames of reference, and performance styles of ethnically diverse students to make learning encounters more relevant and effective for them. It is based on the assumption that when academic knowledge and skills are situated within the lived experiences of students, they are meaningful, have higher interest appeal, and are learned easily and thoroughly. CRT supports self-awareness, culture, sensitivity, and respect for differences. CRT sends the message that all students are valued, and multiculturalism is an asset, not a barrier or a liability. According to Dr. Ladson-Billings, a goal of CRT is to help students embrace and appreciate who they are as well as others who are different. CRT recognizes not only the importance of academic achievement but also the maintaining of cultural identity and heritage.

Why Does Culturally Responsive Teaching Matter?

When children see themselves as part of the school curriculum and can draw on their cultural and experiential knowledge to make meaning, they invest personally and engage cognitively. CRT provides opportunities for students to relate to and talk with some authority about situations in a text. Students see their local funds of knowledge and experiences as useful resources for making meaningful connections with texts. Culturally responsive teaching is a pedagogy that recognizes and responds to the cultural diversity of students in the classroom. It has the following characteristics:

1. Acknowledges the legitimacy of the cultural heritage of different ethnic groups: This means recognizing that the cultural heritage of each student is valuable and worthy of being taught in the formal curriculum.

2. Builds meaningful bridges between home and school experiences: This involves connecting academic concepts with the lived sociocultural realities of students and making connections between home and school experiences.

3. Uses a wide variety of instructional strategies: This means using

instructional strategies that are connected to different learning styles, and adapting teaching methods to meet the needs of diverse learners.

4. Encourages students to know and praise their own and each other's cultural heritages: This involves celebrating and honoring the cultural heritage of each student, and creating a classroom environment that values diversity.

5. Incorporates multicultural information, resources, and materials in all subjects and skills: This means integrating multicultural information, resources, and materials into all aspects of the curriculum, not just social studies or language arts.

CRT is founded on several principles including (1) knowing students well, (2) awareness of personal biases, (3) transformed pedagogy and curriculum, (4) respect and reinforcement of students' culture, and (5) family and community involvement.

Know Your Students – Knowing and understanding students is a key component of CRT. It involves interacting with students and their families to understand their cultural heritage, experiences, and values (Edwards & Edick, 2013). By doing so, teachers can create meaningful connections between academic concepts and students' lived experiences. Building positive relationships with students and families can also increase student achievement and engagement in the classroom. Teachers get to know their students through surveys, interviews, and ongoing communication throughout the school year. It is important for educators to avoid stereotypes and assumptions about students based on their race, ethnicity, gender, or socioeconomic background, and to see the potential for academic success in all students.

Be Aware of Your Own Personal Biases – Merriam-Webster defined bias as prejudice in favor of or against one thing, person, or group compared with another, usually in a way considered to be unfair. It is also "a particular tendency, trend, inclination, feeling, or opinion, especially one that is preconceived or unreasoned." In the context of education, this means the way we teach and the decisions we make regarding student learning, behavior, discipline, and support are impacted by the biases that we may unconsciously or consciously hold about students based on the demographic groups they are part of (e.g., race, ethnicity, gender, socio-economic status, (dis)ability level, etc.). We all have biases, which may exist in many forms and often stem from world views gained early in life. Our beliefs and biases are shaped by education, experiences, family, and friends.

Teaching students from diverse backgrounds requires teachers to set aside their biases and treat each student as a respectable individual. Teachers must delve deeper into where their biases lie to overcome them, so they don't influence teacher-student relationships or instruction. For example, if teachers perceive students of color as not being capable of achieving the same outcomes as their white peers, teachers may lower their expectations and standards for children of color. According to Iruka et al. (2020), correcting teachers' misperceptions of children is critical because perceptions lay the foundation for teacher-student relationships, which we know are key to children's school success. When teachers have positive perceptions of children, they are more likely to have positive interpersonal interactions with them but when they have negative perceptions, they are more likely to criticize children, call on them less often, or offer ineffective feedback. Negative perceptions may lead to teacher-student conflicts and poor student cooperation, which may lead to students underachieving.

Transform Pedagogy and Curriculum – An inclusive curriculum provides the opportunity to learn about perspectives beyond one's own scope and assist in dismantling systems of biases and inequities. Curriculum, content, materials, and readings must reflect the diversity of the students in the classroom as well as the contributors in the field of study. Teachers must also reflect on how their choices of readings, examples, analogies, videos, and other content may be biased or may reinforce stereotypes. Curriculum should be reviewed to ensure there are no hidden forms of oppression and the activities in classrooms should be mindful of the impact they may have on students. Teachers must see student variability and diversity as the norm while making curriculum and teaching methods flexible and designed to meet the needs of all students.

Respect and Reinforce Student's Culture – Each student enters a classroom with a set of behaviors, beliefs, and characteristics that makes him or her unique. Additionally, value systems, languages, religious beliefs, and ways of life contribute to students' self-identity. By valuing students' cultures, we validate them as individuals. Very young children have ideas about how they look and have questions about how others look as well. Educators typically steer clear of discussing race with three- and four-year-old children, but this is the age in which it must be discussed because they are just learning. The issue of race forms very early in a child 's life, whether educators or parents ignore it or dismiss it, the bottom line is it's forming. When we ignore it or suppress it until they get "older" we send a message whether intentionally or unintentionally about how children should think about and understand racial differences at a time when they are very curious and need help in understanding. When we do not intentionally address the subject, children are left to draw their own conclusions about how to think about their own race and the race of others, which is a lot for a young child. This is the very reason why we must not ignore race in the early years of a child's development. Rather, we must explicitly and intentionally explain what children see and guide them using an anti-bias approach in addressing the issues of culture and race.

According to the Anti-Defamation League anti-bias education (ABE) is an approach to teaching and learning designed to increase understanding of differences and their value to a respectful and civil society. ABE aims to actively challenge biases, stereotypes, and all forms of discrimination in schools and communities. It incorporates an inclusive curriculum that reflects diverse experiences and perspectives, instructional methods that advance all students' learning, and strategies to create and sustain safe, inclusive, and respectful learning communities.

Why is this important to reading? In the United States, most of the early childhood teachers are white (Saluja, et al., 2002). Remember early childhood is from birth to eight years old. Wanless and Crawford (2016) stated that classrooms and the educational materials chosen (particularly books) often reflect the values and beliefs prevalent in a traditional white culture. If educators do not notice this or try to counterbalance it, they miss opportunities to teach children that all races must be valued. When educators do not provide culturally diverse learning experiences, they send a message—intentionally or unintentionally— that one race holds privileged status and others do not. If diversity is not valued or respected, we get harmful behaviors like name-calling, bullying, and social exclusion, and all have an impact on reading. Reading proficiently includes mastering foundational skills, but it also means that children must practice reading often. For children to want to read often, they must be motivated and connected to what they read. Children are motivated to read when the content is relevant and meaningful to them. Motivation is half the battle in reading proficiency, particularly with young African American boys.

Family and Community Engagement – CRT means getting families and the community meaningfully engaged in the educational experiences of students. Engagement may include, communication, volunteering, learning at home, decision making, and interest surveys. Teachers must communicate with families throughout the year and not just for discipline issues. Open and honest communication develops greater trust and nurturing relationships. Providing families with resources, transportation, translation, and babysitting to attend school events are ways to engage families as well. Learning about the cultures, customs, and values of families assists in building stronger relationships.

Practically Speaking

When I was in elementary school, I dreaded returning to school after any long break because the typical assignment called for students to write about "the great things" they did and/or "the fun" places they visited. Students had to read their experiences out loud to the class and classmates had the opportunity to ask questions to make comments. The problem was in the wording of the assignment. I, like many students, did not connect with the assignment because I did not do anything great over the break nor did

I visit any fun places. Needless to say, I was petrified by the assignment. What was I going to write about? Therefore, I learned to make up stories. I wrote about places I wanted to visit and passed it off as if I actually visited those places (I did visit the places, just not physically). I wrote about family gatherings and big parties with a lot of food, fun, music, and dancing. These events did not exist for real, but they were real in my mind. When it was time to share my stories, I prayed no one would ask me questions because I was not sure if I could answer them since my stories were fictitious.

I remember one year, the teacher asked me if my story was real and when I said no, she lowered my grade because the assignment called for us to write about a "true authentic" account of our break. However, I did not have an account to write about, I had no content to work with, so I made it up. In retrospect, I wonder if the objective of the assignment was correct grammar usage, sentence structure, punctuation, paragraph formation, tone of voice, subject-verb agreement or was it following directions and determining real vs unreal? My stories became very creative and whimsical over the years. Reading and writing had become my escape, my windows into possibilities that allowed me to express myself safely. The thought never crossed my mind that I would be penalized for being creative. In a CRT classroom, the teacher would have known me, provided me with several options for completing the task, and allowed me to use my frame of reference to make learning relevant for me.

Embracing Culturally Responsive Teaching

There are many schools working to confront inequality, which provides hope for the future of public schools and students. As educators, we are working hard on this sensitive topic and must keep in mind the complex nature of the work when embarking on a path that leads to transformational change around equity. That path must first begin with a shared common understanding about equity because a lack of shared understanding poses a major barrier to real progress. This is why we have well-meaning educators, but misaligned beliefs. As Fullan and Quinn (2016) demonstrated, attempts to achieve equity frequently fail because of lack of coherence. The researchers defined coherence as a common depth of understanding (individually and collectively) about the purpose and nature of improvement work. Educators need a deeper understanding of the goal of educational equity and the level of action required to obtain it. To do this, we must first explore the difference between equity and equality in education.

For years, equality was the term used to ensure success for all, which is a good place to begin. However, equity takes it a step further and tries to address the unique traits of individual children because so many have very different and uneven early experiences. In equal classrooms, everyone is treated the same. They will have the same supplies, assignments, amount of interaction with the teacher, and will learn the same way. Equity, on the other hand, strives to achieve the best possible outcome for each individual child. Instead of giving each child the same, teachers look at each child as an individual and make adjustments accordingly. In equitable classrooms, all children have access to the resources they need, they feel welcome, safe, and able to share their thoughts. In equitable classrooms, all children are engaged in the learning process. Children might be involved in projects, or they may be involved in real-life scenarios where they can apply their knowledge to engage in the learning process. Equity isn't an easy route and teachers may never reach 100%. However, the goal is to make classrooms more equitable than before and keep striving to be better as time goes on. As we work on equity in education, we must also look to liberation where we challenge and remove the barriers that historically kept children of color from gaining access to quality educational experiences in the first place. Those barriers include poverty, racism, inequality, housing, healthcare, criminal justice, economic disparities, and nutrition to name a few.

The systematic marginalization that leads to inequities is a hidden part of any culture. To disrupt the marginalization of certain groups within a school culture, Fullan and Quinn stated that first educators must establish a common meaning of equity. Next, they must understand and become aware of those being marginalized, which requires open and honest conversations that do not shy away from facts. Educators must discuss the root causes of and the actions and conditions that perpetuate inequities. Finally, educators must understand their part in advocating for equity and the differences in the learning opportunities for different groups of students.

The arduous task of reforming instructional practices to make it more equitable for all students is heavy work that begins with teachers. Teachers must begin this work with a self-audit of their biases, explicit and implicit, and examine their beliefs, attitudes, and expectations about others who are different from themselves. They must engage in ongoing critical reflection and learning to create a productive learning environment that meets the needs of all students. To understand students, teachers must first understand themselves. We all have biases, the problem is, we do not always acknowledge them, nor are we skillful at leaving them at the door before entering a public-school classroom.

A self-audit includes acknowledging that our life experiences, values, and assumptions influence the way we see the world and the way we interact with people. The self-audit helps teachers reflect and gain a deeper understanding of how their identity impacts their attitudes and teaching practices. The practice of self-reflection should be included in teacher preparation courses. In a policy brief in 2020 by Jenny Muniz, self-reflection was shown to be a very important practice. Self-reflection is an ongoing process that requires a willingness to challenge one's own assumptions, values, and beliefs. Culturally responsive educators engage in self-reflection to identify and address their biases, improve their practice, and create a more inclusive and equitable learning environment for their students. They also seek opportunities to learn from their students and families, as well as their colleagues, about the cultural backgrounds and experiences that shape their perspectives and beliefs. Through self-reflection, educators can develop a deeper understanding of their own cultural identity, the ways in which it intersects with their students' identities, and the implications of this intersection for teaching and learning. This awareness can help them to build stronger relationships with students, promote their academic success, and foster their social and emotional development.

Teachers continually make decisions, big and small, that can advance or impede equitable opportunities for students, regardless of intention, which happens explicitly or implicitly. Starck et al. (2020) did a lot of work on explicit and implicit bias as they examined the racial biases of teachers compared to other American adults. The results of the study are very disturbing. The researchers found that explicit bias is relatively easy to identify when it occurs. It is obvious and undeniable. Explicit bias refers to the attitudes and beliefs we have about a person or a group on a conscious level. Expressions of explicit bias occur because of deliberate thought and action. With explicit bias, a person is very clear and conscious about his or her feelings and attitudes, and their related behaviors or words are intentional. We have witnessed this throughout the history of the U.S. but in recent years, explicit bias has been running rampant especially with our elected officials. The sheer vitriol, hatred, and venom that one party has toward the other is extremely disturbing and alarming. The name calling, death threats, bullying, taunting, and harassment have been relentless and persistent, all within earshot of young people. Gone are the days of all night debates where opposing views were fiercely argued and deliberated. There was a sense of appreciation of how prepared both sides were at defending their views. There was a level of respect, for the most part, to agree to disagree. Nowadays, lives are threatened, characters are defamed, and careers are jeopardized for having an opposing view. I realize that this has always been the case in the United States but over the last 10 years, explicit bias has been front and center in so many areas of our lives.

On the other end is implicit bias, which is harder to identify. It is where a person is unconscious or completely unaware of his or her biases. Implicit bias can be in direct contradiction to what a person believes or values. It refers to the attitudes or stereotypes that affects our understanding, actions, and unconscious decisions. Implicit bias is often the result of subconscious thoughts, feelings, and perceptions that are formed by the media, our family, childhood experiences and the people we interact with socially in our environment. Implicit bias, or unconscious beliefs, may contribute to stubborn racial disparities in education such as differences in student achievement and school discipline between Black and White students. For instance, teachers' unconscious racial beliefs could produce biased evaluations of students' academic performance, which translates into real implications for educational attainment. Implicit bias is difficult and complicated to overcome and very dangerous because it allows one to form stereotypes about a group based on limited information and perspectives. We know that implicit bias is a problem, and we know that such biases negatively affect teachers' perceptions of children, stifles the teacher-child relationship, and leads to decreased learning outcomes for students of color.

Nelson and Guerra (2014) conducted a study on educator beliefs and cultural knowledge. They found that negative beliefs and stereotypes about certain groups of people, namely people of color and people living in poverty, are well documented in U.S. history. These negative views resulted in discriminatory behavior that was once supported by law and although many discriminatory practices are no longer law, inequitable beliefs and practices remain part of the fabric of the United States culture. Not surprisingly, Nelson and Guerra and other researchers found that teachers, in their study, often held negative beliefs about culturally, linguistically, and economically diverse students and their families. Even educators who were from culturally, linguistically, and economically diverse backgrounds often held deficit beliefs because they have assimilated and adopted mainstream perspectives (Weisman & Garza, 2002). The beliefs of teachers influence the way they instruct students whether positive or negative. Negative beliefs about diverse students and their families lead to lower educational expectations and blame. Rokeach (1968) found that beliefs are deeply personal to individuals and these powerful filters or beliefs shape how they see the world, other people, and themselves.

Educators and other groups frequently attribute inadequacies within culturally, linguistically, and economically diverse students and their families as the source of educational failure. Educators often suggest that the achievement gap is the result of students entering school without prerequisite knowledge, skills, experiences, and parental involvement (Valencia, 2010). This inclination to view certain groups of students as inherently deficient is known as deficit thinking, which results in viewing students who do not adhere to the dominant norms as genetically inferior or socially depraved (Padilla, 1981). In this way, schools construe cultural, social, and linguistic differences as problems that originate in the home. Educators who believe children and families are inherently deficient are reluctant to assume responsibility for students' low achievement and failure (Berman & Chambliss, 2000). When educators do not view themselves as part of the problem, they are reluctant to look for solutions within the educational system itself, which creates a hindrance for educators to engage in real school reform efforts (García & Guerra, 2004). Researchers found that even when reform efforts are mandated, educators who hold deficit beliefs resist modifying their practices because they believe students and families are the source of the problem. Additionally, negative beliefs and deficit thinking often lead to low expectations for students of color.

To turn this around and help students attain academic success and reach their greatest potential, teachers practicing CRT must have high expectations for their students. CRT promotes genuine respect for students, and it believes in their learning capabilities. It also provides instructional strategies and curricula that are driven by standards through the use of challenging, engaging exercises that take place within the context of students' cultural and linguistic backgrounds (Hilberg et al., 2003). Negative beliefs, deficit thinking, and stereotypes are hurting students. For example, teachers who lack cultural understanding often assume students who do not follow expected norms are unintelligent or ill-behaved; thereby, reinforcing deficit thinking. On the other hand, CRT allows teachers to look past their own worldview, better understand the thoughts of others, and form more relevant and well-rounded teaching methods, all of which improve students' learning experiences.

Developing teachers who are prepared to meet the challenges of today's diverse classrooms, require ongoing professional development. However, many teachers, purposefully or unconsciously, find it difficult teaching diverse students and may end up avoiding it altogether. Researchers provided several reasons for this avoidance that included a lack of knowledge regarding issues related to diversity, little understanding of how to foster supportive and inclusive classroom environments, and few skills for handling potentially inflammatory comments (Anderson, 1999). Additionally, difficulties in talking about diversity in a homogeneous environment presented issues for some teachers. Feelings of inadequacy in teaching a diverse student population also plagued many teachers. This lack of knowledge may be the result of teacher preparation programs. Teacher preparation courses may lack quality learning opportunities for teachers to become well versed on issues of diversity and culturally relevant pedagogy in meaningful ways that can translate into practice. Teacher preparation programs must embrace the challenge of developing programs that are not only pedagogically responsive to the needs of increasingly diverse students but are culturally responsive to their needs as well (Irvine, 2003).

Practically Speaking

I marvel at young children—particularly preschool children. They could care less about color, language, status, backgrounds, or family dynamics. All they want to do is play with a friend. They do not get caught up in the mean and hateful rhetoric like some adults. For example, our youngest granddaughter dances for a reputable dance company that is ethnically mixed but when they dance, they are one. It's a beautiful thing to see. I wonder how different things would be if life could imitate art. I also love watching our oldest granddaughter and her teammates interact with each other in a sport where there is little participation from girls of color. The girls and the parents on her team spend a lot of time together. Diversity and exposure to different cultures, races, and backgrounds can help children develop empathy, understanding, and acceptance of others who are different from themselves. It's also important to note that this type of exposure can help combat prejudices and stereotypes that are often perpetuated in more homogenous spaces. As children grow up experiencing diversity, they can develop a broader perspective and become more comfortable interacting with people who are different from themselves. This can have a positive impact on their personal relationships, as well as their professional and social lives. It's great to see the power of diversity and inclusivity in action. I appreciate the fact that our granddaughter and her teammates are breaking down barriers and forming lasting friendships through sports. I hope that more children can have similar experiences that broaden their world view and help create a more just and equitable society.

When I attended Louisiana State University (LSU), I was definitely out of my comfort zone. Up until the time that I attended LSU, I attended school from kindergarten through 12th grade and lived in neighborhoods where I was part of the majority. When I arrived at LSU, I found myself in the minority when I attended my classes. Everyone around me looked different, acted differently, had different experiences, and different backgrounds. I felt uncomfortable, less than, insecure, and afraid for the first time in my life. Initially, I couldn't relate, and I couldn't find my way. I thought I was in over my head but the thought of failing scared me more. I had to pull myself together and walk into my destiny with my head held high. When I realized that while we (classmates and teammates) were all different, we were the same. We had dreams, aspirations, and goals. I was able to see the beauty in people who were different from me. My coaches and teammates were from different parts of the world, and I learned so much from them, even table etiquette, thanks to my good friend Camille. My coaches Loren Seagrave and Gary Sievers never gave up on me. They were men who did not look like me but cared enough to look beyond my background and guided me into my future. I was taken from a homogeneous environment and placed in a heterogeneous environment, and it was the best thing that could ever happen to me.

My LSU experience forced me to grow up, let go of my fears and insecurities, and allowed me to appreciate, respect, and love people who are different from me. We can learn a lot from preschoolers, athletes, and the arts in general. Sports, living in diverse neighborhoods, and attending diverse schools are natural ways to bring people who are different together. It is within these types of environments that we begin to break down biases (especially implicit biases) and walls of hate, to see others for who they are instead of what society purports them to be. If we could only store up the innocence of preschoolers and the special bonds formed in athletics and spread it around, this world would be a very different place.

Culturally Responsive Teaching in the Classroom

Culturally responsive teaching is a student-centered approach to teaching in which the students' unique cultural strengths are identified and nurtured to promote student achievement and a sense of well-being. According to researchers, CRT uses constructivist principles in its approach. It elicits students' prior knowledge and beliefs to connect to new content and knowledge. It also provides ongoing opportunities for students to incorporate new and more complex concepts into existing frameworks (Newmann, 1990). CRT challenges students' mis-concepts, encourages students to conceptualize relationships in complex ways, and recognize multiple causes and consequences (Ashby et al., 2005). Culturally relevant teaching requires teachers to genuinely care about students and every aspect of their lives.

These are the teachers that attend sporting events for their students or provide cupcakes for a student's birthday because the family is unable to do so or provides toiletries for a child to clean up in the morning. These are the teachers that go over and beyond the call of duty. They often wonder if their students are getting enough rest, food, or homework help. They think about different ways to get students engaged in classroom activities. They do not give up on students, rather they push them to always do their best. We often hear teachers say, "I do my job and I go home to my family." In a culturally responsive classroom, the students go home with the teacher (figuratively) because they become family. Dr. Ladson-Billings posited that the goals of CRT are to produce students who can achieve academically, demonstrate cultural competence, and understand and critique the existing social order. CRT requires on-going professional development, deep-level changes rather than surface-level changes, and an adjustment in our mindset.

Culturally responsive teaching requires classroom activities to be presented in multiple ways and scaffolding must be incorporated to gradually build upon the skills that students acquired. Teachers must always consider how curriculum may adversely affect students intellectually and emotionally. Instruction must be inclusive which means that the course work should be meaningful for students and designed to encourage them. Instruction must effectively meet students' needs and invite collaboration. Teachers must ensure that varied and frequent active learning techniques are being used, which include but are not limited to discussions, group work, experiential learning, debates, presentations, and team projects. Additionally, teachers should use books to elicit conversations about diversity and social justice. Use games, songs, traditions from various global regions throughout the school year and begin with the culture of the students in the classroom. No matter the subject matter, teachers must build on the students' life experiences and consistently bring them into the classroom. Current and real-world examples help students connect to the curriculum, allow for deeper engagement, and help students make real connections.

Culturally responsive teaching requires educators to create environments where students learn about and discuss similarities and differences and expand racial awareness. Teachers must become familiar with the backgrounds that all students bring to the classroom and use that information as added value rather than a deficit. Student diversity must be seen as the norm and curriculum and teaching methods must be flexible and designed to meet the needs of all students.

In the area of assessment, teachers must use multiple measures to assess. Students should be invited to share their knowledge in multiple ways which include not only traditional tests but low-stakes quizzes, quick writes, homework, and responses to class questions and group discussions. Additionally, authentic assessments such as life history interviews, personal stories, autobiographical journaling, and portfolios can be used to demonstrate and personalize learning. Any knowledge gaps, challenges, and areas of struggle should be identified early on to provide additional help and to possibly adjust curriculum and/or instruction. Students should be encouraged to self-reflect as well. Giving students the opportunity to reflect on what they have learned can provide insight into progress and areas that may need more attention, but it can also reinforce learning and help students make connections to their life experiences.

Building a strong classroom community is an important aspect of culturally responsive teaching because it creates a sense of belonging and safety for all students. Practicing specific strategies can help to create such an environment. For example, providing opportunities for students to practice new skills with their peers is important because it helps to build their confidence and competence. It also fosters collaboration and teamwork, which are essential skills for success in a 21st century global economy. Individual and whole class meetings can provide opportunities for students to set goals, reflect on their progress, and receive feedback from their peers and teachers. This can help to create a culture of continuous learning and improvement. Encouraging students to help each other is another way to foster a sense of community and support. This can be particularly beneficial for students who are struggling in a particular area, as they can receive help and guidance from their peers.

Allowing students to make mistakes without fear of retribution or ridicule is essential for creating a safe and supportive learning environment. Mistakes are a natural part of the learning process, and students who are afraid to make mistakes may be hesitant to take risks and try new things. Finally, handling conflicts as a community is also an important aspect of creating a strong classroom community. By establishing classroom rules or agreements and holding class meetings to resolve conflicts, teachers can create a culture of respect, collaboration, and problem-solving. This can help students develop important social and emotional skills, such as empathy, communication, and conflict resolution. Creating a strong classroom community is essential for promoting a positive learning environment and supporting the academic success of all students. Culturally responsive teaching strategies can help to create such an environment.

Creating a culturally responsive classroom will take work, patience, and a shift in the mindset of teachers. The key is for teachers to acknowledge the differences between students and themselves and adjust teaching strategies accordingly which often requires nontraditional approaches to teaching and learning. Teachers must believe that all students can learn and more importantly, the environment, the vision, and the mission must reflect this sentiment as well, particularly in classrooms that are culturally and linguistically diverse. Teachers must engage with students to empower them to think critically and to construct meaning from the world around them.

It is important that students hold the beliefs that they are intelligent and full of potential which are central to motivation. Teachers must treat all students as competent and capable learners and focus on fostering a growth mindset rather than a deficit mindset. They must design lessons with their most underserved students in mind and hold all students accountable for learning by building a strong academic environment through a sense of community.

Practically Speaking

I asked my focus group if they were familiar with CRT, and all had heard of the term. I asked how they implemented it in their classrooms. All except one explained what they did in terms of CRT. According to the group, they planned events for Multicultural Day, Black History Month, Women's History Month, and Hispanic Heritage Month. Beyond those events, I did not hear anything that spoke to the practice of CRT. The participants spoke about the importance of being inclusive but there was nothing intentional or ongoing and nothing to connect academics and the culture. There was no plan for using their students' strengths and their cultural backgrounds to help them better engaged in the learning process.

I asked the group about strategies they used to get to know their students and families. Most of the participants stated that in the beginning of the school year, students complete an 'all about me book' that they share with their peers during activities like show-n-tell. I asked about explicit teaching on acceptance, diversity, and empathy. Most of the participants said that it was not "really a part of the curriculum" but they squeeze the topics in when they can via books or real situations that may turn into "teachable moments."

One participant had a different response that surprised me. Her first teaching job was in a predominately African American district and as she reflected on her practice, she realized that she never explicitly taught or discussed inclusion or culture. She said, "I got to know my students as the year progressed, but I did not get to know them beforehand and never reached out to their families unless something was wrong." She further stated that she did not even realize until recently that she only spoke about culture and diversity intentionally during Black History Month. She surprised me when she said, "I was so focused on helping them gain skills needed for the next grade that I didn't think to bring it up. Besides, I didn't think about culture or inclusion because we were all African Americans." I asked about her experience in her new district that is predominantly white. She said, "I have more opportunities to engage in diversity throughout the school year because I typically have two or three students of color per year in my class, so it lends itself to natural conversations about culture, inclusion, and acceptance."

I then asked the group if they thought CRT was important. They were hesitant in saying yes but quick to say, "But we need to ensure that we get those important skills in first." CRT is not thoroughly understood by most teachers; it is seen as something separate and apart from teaching, something that is done in addition to teaching, or something that is done in reaction to a situation. Rather, CRT should be seen as a strategy for teaching and a tool for learning, to move students forward and to help them better engage in the learning process and to feel good about who they are as learners. CRT cannot be an afterthought; it must be intentionally infused in daily teaching and learning practices. The way that the teachers in the focus group practiced CRT was consistent with the practices that were outlined in the beginning of this chapter: cultural celebrations, trivialization, essentializing, and substituting.

"Personalized learning is not what is done to the learner or about tailoring the learning. It is about helping each learner to identify and develop the skills they need to support and enhance their own learning so that agency and self-advocacy can be realized." Kathleen McClaskey

Chapter 9

Student Agency

Excuse Me, Let Me Help

Access to early childhood education in the U.S. has dramatically improved for young children with both state and federally funded programs; however, educational disparities continue (Garcia & Cuellar, 2006). Recent studies have indicated that many elementary schools fail to provide incoming preschool children of color with experienced teachers, appropriate resources (Garcia & Gonzalez, 2006) and adequate, creative, rigorous, and dynamic learning experiences (Fuller, 2007).

Consequently, children of color often leave preschool only to arrive in kindergarten classrooms structured by tasks, worksheets, and instructional lists with little creative and/or critical thinking opportunities (Crosnoe, 2006). Researchers argue that children of color are experiencing a disproportionate amount of strict teaching and learning environments in which children have little or no influence over how and/or what they learn (Fuller, 2007). A specific strategy to ensure the empowerment of all children is through agency. Agency advocates argue that children need dynamic kinds of learning experiences in different subject areas and with a wide range of developmental domains.

In agreement with Genishi and Dyson (2009), educators will learn more about what children know and can do if they provide a diversity of activities, as well as helping them accomplish their intentions, and provide space and time for them to collaborate with others. Instead of using a deficit thinking approach with children, educators must focus on children influencing what and how they learn in order to expand their capabilities beyond what standardized tests measure and categorize (Colegrove & Adair, 2014).

What is agency? One common definition of student agency is being able to make choices and decisions to influence events and to have an impact on one's world. It is a force that promotes learning experiences meant to expand students' capabilities for learning in the early grades. Student agency refers to the capacity of students to take ownership of their learning and be active agents in shaping their educational experiences. It involves personal integrity and a sense of efficacy. In terms of personal integrity, students need to develop a respect for their unique attributes and those of others (Williams, 2019). This can be fostered through an inclusive classroom environment that celebrates differences and encourages students to value their own and others' perspectives. The sense of efficacy refers to students' ability to take strategic steps to achieve their goals. This involves developing skills such as goal-setting, self-regulation, and persistence. When students feel empowered to take action towards their goals, they are more likely to engage in learning experiences that expand their thinking and broaden their capabilities. By taking initiative, being purposeful, and reflecting on their skills, students can develop a sense of agency that drives them to persist in the face of obstacles and make choices that lead to positive outcomes. Interacting with others in their school environment and negotiating their influence can also help students develop their agency by learning from and collaborating with their peers and teachers. Fostering student agency is essential for creating meaningful learning experiences that empower students to take ownership of their education and become active agents in shaping their futures.

According to Vaughn (2019), to promote student agency, teachers must address all three dimensions of student agency, which includes disposition, motivation, and position. They must support students' efforts to define themselves as independent learners. They must ask students to reflect on what they have learned, what has been hard for them, what has gone well, and why. Also, teachers must create a positive classroom environment where norms and rules allow students to make meaningful decisions about what they want to learn and how they want to participate in the group. Essentially, efforts to promote student agency always require a balancing act.

How wide and deep should enabling agency go? Enabling agency is a complex concept that should be approached with care and attention to the needs and readiness of each student. It is not a free-for-all or a hands-off approach, but rather a pedagogical stance that empowers students to take ownership of their learning and make choices that lead to meaningful action. Teachers play a crucial role in enabling agency by providing necessary support, structures, and guidance. This includes being alert to students' readiness to assert themselves and make choices, and scrutinizing classroom structures, materials, and assignments to ensure they allow for student agency. If students are not yet ready to exercise agency, teachers should scale back rather than give up on it entirely. Enabling student agency requires a pedagogical stance that defines the purpose of the structures, systems, and guides we put in place (Williams, 2019). It involves listening to and being responsive to student voice, and ensuring that structures, procedures, rules, and guidelines enhance students' personal integrity rather than reaffirming teachers' authority. Student agency permeates every aspect of the student experience and cannot be switched on and off at the teacher's will. Teachers must be aware of the impact their actions have on each student's beliefs about themselves as learners, and whether their actions communicate a respect for each student's perspective (Lin-Siegler et al., 2016). This is essential for fostering investment and motivation in learning.

According to Poon of the Center for Innovation in Education, agency is not just about acting but about acting in the service of advantageous goals. The Center for Innovation in Education works to advance systems that seek greater equity in how children develop the identity, community, agency, and competency that pave the way for greater equity in our larger society. Goals are contextual and value-laden in ways that affect how people of different backgrounds perform and perceive agency. Poon believes that there is no broad consensus on the definition of student agency. However, he believes that there are common elements found in several definitions which includes: setting goals, initiating action toward those goals, reflecting, monitoring the goals, and self-efficacy. Teachers can help students develop agency by providing opportunities for self-assessment and feedback, fostering concepts like voice and self-initiation, encouraging self-reflection and redirection, and promoting the development of self-efficacy skills. The ultimate goal is to promote greater equity in how children develop their identity, community, agency, and competency, which can pave the way for greater equity in society as a whole.

When students set goals and take action, the question becomes do we identify their actions as valid expressions of agency, or are we biased toward only those actions that are approved by members in power? Whatever definition of agency we adopt, we must seek to understand it based on our country's history of racism which produced structures and systems that constrain some individuals' ability and freedom to enact agency. We must seek to understand students for who they are, including the ways that race, gender, sexual orientation, and other factors influence how they experience and navigate everyday life, which ultimately impacts agency.

One factor in understanding children is to see them for who they are, including skin color. In an article about Confronting Colorblindness, Fergus essentially stated, "If one does not see a person's color, it means that he or she is omitting the basis for some of the lived experiences of that individual." Fergus's argument highlights the importance of acknowledging and understanding the impact of race and culture on individuals' experiences. Colorblindness, or the idea that one should ignore or disregard race or ethnicity in interpersonal interactions, fails to recognize the ways in which historical and societal factors have shaped the experiences of marginalized groups. By ignoring the role that race and culture play in shaping individuals' experiences, colorblindness perpetuates a White cultural frame that fails to consider the diverse experiences of individuals from different backgrounds. For example, it frames how teachers view an argument between a White and Black student in the hallway or when reprimanding Mexican American students for speaking Spanish in the hallway. In those examples, a White cultural frame omits all social realities other than a White social identity. Teachers, in particular, must be aware of how their own cultural biases and beliefs may influence their interactions with students. Color blindness can send a message to children that everyone shares the same cultural experience. For example, if the main characters in the literature that students are exposed to do not include Black or Brown students, it sends a message that Black and Brown people do not play major roles in literature or life. Translating colorblindness into curriculum can also telegraph messages to children that the cultural experience of being white and middle class is the desired standard.

Colorblindness is a complex belief system, that we cannot gloss over. I believe that many people embrace colorblindness with good intentions because they believe that they are moving beyond color to see people for who they are individually. But when individuals refuse to see the elephant in the room (color) they miss or ignore a large part of the experiences (past and present) that shaped and continues to shape individuals of color. This refusal to see color allows groups to deny the presence of institutional racism or discrimination. Pretending that the color of someone's skin has not shaped their experiences in life is not an appropriate response for educators. Rather, educators must be aware of bias-based beliefs and put those front and center as they develop practices and policies. Otherwise, they run the risk of building more educational reforms that see marginalized populations as the problem. This is critical if we want to reform how reading is taught in the early grades.

A major aspect of agency is student voice, which is the ability of children to exert influence in their learning spaces, to transform their own and others' learning experiences, and to expand learning. Student agency does not aim to replace the presence and power of seasoned certified professionals but to insert alongside those experts the experiences, perspectives, and expertise of students (Cook-Sather, 2014). Enacting student agency requires a mindset shift and the sharing of power. When students speak and act alongside credentialed professionals as critics and creators of educational practice, the relationship between "voice" and "agency" is strong. As a growing number of researchers argue, student voice has the potential to open up spaces and capacities for "marginalized youth to play key roles in school reform" (Gonzalez et al., 2017), support more socially just school environments (Mansfield, 2014; Salisbury et al., 2019), ensure that disenfranchised youth are included in decision-making processes (Ginwright & Cammarota, 2006), and foster positive youth development around agency and civic engagement (Brasof & Spector, 2016). Research has demonstrated overwhelmingly that students who have agency in their learning are more motivated, experience greater satisfaction in their learning, and are more likely to achieve academic success (Lin-Siegler et al., 2016). Students with agency are powerful learners who are prepared to engage with the world with sustained, courageous curiosity.

Fostering Student Agency in the Classroom

To provide students with choice and voice in their educational experiences, teachers must harness students' intrinsic motivation to learn. According to Cooper (2017), there are five ways to promote student agency.

1. Creating a culture of inquiry and creativity on the first day of school can set the tone for the entire school year. Teachers can start by fostering a classroom environment that encourages questions, experimentation, and creativity. For example, teachers can ask students to share their interests and passions and then use those as a starting point for inquiry-based learning. Teachers can also introduce open-ended projects that allow for creativity and self-expression. To promote student agency, teachers

must learn to let go and give students more control over their learning. This can involve allowing students to choose their own topics for research projects or giving them options for how they will demonstrate their learning. It is important for teachers to support students through the learning process, even when they are struggling, and to help them see the value in the struggle. Explicitly teaching collaboration skills can also help create a culture of agency in the classroom. Teachers can model effective collaboration by working with colleagues or sharing their own experiences with collaboration. They can also have students work together to establish norms for effective collaboration and provide opportunities for students to practice those skills.

2. Emphasize relevance over engagement. When students are able to connect what they are learning to their own lives and interests, they are much more likely to be motivated to learn and to retain what they have learned. It is important for educators to recognize that students come to the classroom with their own unique backgrounds, experiences, and interests. By designing learning experiences that are relevant to these individual factors, educators can tap into students' intrinsic motivation and create a sense of ownership over the learning process. In contrast, when learning experiences are based solely on the teacher's interests or preferences, students may feel disconnected from the material and disengaged from the learning process. While initial engagement may be high, it is likely to be short-lived and may not lead to long-term learning outcomes.

3. Share learning targets. When students have a clear understanding of what they are expected to learn and what they need to accomplish, they are more likely to take ownership of their learning and to be motivated to achieve the desired outcomes. Learning targets help students focus on the most important aspects of a lesson or unit, and they provide a clear roadmap for what they need to do to be successful. By sharing learning targets with their students, teachers can help reduce ambiguity and confusion, and can provide a sense of structure and direction to the learning process. In addition, when students have a clear understanding of

the learning targets, they are better able to assess their own progress and take responsibility for their own learning. This can help to foster a sense of independence and self-efficacy, which are important skills for success both in school and in life.

4. Provide constructive comments. Feedback serves as a tool for students to understand where they are in their learning, what they need to do to improve, and how to reach their goals. Effective feedback can help students to develop their skills and knowledge, and to build their self-confidence and self-efficacy. In the classroom, feedback can take on different forms, including teacher to student, student to student, and student to self. Each of these forms of feedback can be valuable, and they can all contribute to student learning and growth.

5. Allow time for reflection. To promote student agency and ownership of learning, it is important for teachers to prioritize student-to-self feedback. When students are able to reflect on their own learning, set their own goals, and assess their own progress, they are more likely to take responsibility for their learning and to be motivated to improve. To create the conditions for student-to-self feedback to be the norm, teachers can incorporate regular opportunities for reflection and self-assessment into their instruction. They can also provide students with clear criteria for success and encourage them to set their own learning goals. In addition, teachers can model the use of self-assessment and reflection by regularly sharing their own reflections on their teaching and their own professional growth. This can help to foster a culture of continuous learning and improvement in the classroom. However, teachers must intentionally allow for reflection and create time for students to do nothing but analyze where they are in relation to the learning targets. Teachers can assist students by giving them reflective questions: What additional questions do you have about this topic? What strengths can you identify in your work? What are you most proud of? How could you improve your work? What would you do differently next time?

Dr. Caitlin Tucker believes that providing students with the ability to make key decisions about their learning is a powerful motivator for students. Tucker's approach to encouraging student agency involves giving students the opportunity to answer the **what**, **how**, and **why** of a lesson, assignment, or project. This approach helps to engage students in the learning process by allowing them to focus on topics that interest them, think critically about how they will approach a task, and articulate the value of their work.

In the "**what**" phase, students choose what aspect of a subject or topic they want to focus on for a lesson, assignment, or project. This helps to create personal investment in the task and invites students to focus on an aspect of the subject that interests them. This approach also helps students develop research skills, design a presentation, and present for the class. In the "**how**" phase, students decide how they will accomplish a task. This challenges them to think critically about what they are being asked to do and how they would approach solving a particular problem. This approach encourages students to think through a task and articulate their own path for completing the work. In the "**why**" phase, students articulate why a task, assignment, or project is valuable. This helps them understand the purpose of the work they are doing and make informed decisions about what they want to produce to show what they learned. Allowing student agency about what they produce or create is another way to engage even the most reluctant learners in the learning process. Providing students with agency over their learning is a powerful motivator that can help to engage students in the learning process, increase their investment in their own learning, and improve their academic outcomes.

Zeiser et al. (2018) outlined three primary factors identified by teachers for deepening the use of instructional practices that promote student agency: supportive school processes, teacher collaboration, and professional development. These factors are crucial for promoting student agency and ensuring that instructional practices support students' development of agency. Supportive school processes can help create a culture that values student agency and encourages its development, while teacher collaboration can provide educators with opportunities to share effective practices and learn from one another. Professional development can also help teachers to develop the skills necessary to facilitate student agency effectively. These factors can help ensure students are able to take ownership of their learning and develop the skills and dispositions necessary for success in school and beyond.

Williams (2019) found that recreational reading and other literacy activities are powerful ways of exercising student agency as well. Recreational reading is defined as students choosing what they want to read, when they want to read it, and where they want to read it (Krashen 2011). By definition, recreational reading implies the complete handing over of key choices about reading to the student. It also implies relinquishing teacher control: no grading, no testing for comprehension, no book reports, and no rewards for their reading. This release of control is not easy for educators. However, when students have this level of agency they read more; they read longer; they read later into life; they learn more; their reading, writing, and mathematical skills improve; their spelling improves; their vocabulary expands; and their knowledge builds (William, 2017). All these benefits are gained just from reading for fun.

Additionally, teachers should allow students to create citations for their own work. For example, if a student takes a photo for an exhibition or interviews a peer for research, creating a citation that accurately communicates the student's role builds his or her identity as a creator and builds a sense of accomplishment. Also, teachers should talk about literature choices with students and as they get to know their students, they may find more creative ways to introduce them to more-accessible texts and provide more opportunities to enable moments of discovery. Therefore, through affirming students' choices and keeping communication open, they build student agency in their reading and retain future opportunities for learning. Another fun idea is to provide opportunities for students to create their own books. Creating books is a powerful affirmation of student agency because students get to catalog, barcode, and display their own books for others to enjoy. Teachers do not need to edit them, rather they just need to have genuine conversations about the books by inquiring about what students created and the process they went through to create their books. Williams found that cataloging books together creates opportunities to discuss subject matter, genre, target audience, summaries, and why students think their peers may want to read their book. Agency is "a fundamental human desire" (Johnston, 2004). Our conversations with students and how we interact with them may help students build bridges between their actions and results, reinforcing a sense that they can accomplish anything.

Challenges and Obstacles to Student Agency

While the benefits of enacting student agency are numerous, there are challenges and obstacles that are associated with implementation. The results of a study conducted by Zeiser et al. (2018) found that the challenges associated with enacting student agency included lack of support from administration or school leadership, lack of resources or materials needed to implement agency-supporting instructional practices, resistance from some students who may be accustomed to more traditional, teacher-centered instruction, and challenges related to measuring student progress and growth in areas such as critical thinking and collaboration. Despite these challenges, it is important for educators to work towards promoting student agency as it has the potential to improve student engagement, motivation, and learning outcomes. Addressing these challenges may involve providing teachers with more professional development opportunities, encouraging collaboration among teachers and students, and creating a supportive school culture that values and prioritizes student agency.

Vaughn (2019) found additional obstacles in fostering student agency in schools. First, test-based school accountability creates pressure on teachers to provide highly directive instruction, which prevents them from offering a lot of opportunities for students to make choices about what they learn and how they learn. Even if students are encouraged to choose topics, texts, and activities that meet their linguistic, cultural, and instructional needs and interests, their decisions can easily be vetoed by supervisors who may insist students and teachers follow a prescribed curriculum. Stires and Genishi (2008) argued that teachers are often unable to create their own schedules, select their own materials, lesson plans, or assessment tools, because they are teaching and learning in a highly compressed way. In extreme cases, teachers are given a curriculum and each day they must follow a pacing guide and stay in lock-step with other teachers in the same grade level. In these types of environments, student agency is difficult to foster, which is why student agency must be a school wide or even a district wide agreed upon approach. Second, Vaughn found that even if teachers agree in principle that students should have opportunities to enact agency, they may struggle to translate that goal into classroom practice.

Moreover, many teachers worry about a loss of control when it comes to student agency as well. However, student agency does not mean students make all the decisions, but it does mean they get to make some of them. The more teachers release control of the learning to the actual learners, the more rewarding the learning is for everyone. Building student agency is a lifelong endeavor for everyone, but the results are worthwhile. When we empower students to drive their own learning, show them possible destinations, let them chart their own course, and help them redirect along the way, they build a sense of self-efficacy. They develop not only the skills and knowledge required, but also the confidence from knowing they found success themselves.

Disparities in What Children of Color Experience at School

"Student agency boils down to students having a voice in the classroom."
Laurie Manville and Dr. Ava Lafevre

I was fortunate enough to participate in a book study with the authors of the book *Segregation by Experience: Agency, Racism, and Learning in the Early Grades.* The two authors, Jennifer Keys Adair and Kiyomi Sanchez-Suzuki Colegrove hit the nail on the head from page one as they shared first-hand experience of a teacher providing opportunities for her students to enact their agency, which was not the practice of the school at large. The first few sentences of the book are typical of what we see in schools largely populated by Black and Brown students from low-income families. In the words of Adair and Colegrove, "In schools across the United States, many young children of color are forced to walk in prison-like lines with silent 'bubbles in their mouths' and hands behind their backs. They go through much of the day disconnected from their real lives, asked to submit to significant controlling mechanisms such as behavior charts, monolingualism, punishment systems, and the denial of movement. In other schools, meanwhile, young white children walk in zigzag formations, taking their time, chatting, joking, and sometimes singing with their friends. They read and hear stories that reflect their realties and comfort. What makes it 'acceptable' for children in the United States of America to have such different kinds of schooling experiences, especially in the earliest grades?"

What a powerful and accurate picture of what goes on in so many of our schools today. I often say the difference between children of color and their white counterparts is experience and opportunity. There are educators who are adamantly opposed to giving up power and control to allow students to enact agency. These teachers do not believe in classrooms where students are free to talk, free to get up to get materials that they need on their own, free to walk over to a friend for assistance, free to work on a project either alone or with a group of students, free to laugh out loud, or call out answers without having the label of "out of control" attached. Once more, teachers who allow children to exercise student agency are seen as teachers who cannot control their classrooms, or teachers who allow students to "run over" them. Teachers who share control with students get the "side eye" from colleagues because their students are not as quiet in the hallway, they do not walk in a straight line with their hands behind their backs, and they speak to others while in the hallway. These teachers are the subject of conversation in the teacher's lounge. These teachers receive partially proficient ratings on their observations and are handed resources for classroom management. The act of relinquishing some control over to students is a heavy price to pay, but it is so worth it.

The authors (Adair and Colegrove) conducted a study where they spent a full year observing first grade classrooms. The children were mostly children of color (Black and Latinx) and from low in-come families. The authors set out to identify as many forms of agency as they could to make a video. Agency, as defined by the two authors, is the ability to influence and make decisions about how and what is learned to expand capabilities. The authors created a video of the children and the teachers during typical classroom experiences and showed the same one-minute portion of the clip to over 250 educators, parents, teachers, and young children to see what forms of agency they noticed and valued. The twist that shocked the authors and totally threw me off guard was that people did not respond in a manner that was expected. The authors thought that people would be "excited and inspired to see young children of color acting as scientists, formulating questions, working deeply and collaboratively, thinking carefully, and being engaged in their learning." But they were not. In fact, many admired the practices exhibited in the classroom but did not think that those practices would work for the children in their schools, who by the way, had the same demographic make-up as the children in the video. In the next sections, I summarize some of the forms of agency exhibited in the video followed by the stunning reactions of educators and students. This section is ends with the meaning of segregation by experience.

Student Agency in Ms. Bailey's Classroom

Ms. Bailey is an immigrant from a country in East Africa who speaks four languages. Her classroom was made up of 22 students: thirteen boys and nine girls with fifteen students self-reporting as Latinx, three as African American, and four as White. Ms. Bailey offered her students something very different than colleagues in her school; she offered students "dynamic, sophisticated learning experiences connected to the reality of their lives." Each child brought their unique personalities to the classroom as well as their family life to create an inclusive learning community. Research has proven time and time again that children learn best through movement, discovery, observation, helping others, collaborating, and exploring in shared endeavors over time with peers and caring adults (Gopnik 2012; Paradise and Rogoff, 2009).

What Adair and Colegrove pointed out is that in Ms. Bailey's classroom, children of color were offered all these experiences regardless of their behavior, language spoken, family makeup, or economic status all while in a classroom governed by state standards and testing pressures. The children in Ms. Bailey's classroom did not have to "earn" these experiences like so many children in United States public schools. The children in Ms. Bailey's classroom had the opportunities to move around the classroom, usually at will, "talk to one another often, and use initiative because they had the space and time to do so." At times, they were able to select their own topics of study and they made many decisions about what and how they learned. The opportunities to move around, talk to one another, notice new things, contribute effort, and share ideas led to a range of developed and practiced capabilities across social and academic domains. These opportunities were justified and motivated by Ms. Bailey's belief that "children need to own what they are doing so that they can be empowered learners throughout their lives."

The children in Ms. Bailey's classroom supported each other. They were engaged in the learning process, and needless to say, they were not always quiet during their learning experiences, which I am sure annoyed colleagues. However, the "noise" included discussions, chatting, debates, stories, and questions. The children used noise to be social and to engage one another. More importantly, the authors suggested that noise in the classroom offered children many ways to interact with the content and with one another's knowledge.

Ms. Bailey believed in the concept "own what you are doing", which is a recognition that children learn through using their bodies. Ms. Bailey gave children some control (not complete) over how, what, when, where, and the why of their learning. So many teachers often disregard student agency because they do not want to give up control and they fear that children will be out of control. However, according to the authors, giving up control resulted in specific kinds of learning experiences that became everyday normalized parts of the day, including noise, movement, time, and collective work. Ms. Bailey took a lot of heat from her colleagues as she received 'the look', whispers, and was certainly the topic of conversation in the "teachers break room." Nevertheless, Ms. Bailey forged forward because she believed that all children deserve to have a voice and choice in their learning experience. Who would not want their child in Ms. Bailey's class?

Reactions to Student Agency from Educators

The authors created a video that captured different forms of agency depicted in Ms. Bailey's classroom and showed it to educators. Before showing the video, the authors made two points. The first point was that the study was about the type of educational experiences children should have in the early years, but the video was not meant to depict best practices only to elicit discussion and opinions about the variety of practices in the video from educators. The second point was that Ms. Bailey's classroom was similar to their classrooms regarding demographics. These points did not sit too well with the educators in the discussion group and their reactions were revealing. First, the educators liked the fact that the children in the video had the opportunity to talk to one another, they admired the types of discussions, the classroom community concept, and that children had the opportunity to call out for help and get it on their own. Educators also liked that children could choose who they wanted to work with, the materials they wanted to use, and the opportunity to build upon their interests and curiosity. However, the educators in the study fundamentally disagreed with Ms. Bailey about *when* children should be able to ask questions, act on their curiosity, follow their interests, feel ownership, and experience freedom like what they saw happening in the video clip.

According to Adair and Colegrove, teachers in the study group felt that children needed to "prove" themselves first. This absolutely blew me away. The conundrum is that the educators believed that the practices displayed in the video were good for students in general but not for their students because the type of experiences in the video must be earned, not freely given or experienced. The educators believed that "children should not be given control over themselves or their environment before they had proven their ability to be efficient and obedient." Children needed to be trained to know how to be obedient enough to learn. Self-control and self-regulation were two terms that educators in the study used in reference to children being able to control their bodies into compliance and do what the teachers say. The educators in the study emphasized a period of "training" for students to be afforded with the privilege of student agency. The training takes place during the first few weeks or months of school. The educators thought that since the children in Ms. Bailey's classroom were all over the place, they thought that the video clip was done in the beginning of the school year, when children were not "trained." This would account for why children were moving around and goofing off because they had not been trained (according to the educators in the study).

When the educators were told that the video clip was done in December, the teachers believed that Ms. Bailey had not properly trained the children. Adair and Colegrove pointed out that the educators in the focus group made negative comments and assumed that everyone would see Ms. Bailey's class as less than ideal. "Kids can just get away with playing around in corners and not getting anything done." "Maybe she hasn't set the ground rules yet, or maybe they're still in training." Safety was a concern for some of the teachers as well. One preschool teacher stated, "You just don't want them all over the place bumping heads or whatever. Accidents happen while running. I do it that way because it feels secure." The teacher was referring to her strict classroom rules. Basically, according to the educators in the study, agency was a privilege, not necessarily a part of learning.

The educators in the study also pointed out that the practices that the students in Ms. Bailey's classroom experienced, although good, would not work for their students because their students were not "prepared for such a privileged set of learning experiences." Some of the educators in the study stated that the educational system and its unfair emphasis on testing that disproportionately burdened communities of color needed to change before they could offer the learning experiences in Ms. Bailey's classroom. They also thought that families did not prepare their children well enough before they entered school so that students could handle decision-making, problem-solving, relationship-building practices like those they admired in Ms. Bailey's classroom. Teachers could not allow their children to talk more in class and have deep conversations or discussions because all classes in the same grade level had to be on the same 15-minute increments, which is a school mandate. In other words, pacing dictated the schedule for teachers. Therefore, since teachers could not control their time, students could not control their time. Educators in the study also stated that their children lacked appropriate vocabulary to handle the interactions, discussions, and peer conversations that they observed in Ms. Bailey's class.

Educators blamed families for the lack of vocabulary and for children's lack of preparedness when they enter school. Consequently, the reaction from the parents that observed the video clip was basically the same as the educators. The parents liked what they observed but did not think that their children should be engaged in what they saw. Educators and parents agreed that what they observed: hands on learning, deep conversations, students helping each other and caring for one another, appreciating different cultures, and students exercising voice and choice were all good for students in general, just not their students.

Reactions to Student Agency from Students
(First Graders)

First grade students had the opportunity to view the same one-minute video clip as the educators and parents. To my surprise, every single student in the study had negative reactions to what they observed in the video clip. Some students became angry at the children in the video because "they should know better", meaning the students should know the rules of the classroom. Several students covered their eyes and made statements like "they are bad", "they are going to get in trouble", "they don't know how to act", or "they talk too much." Overall, the students' focused on three issues in Ms. Bailey's classroom: movement, noise, and acting without permission. The students in the study believed that the students in the video moved around too much, like getting out of their seats or lying down on the floor to read without permission. These types of actions were labeled 'bad' by the students in the focus group.

The authors asked the students in the study if they had the opportunity to select where they wanted to work or if they needed something in the classroom, could they get up to get it? All the children responded with a resounding no. In the video, there was a scene where one student helped another student and the students in the focus group said it was wrong unless they had permission from the teacher to do so. To the children in the study, learning involved following directions, listening to the teacher, and generally working independently. As the students watched the clip, they could be heard saying, "Keep your mouth zipped, eyes watching, ears listening." They were repeating what they had been exposed to in their classrooms. The students in the study group were conditioned and, based on what they were used to, they could not understand why the students in the video clip were not conditioned or trained as they were. What the students in the study group observed in the video clip was not the norm for them, rather it was the total opposite, and they expressed as much.

The second issue that bothered the students in the focus group was the noise level. The students expressed that the students in the video were loud, and they talked too much. "They needed to be quiet," said one student. Conversations, sharing stories with classmates, or any kind of spontaneous discussion was not acceptable because, according to the students in the study group, "It was not good for learning." In fact, one student said, "If we talk, our thoughts will leave our heads." I wonder where that came from. To the students in the study, learning involved using quiet or low voices and not talking to their classmates while working. One student in the study said, "If you are talking with someone, you can't do your work, and this is not good for the teacher." Recess and lunch were the only times students could talk with their friends, but if they talked in class, the teacher would take recess away and they may not be able to talk with their friends at lunch. Students in the study also referred to hierarchical punishment systems for misbehavior. The hierarchical punishment approach to classroom management uses a tiered system to approach discipline. Most hierarchical systems have three or four general tiers. Tier one is for a first infraction of a behavior, and usually results in a nonverbal reaction from the teacher. Tier two usually involves a verbal warning. Tier three involves consequences for misbehavior and the consequences depend on the teacher and the behavior. Teachers start at the bottom for small infractions and move up if the student continues to misbehave. I am sure that the students in the study group believed that Ms. Bailey's students were all on tier three and needed serious consequences.

The last issue that bothered the students in the study was that the students in Ms. Bailey's class acted without permission. The students in the study were annoyed that the students in the video clip moved around on their own without permission from the teacher. The students felt that the teacher was the one who decided who moves and when and that moving without direct permission from the teacher was not good. When asked if they could move to get materials and supplies, the students responded by saying that teachers select and distribute materials and supplies even the books that they read during choice time. Never once did the students in the study mention anything about what the students were learning or the fun they were having while learning. To them learning was not fun, it was serious business that required them to be quiet, still, and focused on the directions from the teacher, which were the sentiments of the teachers and the parents in the study.

The message students received from being denied a range of dynamic, meaningful learning experiences was that learning was about compliance, not agency. Educators in the study were reluctant to give students opportunities to make decisions, choose their partners, or follow their interests unless they had earned them through their obedience. Adair and Colegrove stated that it was hard to hear students of color responding so negatively to the video. The video showed children of color having fun, laughing, playing, talking, moving around, and enjoying learning. But to the students in the study, the behaviors in the video went against how they experienced and understood the learning process. The students in the study believed that discussing, trying things out, moving around, and initiating activities were not indicators of how a first grader becomes a good learner.

In this respect, the students had internalized, adopted, and defended what effective learning looked like based on what their teachers exposed them to. Quiet, still, and rigid classrooms with little decision making or problem-solving opportunities are the norm in many public schools serving largely students of color, but the sad part is that some educators, parents, and students believe that those qualities are necessary for learning to take place.

Practically Speaking

I turned to my focus group of educators and asked their opinion about several topics such as talking in class, movement, rules, training, walking the hallways, etc. All the teachers in the group except one had some of the same sentiments as the educators in the study. Some responses included, "You must gain control on the first day of school and let them know who is in charge and lay down the law in the beginning because if you don't, you will be in trouble later." Another educators said, "It may sound cruel, but you almost have to be mean or strict for the first few weeks of school just to establish order; once you see that they have caught on, then you can ease up a little." Most of the teachers that I interviewed agreed that students must raise their hands to speak in class out of courtesy and respect.

Almost all the teachers agreed that too much noise was not conducive for learning because it's distracting. They also agreed on very little movement in class because "once kids begin moving, they like to play around and won't finish their work." Regarding materials and supplies, a few teachers said they distribute what children need to complete their assignments because, "if you let them choose, they take too long or they end up arguing over who got what." All agreed that classroom rules (created by the teachers) were for order and safety, and each had a unique behavioral system that students and parents understood and signed off on. Most had a visual chart with each student's name on it and columns that indicated thumbs up or thumbs down for behavior, or students collected tokens throughout the day for being 'good' and at the end of the week, students with tokens had the opportunity to shop in the classroom treasure chest. The teachers all agreed that students really needed recess; therefore, they only took it away when children were really "acting up."

I asked about uniforms and hallway etiquette. Teachers thought uniforms were a great idea because they are not expensive for families, and it reduces teasing, bullying, and students feeling bad about themselves if they do not have trendy clothes. However, in full transparency, I have yet to come across research to support such claims. When asked about students moving in the hallways, one teacher spoke for the group: "All I have to say is 'line up' and the children know exactly what to do." I asked the teacher to explain further. She said her students know the line-

up routine. They line up on the numbers, place their hands behind their backs (so that they do not touch anything), eyes are straight ahead, and they must catch a quiet bubble (to be quiet in the hallway because other children are learning). Another teacher added, "—and they know how to keep a straight line." The other teachers laughed out loud. These routines are very similar to what the educators in the study group shared about the children in the video clip. I have been in education for over 25 years, and I am still perplexed with the straight-line issue. It is a serious thing. I observed teachers standing still, without saying a word, while students checked themselves to see if they were straight and they positioned peers who were slightly less than straight. I wonder why students cannot walk from point A to B without being conscious of being in a straight line.

When a group of adults walk in the hallway, they do not walk in a straight line because it isn't natural. I also wonder if we could just ask students not to touch items in the hallway and remind them beforehand instead of making them put their hands behind their backs. Who walks with their hands behind their backs, except those in handcuffs? Can we ask students to keep a low voice while in the hallway to respect others who are in their classrooms so that students are free to say hello to their friends, siblings, or other teachers in the hallway instead of catching a quiet bubble. It is not natural to see someone you know and not speak; in some cultures, it could be considered rude and disrespectful. I have observed students staring at siblings or friends but cannot say hi—not even a simple wave of the hand. However, the same teachers who want their students to catch a bubble are the ones calling across the hallway to a colleague about something that has nothing to do with school. Adults could walk in the hallways and see students from previous years and the students will not say a word until the teacher grants them permission to, "say hi." Our students are growing up in unnatural environments. When we see people we know, we typically greet them, but not our students, they must be quiet with a big bubble in their mouths. We ask students not to talk for pretty much an entire school day (except for lunch and recess, if they are good), this is unnatural. We were born to interact and socialize with others. How many adults can make it through a typical day without accepting a text, phone call, email, or social media notification from a friend? Not too many, but we ask this of our students.

The one first grade teacher in my focus group had a different experience than the other teachers as she taught in a very affluent school district. She said, most classrooms in her school are pretty loud, and there are no uniforms. She said students come to school in "old pajamas and ratty sneakers half the time." Students are not required to walk in a straight line, and they are free to talk and socialize while in the hallways as long as they respect others who are learning by keeping their voices down. In the classrooms, students are allowed to move about without permission from the teacher because most of the time they are working on projects that are self-directed and self-initiated anyway. Students select their own materials and supplies as needed. Scores on the statewide assessments were high and students have a lot of say in what they learn and how they learn.

The interesting thing about this teacher was that she spent 7 years in an urban school district where most of the students were Black and Brown and when she moved to a suburban district, she had to retrain her mind because she thought things were "too loose and relaxed." She didn't think "children could learn in such chaos." She shared that she had to change her entire teaching practices and thoughts about quality teaching and learning experiences and when she did, she realized the disservice she provided her students of color for seven years. She stated that students of color in her old district were not receiving the same meaningful, relevant, and rigorous learning experiences as her more affluent students in her new district. Her first observation stated that she was too "rigid and firm" with the students. I can only imagine the content in Ms. Bailey's first observation.

Why are many Black and Brown students receiving inferior learning experiences in our public school system? The basic premise of the book *Segregation by Experience: Agency, Racism, and Learning in the Early Grades* shows a classroom that had many rich experiences and how everyone viewing the video struggled to appreciate the experiences that students of color were exposed to. The responses to the video from Ms. Bailey's class are indicative of a broken system where the same behaviors of students could be viewed and labeled differently depending upon who is viewing the video. For example, I can name a few labels that some would assign the students in Ms. Bailey's class: misbehaved, undisciplined, talkative, misguided, unruly, disrespectful, uncooperative, uncontrollable, wild, and uncaring. If those same behaviors were evident in an affluent school district, the labels would be very different: leader, resolute, strong-willed, persuader, collaborator, thinker, high energy, eager learner, scholar, intellectual, and knowledgeable. The labels we assign to students matter and can be detrimental to their overall development and success in school.

Another example, if a student yelled out an idea in one district, he/she may be praised for having a good idea and taking the initiative to push it forward. If the same behavior occurred in a different school district, the student may be sent to sit in the back of the classroom or sent to the principal's office for being disruptive. The book is a clear example that we do not know what good learning looks like, sounds like, and feels like. Students learn who they are, what society expects of them, and what it means to be a learner in the early years of school. They learn largely who they are as learners based on their experiences in school. We must normalize the types of experiences observed in Ms. Bailey's classroom to overcome inequities that are prevalent in many public school classrooms.

The Impact of Unequal Experiences

A concern of Adair and Colegrove is the messages students receive from being segregated from dynamic, active, and sophisticated learning experience. They believe that "how students experience school, teaches them about the process of learning and about being a learner. When schools prioritize compliance and rigidity, students formulate a theory of school learning that demotes them to a passive role in which the main objective is to obey (Love, 2019). Why do children of color typically have to earn the privilege of learning in culturally relevant ways that lead to increased freedom and self-rule. Many students of color do not have opportunities to exercise their agency, rendering their learning experiences different from that of their white affluent peers, this is what segregation by experience means. Why do adults think that students cannot handle an environment like Ms. Bailey's? We have seen our early grades transform into training camps for the higher grades where many students do not experience a range of talking opportunities, authentic discussions, movement, or learning activities that are not authorized or directed by the teacher. Why are students of color controlled by silence and labeled as a problem if they are too loud? As Adair and Colegrove states, "The routine denial of agency to young children of color at school goes unnoticed and the constant reprimands, harsh controls, and prisonlike lines are normalized." The preschool to prison pipeline phrase is very real. Fostering each student's sense of agency is more than providing them with choices. When students have a sense of agency, they feel more in control of themselves and develop an understanding of their influence on the people and spaces around them. When we listen with respect to children's voices, their words, and their ideas, we model trust and collaboration, and we confirm that they are heard and what they think and feel matter. Teachers ultimately control opportunities for students to exercise their agency, which is largely based on how they view students, their background, family, and the community. Teachers' views are based on who they are, how they were raised, personal and professional experiences, beliefs, values, and morals. A teacher's lens will dictate who is worthy of having agency and the types of experiences students will have in the classroom. I am a firm believer that in the early grades, when we exert so much control over children, they lose the opportunities to develop self-control because someone is always in control of their lives.

To back up my claim, researchers Durkin et al. (2022) conducted a study on children's achievement and behavior through sixth grade. One surprising finding was that behavioral control exerted by adults in preschool settings was associated with a decrease in children developing internal self-control skills necessary for long-term development. Children need boundaries and there must be rules or agreements in place for safety reasons. However, too much control may be detrimental and could lead children in the opposite direction of our intent, which is self-control. By the time they move into the higher grades and begin to experiment and challenge rules, they may not have enough practice or experience with self-control to actually control themselves when needed. In fact, some children may look for or expect the adult to step in and 'control' the situation, which usually means a trip to the principal's office, in-school suspension, Saturday detention, or missed recess. Young children eight and under are still developing and are easily conditioned; therefore, teachers and caregivers must be mindful that children can be positively or negatively conditioned during these early years. Good intentions may sometimes lead to unfavorable outcomes.

This study was an eye-opener, and it demonstrated the serious inequitable school offerings that some students experience. Many white students experience school as a place that welcomes their ideas, identities, and curiosity, while students of color experience school as a place that insists on compliance, order, and efficiency. Transforming schools is not easy but meeting the needs of students of color who are the most disenfranchised within them, must be a priority. Educators must create safe and trusting environments that are respectful of students' culture and voice. According to Adair and Colegrove, "segregation by experience results in short- and long-term injustices that perpetuate an intentional denial of access and opportunity" to students of color who are already marginalized. How does this impact reading proficiency? How teachers view teaching and learning and student's capacity to learn will dictate the type and quality of instruction they receive as well as the quality of interactions between teachers and students. These are all important qualities for students to thrive in learning environments and to reach their greatest potential.

This quote by Adair and Colegrove sums things up for me, "Seeing what is possible as opposed to what actually ends up happening to many young children of color during the early years of schooling should give us pause, and hopefully provide fire in our bellies." We can do better by young learners of color.

"If we as a nation do not get children on track for reading proficiently, they stand to become our nation's lowest income group, least skilled, and systems dependent citizens in many generations, thus adding to generational poverty and illiteracy problems."

- Dr. Jacquelyn Bobien-Blanton

Part IV:

Contributing Factors in Reading Fadeout

"Reading furnishes the mind only with materials of knowledge; it is thinking that makes what we read ours"
- John Locke

Chapter 10

Reading Fadeout

Stalled Skills

Reading proficiency does not happen overnight, nor does it magically happen in third grade. It is a process that is built over time and begins at conception. There are several factors that occur in a child's life between conception and third grade that historically could impact reading development. I place all of them under the umbrella term 'reading fadeout'.

Specific to reading, fadeout occurs when children gain reading skills at one level or grade and those skills slowly fade over time because they are not supported or nurtured through third grade. Essentially, the skills all but disappear or stay stagnant. There are several major research studies regarding preschool reading fadeout, although reading fadeout may occur in any of the early grades.

Researchers studied the academic achievement of children who attended preschool programs and those who did not in several landmark studies. The researchers found that the academic gains made in preschool disappeared by the end of third grade and in some cases by the end of kindergarten (Jenkins et al., 2015; Lipsey et al., 2018). A significant finding in these studies was that in first through third grades, the non-preschool group caught up to the preschool group by second grade, and in third grade, they surpassed them in all achievement tests, including the third-grade state test. After the first or second grade, the differences between children who attended preschool and children who did not had almost disappeared. The phenomenon of reading fadeout is relatively new but may explain why so many children are not proficient readers by third grade. Unfortunately, a significant number of children experience fadeout in elementary school (Yoshikawa et al., 2016).

Learning to read is important and once children fall behind, it is very difficult for them to catch up (Austin et al., 2017). It is essential for elementary schools to build on skills from year to year for reading to persist through third grade (Ehrlich et al., 2018). Knowledge of the developmental continuum of reading from grade to grade is important for children to be successful readers. Learning is a cumulative process in which new knowledge is depended on previously acquired knowledge and happens over time. Examining the factors that contribute to reading fadeout is essential to reading proficiency in the early grades. The teachers in my focus group had experience with reading fadeout in their respective districts. Most of the teachers agreed that reading fadeout typically began in first grade.

Attending Preschool

In January of 2015, U.S. Secretary Arne Duncan summarized the preschool challenge we face as a nation. He stated that each year, about four million children enter kindergarten in the United States. Before they enter kindergarten, families hope their children start school ready for success by seeking supportive and high-quality early learning opportunities. However, the grim reality is that not every family finds those opportunities, because access to quality preschool differs based on geography, race, and income. As a result, too many children enter kindergarten a year or more behind their classmates in academic and social-emotional skills. Duncan further stated that for some children, starting out school from behind can trap them in a cycle of continuous catch-up in their learning. Children who do not experience preschool may enter kindergarten with less developed skills than those who attend preschool (Mantei & Kervin, 2018). As a nation, we must ensure that all children, regardless of income or race have access to high-quality preschool opportunities.

Advances in neuroscience and research helped to demonstrate how critical the early years are in children's learning and development (Yoshikawa et al., 2013). For example, children's language skills from age one to two are predictive of their pre-literacy skills at age five (Kuhl, 2011). A robust body of research shows that children who participate in high-quality preschool programs have better health, social-emotional, and cognitive outcomes than those who do not participate. The gains are particularly powerful for children from low-income families and those at risk for academic failure (Shonkoff & Phillip, 2000). Children who attend high-quality preschool programs are less likely to utilize special education services, be retained in the early grades, and are more likely to graduate from high school, go on to college, and succeed in their careers than those who have not attended high-quality preschool programs (Center for Public Education, 2008).

During these early years, significant growth and development in critical pre-reading skills occurs. Pre-reading skills obtained in preschool lay the foundation for more advanced reading skills in elementary school. Achievement in foundational reading skills lead to increased reading fluency. Mastering pre-reading skills by the end of kindergarten or the start of first grade is a strong predictor of later word recognition and reading comprehension. It is not enough for children to attend preschool, rather they must attend a quality preschool program that engages children in pre-reading experiences. Ongoing intentional access to pre-reading skills will determine if reading persists through the early grades or fade because reading is a cumulative process. The research is clear about the benefits of attending a quality preschool program. The question is, why do we still have children experiencing reading fadeout even after attending quality preschool programs? The causes of fadeout are numerous and must be examined to reach the goal of reading proficiency by third grade.

Quality Elementary Schools and Instructional Practices

State-funded preschool programs throughout the United States grew between 2000 and 2015 as many states provided full funding for many three and four-year-old children to attend. Given the increased enrollment rate in preschool programs and the research on the academic advantages, we must examine the reasons why children are still failing to read proficiently by third grade. One reason why children are underperforming in reading after attending preschool may be the quality of the elementary schools they attend. As children move into elementary schools, teachers must assess and monitor the ongoing development of children's reading skills to avoid spending time covering material they already mastered or that was too advanced. The diminished impact of preschool and pre-reading skills overtime may be the result of teachers who neglect to differentiate instruction for their students.

If teachers do not support and build on the pre-reading skills developed in preschool, those skills might fade over time. The quality of elementary schools and the reading instruction children receive in the first few years are important for reading sustainability. Early elementary school teachers must adapt their instruction to reflect the growing presence of children who have quality early learning experiences. Children who have pre-reading skills when they enter kindergarten, benefit from teachers that provide academic instruction at the children's current level. Reading fadeout occurs when children do not receive reading instruction at their current level. Children need consistent exposure to more advanced skills and content after preschool to bolster new skills.

There is a large body of research on the quality of reading instruction in the first few years in elementary school. For example, elementary school teachers who taught content that children already learned the year before, curtailed their academic growth and tempered achievement gains (Bailey et al., 2017). Maniates (2017) found that children wanted to participate in reading activities as they developed their interest in texts, their identities as readers, and their proficiency with reading; however, they were denied or limited at times by teachers who blocked or limited them from full participation. This happens when there is exposure to a narrow curriculum that assumes an idealized middle-class knowledge base, which creates barriers to learning by excluding children from under-resourced communities from using their culture and experiences to connect to new concepts (Gershenson et al., 2016). Rubie-Davies and Peterson (2016) found that teachers who had low expectations of students' abilities provided lower-level skill-based activities and slowed the pace of their lessons, which reduced children's opportunities academically.

Timmermans et al. (2016) found that students in low ability groups were less likely to engage in reading activities, more likely to dislike reading, and typically developed anxiety for reading. Ramirez et al. (2019) found that children who experienced reading instruction that included reading out loud in front of others in the beginning of the school year while they were acclimating to their teachers, classmates, and learning environment, experienced increased anxiety about their reading ability and performance. Overall, children generally begin kindergarten with a positive attitude about reading, but according to Ramirez et al. (2019), the positive attitude declines with advancing grade levels. Early setbacks in reading achievement could influence children to adopt a negative personal narrative about their abilities in reading, which could create reading anxiety (Gao et al., 2020). Children also develop reading anxieties by engaging in different processes and situations in reading that involve evaluative reading measures like oral fluency and comprehension tasks that are conducted in the presence of peers and teachers (Piccolo et al., 2017).

Practically Speaking

Unfortunately, many students have major anxieties about reading, which impacts academic achievement. Reading instruction that builds children's confidence in their reading ability is important for later reading success. Confident readers engage in reading more, which is critical for students' reading performance and has a significant impact on reading skills. For children to develop strong reading skills, they must practice more and engage with increasingly longer and more challenging texts. Instruction must promote reading resiliency, which leads to life-long learners. Additionally, to reduce reteaching skills that children have mastered and help them stay engaged or gain confidence, we must know where they are on the reading developmental continuum. Therefore, reading asssessments are critcal.

I asked the focus group teachers where they begin instruction in September when the children enter their classrooms. There was no standard response. Some said they assess the children to determine where they are developmentally, others said they wait until a few weeks into the school year to get to know the children a little more. Three of the teachers said they begin at the same place with all their students because, "most need a review." I asked about the children who may not need a review, two of the teachers said they review anyway just to see how much they (children) know. One participant explained that students who have a good grasp of the concepts will serve as peer helpers in the beginning of the school year, which helps to "build a positive classroom community." When asked how long the review process takes, most of the participants responded by saying it depends on where the students are developmentally, but the review could last for a few weeks or a few months for some students.

One teacher said she almost always spends at least two months reviewing because most of her students "turn off learning during the summer" and "forget everything they learned the year before." By my account, students in her class get less than eight months of instruction on new material after accounting for all the days schools are closed for holidays or breaks. The teacher in the predominantly white school district said she does not review because almost all her students complete the summer assignments which are good indicators of where they are developmentally; therefore, she begins class with grade level content within the first week or so of school. If students need help, the teacher said she works with them one on one or she may send extra work home, but according to the teacher, "With extra time and help from their parents, they usually catch-up rather quickly."

Why do so many students of color miss weeks or months of school in the beginning of the school year reviewing old content? Is reviewing necessary for students or a habit for teachers? What typically ends up happening is after reviewing for long periods of time, teachers end up cramming grade level content into a shorter school year, which could impact students' ability to master skills. As the research demonstrated, students who are presented with the same or similar content they learned in the previous grade for weeks or months, may experience boredom and disengage with school. If they disengage with school this early, it may be difficult for them to re-engage, which could impact the development of early foundational skills.

Preschool through Third Grade Alignment Practices

Transition refers to the process of a child moving from one program or setting to another. For example, when children make the transition from preschool to elementary school, they must adjust to new settings and situations, new rules and expectations, new ways of learning, new relationships with peers and adults, and new physical surroundings (Dunlop & Fabian, 2007). The earliest years are the cornerstone of an effective educational system and the foundation upon which subsequent learning is built. Preschool to Third Grade (P-3) transitional practices aim to level the academic playing field for all children. Transitional practices include the alignment of pre-kindergarten through third grade with respect to curricula and assessments, teacher preparation in alignment practices, and developing sequential learning experiences for children as they move from pre-kindergarten through third grade. The P-3 approach represents the potential for a well-integrated educational experience for children in the first several years of public school. This integrated experience would embody different developmentally appropriate practices, based on scientific research. The goal is to be intentional in providing all children with equitable opportunities to succeed in school.

Learning and development for young children is a rapid and cumulative process and if the public school system, particularly the early elementary grades, is not equipped to sustain and build upon the benefits gained from grade to grade, skills will fade over time. The fadeout of reading skills can be detrimental to a child's academic journey. Dunlop and Fabian (2007) found that inadequate transition practices from preschool through third grade can result in children experiencing high levels of stress, which can interfere with their academic performance and emotional adjustments. Furthermore, ineffective transitions can also lead to poor social adjustments, which may lead to negative consequences like chronic absenteeism and failure to make the academic gains necessary to succeed by third grade and beyond.

On the other hand, McIntyre et al. (2007) found that when a young child transitions successfully, he or she is more likely to enjoy school, show steady growth in academic and social skills, and have families who are more actively engaged. Intentional transition programs and practices provide several types of support to the child, as well as the child's family, and engage all teachers in regular communication about children's progress, including their assessment data. Children who attend elementary schools with a concrete and specific transition plan inclusive of curricula, instructional practices, and assessments, experience higher reading achievements at the end of kindergarten (Onyango & Gakii, 2017).

Developing a P-3 transitional plan is not easy work, and it takes a lot of coordination between various people and organizations. Three critical areas in building a strong P-3 plan include creating a vision for early learning, continuity of practices, and building the capacity of all staff. First, school districts must create a P–3 vision by establishing a culture that is inclusive of the different learning opportunities children have prior to kindergarten. Everything that is done in the school district and at the school level must be driven by the vision and the mission for early learning. All staff must understand the vision and mission and must align all programming for children and families accordingly. Operating outside of the vision and mission could create misaligned practices in the early grades as well as gaps in the academic programs. All stakeholders, including families, staff, administrators, community members, and students must have a role in creating the vision and mission for ownership and buy-in.

Second, school districts must develop continuity of practice and integrated service support. Districts must align curricula and instructional practices across the P–3 grade band to ensure continuity and differentiated learning for students along the developmental continuum. In the words of James Heckman, "too often government officials design programs for children as if they lived their lives in silos, as if each stage of a child's life were independent of the other, unconnected to what came before or what lies ahead." Early gaps in school readiness magnify over time and contribute to disparities in achievement proficiency and school completion. To realistically address these challenges, multiyear and multicomponent approaches that integrate services are needed.

The lack of coordination of curricula from grade to grade can create gaps that may hinder children's growth in reading. Atchison & Pompelia (2018) found that alignment within a program may highlight the interconnectedness between standards (what children are expected to know and do), curricula (what children are taught), instruction (how children are taught) and assessments (what and how children's progress is measured). Aligned experiences include all areas of learning (social, emotional, physical, and cognitive) that are developmentally appropriate and correlated to the individual abilities of the child. Intentional alignment of these interconnected pieces increases the consistency of children's experiences across and within grades to create a continuum of learning that builds on the previous year (Atchison & Pompelia, 2018).

For reading skills to persist, our educational system must create a more seamless system of education that is "connected from one stage to the next;

thereby, reducing the chances that students will be lost along the way or require remedial programs to acquire skills or knowledge they could have learned from the start" (Olson, 2007). By aligning standards, curricula, instruction, and assessments from grade to grade, beginning with preschool, children can experience a seamless transition that may set them up for future success. If transitions do not go well, children may be turned off to learning and school at an early age. Additionally, continuity of all programs, initiatives, policies, and legislation at the state and federal levels must work in tandem to improve quality and coherence across the P–3 continuum. This is important in ensuring coherent support for early grades. Continuity is achieved by aligning care and learning vertically over time as children progress through home visits, infant and toddler care, preschool, and the early elementary grades. It is achieved horizontally as children and families experience multiple services and support at each stage of development. Vertical alignment addresses standards, curricula, assessment, instructional strategies, environments, and transitions so that new learning experiences build on competencies developed earlier, and the dosage of high-quality experiences increases over time. Horizontal alignment requires communication and coordination across the providers serving the same children and families so that services are mutually reinforcing and, thus, more effective, again increasing the dosage of high-quality experiences.

Third, school districts must build the professional capacity of all instructional staff in the early grades. Teachers must have supportive, rigorous, aligned, and ongoing professional learning opportunities that reflect current knowledge of child development and effective, high-quality instructional practices. Additionally, district administrators must reduce the turnover rate for kindergarten through third grade teachers and refrain from moving teachers into that grade band without knowledge, professional development, coaching, and support. The early grades are where children learn important foundational skills like reading and we must ensure that the right teachers are in place for this arduous task. It is a common practice in some school districts to move teachers from higher grades to the lower grades based on unfounded and incorrect assumptions and thought processes about teachers that include "they will do less damage", "these are not the testing grades so they can't do too much damage", "it's easier to teach little kids", or "to frustrate a teacher to resign." These reasons are not based on research or best practice and more importantly, they hurt children's chances of developing important skills for academic success.

The P-3 grade band of teachers must be energetic, patient, kind, fun, exciting, and must possess a deep understanding of the developmental sequence for early learners. Also important, teachers must not view each of the early grades as isolated experiences for children; rather they must view learning as a continuous process that builds from grade to grade. Research shows that variability in teaching proficiency leads to different outcomes for children. Therefore, it is important to assess teachers' instructional behavior in the classroom and how they support children's learning. Evaluations focusing on both the teacher and child will provide better information to inform instruction.

Under the existing K-12 educational system, achievement gaps are evident at kindergarten entry, and persist through third grade. Children differ in their readiness to begin kindergarten, due to different experiences prior to kindergarten entry. Many struggling readers in first grade continue to struggle in fourth grade if deficiencies are not properly addressed. The research is clear, young children are ready to learn at birth and they seek stimulation to further their development. If channeled in appropriate ways, and if educational settings are better organized to build on existing concepts and skills, children are less likely to fall through the cracks. With developmentally-appropriate scaffolding in the early grades, children are more likely to flourish socially and academically. The key for student success is to put a greater emphasis on the continuity in the early grades and creating predictable learning environments with familiar rules and routines that ease the transition from one grade to the next.

Motivation to Read

The Oxford dictionary defined motivation as the process that initiates, guides, and maintains goal-oriented behaviors. It is what causes one to act, like reading a book to gain knowledge. Motivation involves the biological, emotional, social, and cognitive forces that activate behavior. Factors important to reading motivation include self-efficacy skills, (i.e., confidence in one's ability to accomplish different tasks), value of reading, choice, time spent talking about books, and types of texts. Research confirms that student motivation is a key factor in successful reading. Reading motivation is a known predictor of reading achievement and comprehension (Hebbecker et al., 2019).

For example, when students are confident at a given task, such as reading, they perform optimally. Students with greater self-efficacy skills see difficult reading tasks as challenging and work toward mastering them productively using cognitive strategies in the process (Schunk & Pajares, 2009). Students who value choosing their own books develop elaborate strategies for selecting books and are more motivated readers. Motivation increases when reading instruction integrates motivational practices such as relevant text to students, text selected by students, and text collaboration with peers. Additionally, motivation increases when text reflects and confirms a student's culture, and when they engage in social interactions with their peers around familiar texts (Nevo & Vaknin-Nusbaum, 2019).

The two common types of motivation found in reading research include intrinsic and extrinsic motivation. Schaffner et al. (2016) defined intrinsic motivation as the willingness to read because reading is satisfying and rewarding. Students' extrinsic motivation related to the use of surface strategies (e.g., simple rehearsal or memorization) for reading and the desire to complete a task for a reward. Extrinsically motivated students depend on outside reasons for reading such as grades and praise. Although extrinsic motivation is associated positively with grades in reading, it is less likely to positively influence reading comprehension. Students who are intrinsically motivated engage in the reading process more, they enjoy reading, they are interested in the text, and they invest time in using reading strategies to develop a deep understanding of the text (Hebbecker et al., 2019). Intrinsically motivated students are more likely to read recreationally, which creates more opportunities for them to improve their reading skills and experience exploration and excitement because they enjoy reading. Elementary schools that focus on isolated skills, test preparation, and incentives for reading, impact children's intrinsic motivation to read.

A student's intrinsic motivation correlates positively with their reading achievement over time.

Reading Assessment and
Differentiated Instruction

Stover et al. (2017) posited that teachers must assess and monitor the ongoing development of reading skills to avoid children spending too much time on material they already mastered or material that was well over their heads. Too much redundancy or lessons that are too advanced inadvertently interrupt educational progress and stalls development (Phillips et al., 2017). Danish et al. (2016) found that students will persevere with appropriate scaffolding and when they have learning tasks that are within their zone of proximal development.

The zone of proximal development is defined as the space between what a learner can do without assistance and what a learner can do with adult guidance or in collaboration with more capable peers. Scaffolding is directly related to the zone of proximal development in that it is the support mechanism that helps a learner successfully perform a task within his or her zone of proximal development. Typically, this process is completed by a more competent student supporting the learning of a less competent student.

Practically Speaking

When I asked the teachers in my interview group about the term zone of proximal development, none of them ever heard of it. I asked about their process for designing differentiated learning experiences for their students. All defined the term appropriately and stated how important it is to differentiate instruction. One teacher explained how she uses formative and summative assessments to inform her instruction while the others said they "know" their children and provide instruction accordingly. However, when pressed for examples, most of them could not provide sufficient examples.

One teacher became very uncomfortable and defensive and stated, "I have been teaching for over 20 years and if I don't know what to do for students by now, then I don't need to be teaching. I don't need numbers or outsiders telling me what my students need. I am with them all day, every day." However, I was not successful in obtaining recent specific examples of differentiated instruction from anyone in the group. One thing that I have learned as a school administrator is to never assume anything about the capacity of staff. I believe in differentiated professional development for adults, but I also believe that everyone must have common knowledge, understanding, and language for essential and common terms to alleviate wrong assumptions, which could impact instruction and assessment. Differentiated instruction is not easily defined and a challenge to execute. However, in preschool, differentiated instruction is the norm, it is not something that teachers must think about, it is an automatic practice. In fact, in many Head Start programs, each child has an individualized learning plan that is created and followed by the family and the teachers.

The Office of Head Start helps young children from low-income families prepare to succeed in school through local programs. Head Start programs promote children's development through services that support early learning, health, and family well-being. Elementary school teachers who do not make differentiated instruction essential, could learn a lot from preschool teachers. Data-informed instruction is necessary for monitoring reading development in children. Knowing children's specific reading levels allows teachers to place them in appropriate reading groups and to create lessons that promote specific skill development, rather than assuming which skills children lack. Ongoing assessment data allows teachers to adjust their instruction for children to make optimal progress by identifying skills that need further development and skills that children have mastered (Stover et al., 2017).

Differentiation of instruction occurs when teachers intentionally modify curricula, teaching methods, resources, and learning activities to address the diverse needs of individual students (Tomlinson, 2017). Teachers who do not use assessment data to differentiate instruction may struggle to meet the needs of their students. There must be a clear understanding of the developmental levels of children to build on their current skills. In the book *How to Differentiate Instruction in Academically Diverse Classroom* by Carol Ann Tomlinson, differentiated instruction occurs by content, process, product, or environment to meet the needs of students. Differentiating access to content includes curriculum topics, concepts, or themes. It involves providing students with choices to add depth to learning and to provide resources that match their levels of understanding.

To differentiate content, teachers may use 'hands on' activities for some learners to help them understand a new idea. Teachers may use texts or novels at more than one reading level, or tape recordings, computer programs, and videos to convey key concepts to different learners. Differentiating process refers to how students make sense of information, ideas, and skills being studied. It also reflects student learning preferences. Differentiating process involves providing varied options at different levels of difficulty, providing options based on student interests, giving choices about how students express their understanding, and varying the learning process depending upon how students learn. To differentiate the process, teachers may use tiered activities through which all learners work on building the same important understandings and skills but proceed with different levels of support or complexity. Teachers may provide interest centers that encourage students to explore subsets of class topics that are of interest to them. Teachers may elect to develop activities that target auditory, visual, and kinesthetic learners or they may establish areas or stations for inquiry-based, independent activities.

Differentiating products involves the tangibles like reports, tests, speeches, and performances that reflect student understanding; it involves providing challenges, variety, and choice. Differentiating by product also involves giving students options about how to express what they have learned, for example, students may create a puppet show, write a letter, or create a diagram. To differentiate products, teachers may encourage students to express what they have learned in various ways, allow students to work alone or with a group, or provide the use of various types of resources in preparing products.

Finally, differentiating the learning environment involves the climate of the classroom as well as the operation, and tone (i.e., class rules, furniture arrangement, lighting, procedures, and processes). It involves the look and feel of the classroom, whether it is a safe and positive environment for learning, and whether it allows for individual and group work preferences. To differentiate the learning environment, teachers must ensure that there are places for students to work quietly and without distraction as well as places that invite student collaboration. Teachers may provide materials that reflect a variety of cultures and home settings. Classroom management should include routines that allow students to get help when teachers are busy with other students and cannot help them immediately. Also, teachers must help students understand that some learners require different options to learn, for example, some students may need to move around to learn while others do better sitting quietly.

Differentiating by content is usually seen in many classrooms, but unfortunately, process, product, and the learning environments are not as prevalent, but they are equally as important in creating supportive learning environments that meet the needs of all students. One thing I repeatedly heard from the teachers whom I interviewed was the phrase "my classroom" or "in my classroom." Those words are not inclusive, and they leave student voice and choice out of the equation. I heard teachers say, "It's my way or the highway—I'm not running a diner." Words matter as they send signals to students regarding their learning space, the facilitator (the teacher), and who they are as learners. Words and phrases that put the teacher solely in charge and do not allow students to be part of the learning process may stunt the academic and social and emotional growth of students. It goes back to teachers being afraid of shared control.

When we treat students with respect, honor the experiences they bring to the classroom, and give them choice in what and how they learn, students will thrive, they will be engaged, and they will be enthusiastic about learning. When provided with the right learning environment, coupled with opportunity and experience, students will show how incredibly intelligent they are. How does this relate to reading? Differentiated instruction allows teachers to see and understand the development of individual students. Assessing student's reading levels and differentiating instruction, assist teachers and students in making informed decisions about reading instruction, which could support reading sustainability.

Chronic Absenteeism

If students are not in school, learning the curriculum content could be challenging. Whatever great learning experiences that schools may have to offer are all for naught if students do not show up. The early grades are the most critical years for learning as they build the foundation for more advanced learning. According to the U.S. Department of Education, on average, more than eight million K-12 students are chronically absent per year. Chronic absenteeism is defined as students missing 10% or more of a school year, which is roughly 18 school days or 117 instructional hours. Additionally, students in the earlier grades and African American students are significantly more likely to be chronically absent than their white peers according to the Civil Rights Data Collection (2014).

Ansari and Purtell (2017) and Robinson et al. (2018) found that absenteeism in urban communities is rampant among preschoolers and elementary school students. The adverse effects of absenteeism are compounded for students from low socioeconomic backgrounds because these students face additional barriers that prevent them from accessing the extra services needed to compensate for the lost school time (Gottfried, 2019). For younger students, research has shown that chronic absenteeism in kindergarten is associated with lower achievement in reading and math in later grades, even when controlling for a child's family income, race, disability status, attitudes toward school, socioemotional development, age at kindergarten entry, type of kindergarten program, and preschool experience (Romero & Lee, 2007).

Sawchuck (2021) stated in an Education Week article that getting students to attend school regularly is not a silver bullet for achievement. Learning hinges on developing relationships with students and providing them with a powerful instructional program—but those are impossible if students do not show up.

There are families who think that missing school in the early years will not hurt children as much because they are young, and they have years to catch up. What they fail to realize is that missing school means that students are not building the foundation they need to be successful in the higher grades because they are missing critical instructional time. We must not think of children's educational journeys in silos; rather it is a long cumulative process that builds on itself from year to year. Attending school consistently is important no matter the grade level, but it is crucial in the beginning years. Children this young cannot put themselves on routines like going to bed on time, reducing screen time, getting proper nutrition, laundering clothes, completing homework, waking up on time, and walking to school. They need the assistance of the adults to make this work. If we are looking for areas that are within our control regarding reading proficiency, controlling student absenteeism is a place to start.

Children who miss many days from school have the lowest skills and fewer opportunities to catch up to their more skilled peers (Ehrlich et al., 2018). Frequently absent students receive fewer hours of instruction and are consequently more likely to require remediation when returning to school. Chronic absenteeism may lead to students feeling alienated from their classmates and teachers and it may also influence significant frequencies of negative interactions and social disengagement when returning to school (Gottfried, 2019). Ansari and Purtell (2017) found that in addition to missing instructional hours, students who are absent a lot miss the opportunity to develop supportive relationships with teachers and other students because absenteeism limits how often students interact with others.

Gottfried went further to state that chronic absenteeism not only had a damaging effect on those individuals missing excessive school days but also has the potential to reduce outcomes for others in the same educational setting. This happens because teachers may end up spending more time with students who are chronically absent to 'catch them up' and less time with students who are typically present. The bottom line is young children who are chronically absent from one year to the next during the early elementary school years, reduce their chances of reading proficiently by third grade because they receive fewer hours of instruction. To improve attendance, we must examine the culture and climate of schools. Are schools genuinely welcoming, inclusive, supportive, academically rigorous, fair, fun? Chronic absenteeism is not an issue for families alone; schools must take some accountability as well. When we create places and spaces that are exciting, fun, challenging, and student and family friendly, students will attend, and they won't want to leave.

Summer Slide

In the United States, school calendars run nine to ten months out of the calendar year with a two-to-three-month summer break. Former Secretary of Education Arne Duncan stated that the school calendar was "a legacy of the farm economy" that dates back to farm cycles and harvests. Kenneth Gold, a historian at the College of Staten Island, disagreed with the former secretary in a PBS documentary in 2014. Gold found that children in rural agricultural areas were needed in the spring, when most of the crops had to be planted, and in the fall, when crops were harvested and sold. Historically, many students attended school in the summer when there was comparatively less need for them on the farm.

On other hand, urban schools had a very different school schedule, but also included summer. School was essentially open year-round, but was not mandatory, and students came when they could. In 1842, New York City schools were open 248 days a year. In the days before air conditioning, schools and entire cities would be extremely hot during the summer months. Wealthy and eventually middle-class families usually made plans to flee the city's heat, making those months the logical time in cities to suspend school. By the late 19th century, school reformers pushed for standardization of the school calendar across urban and rural areas and a compromise was struck that created the modern school calendar. The thought was that a long break would give teachers needed time for professional development and give students a break. While summer was the logical time to take off, the cycles of farming had nothing to do with it, according to Gold. Whatever the historic reasons for the current school calendar, it hasn't changed, despite concerns that a two-to-three-month break from education may lead to significant deficits in student's knowledge and skills. Long summer breaks have been shown to cause students, especially students from lower income families, to lose ground academically. This phenomenon is known as "summer slide," where students return to school in the fall having lost a full month or more of learning, on average (**Cooper et al.,1996**). There is a considerable amount of research that confirms the existence of knowledge and skill stagnation during the summer (Alexander et al., 2007; Lindahl, 2001; Lynch & Kim, 2017; Shinwell & Defeyter, 2017).

Researchers found that students learn best when instruction is continuous because long periods of time away from school may lead to them forgetting important concepts (Caputo & Estrovitz, 2017). Consequently, teachers must spend a significant amount of time reviewing previously learned material when the students return to school rather than moving ahead from where they left off. Students who do not participate in reading experiences over the summer for multiple years have an academic achievement gap that may grow over the elementary school years (Caputo & Estrovitz, 2017). To become proficient at reading, students need to read a lot; however, McClanahan et al. (2016) found that students from low-performing schools read less and have less exposure to text. For example, children who are behind their typically developing peers in reading during the regular school year are less motivated to read during the summer months, which impacts reading development (Cantrell et al., 2017). These issues raise concern about the consequences of summer slide. Not only are students ultimately forced to invest extra energy at the beginning of the school year, but the effect is also acutely experienced by teachers. When students must invest extra effort and energy in learning, it may affect their motivation and desire to learn but it may also have a cumulative effect on the classroom whereby teachers are forced to spend time reiterating or reteaching part of the curriculum from the previous year. Researchers have argued that when students experience summer slide issues continuously, it may set them back over time, ultimately expanding the achievement gap and impacting their future academic success (Alexander et al., 2007).

In the U.S., these findings have fueled a discussion on shortening the summer break, thereby increasing the amount of time students spend in school (McCombs et al., 2011). It has been argued that simply increasing "school time" by itself will not help; instead, what matters is increasing "academic learning time", which is time that students spend actually learning material that is relevant to them at that time (Aronson et al., 1998). Not all children suffer issues from summer slide to the same degree. Some children might continue the learning process to some extent during the summer break, which may lessen the impact of summer slide.

Some researchers found that school is like a "faucet" that pours out resources during the academic year, enabling all students to make learning gains (Entwisle et al., 2000). When school closes for the summer, the faucet shuts off. Presumably, that means less learning opportunities for students from disadvantaged backgrounds, while wealthier students have access to other learning opportunities. Needless to say, this theory impacts children of color as so many disengage with academics during the summer months.

To combat summer slide issues, many states are looking for alternative programs. Based on an article written by Lauren Camera for U.S. News in 2022, Education Secretary Miguel Cardona called for state education officials and school leaders to offer intensive summer learning programs and afterschool programs for students who have incurred academic hardships due to chronic interruptions to learning during the pandemic. However, I would argue that we must re-image the after school and summer programs that we offer our students. These programs cannot be an extension of what students receive during the typical school day or school year, which is why many students opt out of attending. If students did not get the concepts or skills during the regular school hours, why would educators think they will magically occur during after school or summer programs, especially if the same type of learning experiences are offered. Who would be enthusiastic about doing the same type of work after school or during the summer? If we want to spark an interest, we must find a different approach for students to access curricula content during these supplement programs. If we do more of the same, we will get more of the same regarding results. It might be a good idea to package after school programs and summer school programs differently and offer other types of learning experiences to get students interested and motivated to learn.

It's difficult to offer various types of learning experiences during the school year because of class size, pacing, and the different academic levels of students. However, the lesson plan book opens up when students have access to one-on-one tutors and small group learning opportunities. Teachers and facilitators can offer more engaging, hands-on, project-based learning experiences that may motivate students a little more. I mentioned facilitators because we must preserve teachers because their shelf life has an expiration date. If we continue to use the same teachers for before and after school programs, during winter and spring break sessions or summer school programs all while teaching a full load during the school year, burnout is sure to occur. Rather, we must utilize outside resources to get the job done. For example, college students who are enrolled in teacher prep programs may be a good resource to tap into. They have fresh, innovative approaches, and different perspectives when connecting with students. Similarly, community members, organizations, and outside reputable tutoring services maybe another option. The bottom line is teachers need a break. They need time to reflect, recuperate, revive, and return to school rejuvenated and ready to teach and learn. However, for so many teachers, they take on these extra positions to supplement their salaries even though they are tired. You cannot perform at a high level and you cannot give your best when you are tired and worn out. No matter how much money is spent on afterschool and summer programs and how much planning goes into these programs, they won't work if they are not re-packaged.

While the federal pandemic aid is pouring in now, it will dry up soon, and then what? The extra funds are needed to stop the bleeding, but we need a plan for when the band-aid comes off. The educational system needs systemic changes not only to recover from the pandemic, but for sustaining power far after the pandemic is over. It is silly to think that the money being poured into schools now is enough to close the long-standing achievement gap and miraculously get all students performing at or above grade level in their core courses by 2024. The research is clear, "high dosage" tutoring either one-on-one or multiple small-group sessions per week coupled with the right instructors and learning experiences are most effective for student improvement

The factors outlined in this chapter aren't new, but they serve as a reminder that reading proficiency is attainable and that some factors that exist in prohibiting reading proficiency are within our control. There are no legitimate reasons why typically developing children should not be proficient readers by third grade. Reading does not happen all of a sudden when children enter elementary school, rather it begins at birth and continues through the early years with each year building upon the year before. Reading requires much more than teachers, reading curriculum, and reading programs. Reading requires a village.

Conclusion

Why Johnny Can't Read… is part of a book title, but it is also a loaded question that requires a multilayered response. In the famous book released in 1985, Rudolf Flesch stated, "Ever since 1500 B.C., wherever an alphabetic system of writing was used, people have learned to read by simply memorizing the sound of each letter in the alphabet, except 20th century America. We have thrown 3500 years of civilization out the window." Flesch suggested that we "go back to the ABC's and teach children the 44 sounds in English." He was surely on to something. Why can't all students of color experience the freedom to learn in their classrooms and act like scientists and formulate their own questions and inquiries, or work deeply on a project collaboratively with their peers, or be engaged in learning experiences that they are interested in? Why must they earn the right or be trained first before receiving these types of learning experiences, which are so freely given to others? Why are so many students of color silenced with bubbles, conditioned to speak only with the teacher's permission, or walk with their hands behind their backs as they walk down the hall? Why are the learning experiences so different for some students? Why do we constantly yell, scream, and harshly punish young students of color simply because they are "used to it" or because "it's the only way they will listen." I have heard teachers say both.

For years, there have been false beliefs that students of color were incapable, less than, and unworthy of learning experiences that included critically thinking, voice, choice, or the freedom to challenge the status quo and think outside of the box. The sad part is that there are educators, parents, and even students who have been conditioned to believe the same. Somehow teachers think that the children they teach are different and require different teaching and learning experiences, but development isn't different. It's hard to recognize and break the generational grip of segregated experiences when parents and their children have been educated the same way. To change this narrative and this toxic belief system, we must understand what good teaching looks like and make it a norm for all learners. It's insane for us to continue doing what we have been doing and expect different results. Parents and teachers must understand that there is another way and a better way to teach and learn. We must demand a paradigm shift where we move from equality in education and equitable educational experiences to total educational liberation for children. For decades, we have failed our youngest learners and it's time to make a change. Our children deserve it and our society needs it.

Why can't our children read proficiently by third grade? The United States Congress established national education goals, and one goal is to have all citizens literate and reading at a very high level. While this is an important and lofty goal, I wonder if it really applies to all citizens. Leaving some folks behind is profitable and necessary for a society that is consumed by power, money, greed, racism, hatred, and individualism. In this type of system, it is hard to imagine everyone enjoying a piece of the American dream because there will always be a group that wants the whole dream and sharing is not part of the plan. Therefore, systems are created to suppress, ignore, mistreat, and malign those who do not conform and those who are different from mainstream America. By keeping some groups down, others are able to rise. So, again I ask, is the goal of a literate society a goal for all citizens? I challenge the premise of the goal because we still have an alarming number of students who are not proficient readers, and many are students of color. We know based on the science of reading and reading statistics that we can and must do better for students in reading instruction.

For decades, reading instruction was held captive by the never-ending reading wars which were detrimental to young children; especially Black and Brown children. Unfortunately, those wars still exist even with the abundance of research regarding reading instruction. If we peel back the onion to answer the question *Why Johnny Can't Read*, we find that there isn't just one reason, in fact, there are multiple reasons. When a child fails to read by third grade or is retained because he or she is not proficient in reading, we cannot place the blame squarely on the shoulders of an eight-year-old; rather, we must take a deep dive into the child's ecosystem to ascertain what occurred in such a short span that prohibited the development of skills necessary for reading proficiency.

The title of the book *It Takes a Village to Raise a Reader* demonstrates that pre-reading skills are developed long before a child enters kindergarten. The years between birth and five are critical for young children and will dictate kindergarten readiness. The premise of this book was not about reading, per se, but about systems and habits that children have no control over but are predictive of their future reading achievement. When a child enters kindergarten, he brings five years of experience with him on his resume that has little to nothing to do with the K-12 public school system. The resume will detail if the child's experiences are sound enough to support more advanced skills in kindergarten and beyond. How prepared children are when they enter kindergarten is based on the environment and experiences they were exposed to in the years prior to kindergarten. It is incumbent upon those in the medical field, especially pediatricians, to be intentional and specific in educating parents about early brain development and the connection to school achievement.

If parents are better informed, there is a chance they will provide home learning environments that are conducive for healthy brain development. Information during wellness checks about child growth and development and the connection to school readiness is critical during the first three years of life because of the sensitive periods in the brain. If the brain does not get the right type of stimuli during sensitive periods, the architecture changes. There are specific and simple strategies that parents can do, free of charge, to stimulate the brain and prepare it for school success. For example, parents must talk to and interact with their children daily. It sounds simple, but it is critical to development. The serve and return phenomenon where children communicate via coos and babbles and adults respond accordingly is important for social, emotional, attachment, and language development. Not only must parents communicate with their children, but they must play with them. Who would have ever thought that playing a simple game of peek-a-boo would be so important for the developing brain? Reducing screen time and providing children with ample time to get outdoors and experience nature does wonders for young children.

Around three years old, if some families are fortunate, they may have access to preschool. Research has shown how important preschool is and how beneficial it is for children to attend. However, quality preschool programs are hard for some families to afford. As the title of the book intimates, it takes legislators, school officials, community members, and other stakeholders to chart the course for all children to have access to high quality early childhood programs (including infants and toddlers' programs). High quality early programs have staff who are knowledgeable about brain development, child growth and development, developmentally appropriate practices, and equitable experiences and opportunities for all children, no matter their skin color, language spoken, family dynamics, zip code, or differing abilities.

Quality early childcare programs value children's cultures, traditions, interests, ideas, and families. They provide children with hands-on, meaningful, and relevant learning experiences through play. Early childcare programs also focus on building and fostering relationships. The preschool years are critical as they lay the foundation for more advanced skills. A weak foundation will not support advanced skills. Learning is a cumulative process and for it to stick and become a permanent file in the brain, we must build a strong foundation from the beginning. There is an old Chinese proverb that says: "Your future at 80 was decided when you three." The early years are critical for later school achievement and success in life.

As children move into the elementary school years, it is important that they do so with the expectation that learning will begin at their current level, taking into consideration the resume that they bring. If elementary schools cannot build on and extend children's learning, skills will fade over time. Schools must be ready for children at all levels. Teachers must be skilled, and knowledgeable about differentiated instruction and they must be trained in the science of reading. District leaders and school-based administrators must turn to science to ensure all children, no matter their resume, will have equitable experiences and opportunities to read proficiently by the end of third grade. Teachers must provide children with voice and choice for them to engage in the curriculum optimally. However, it does not matter how prepared teachers are, or what type of lessons they prepare, if students do not come to school. School cannot be an afterthought or a babysitter; it must be a priority.

Our commitment and responsibilities rest with our students, not curriculum developers or reading programs. When we fall down and break a bone, we trust the science behind the skills of doctors. Similarly, we must trust the overwhelming science behind reading and put our children on a path for success. We need college professors, teachers, and administrators to read what the science says about reading instruction and prepare future teachers accordingly. If we are serious about closing achievement gaps and giving all children, regardless of race, family income, or zip code, the opportunity to truly succeed in school, we must translate the knowledge about reading into action. We do this by building a commitment for a solution, mobilizing all stakeholders, and enacting change. Dorothy Height once said, "We have to improve life, not just for those who have the most skills and those who know how to manipulate the system, but also for and with those who often have so much to give but never the opportunity."

We cannot continue to rob our children of the future they are destined to have by vacillating over reading curricula, programs, and instruction. Let's follow the science, train teachers and professors, and do right by all children. Philanthropists, legislators, and educational reformers, if we want to close the achievement gap, we must place greater emphasis on the early years and build the whole child from the foundation up. Reimagining the current educational system is not easy and it's time consuming but as the late Supreme Court Justice Ruth Bader-Ginsburg stated, "Real change, enduring change, happens one step at a time." Yes, it takes a village to raise a reader.

This book is dedicated to our young, bright, beautiful, smart, creative superstars of the future. We have the power, the opportunity, and in some cases, the funds to change the reading narrative for all children. We have the tools to alter their path, to be champions in their lives and push them toward greatness. We have the power to close the achievement gaps and put an end to generational poverty and illiteracy. But in doing so, we must not come down so hard on teachers as they are trying their best to work with the resumes of students that are in front of them and some of those resumes are tough to look at and hard to digest. More teachers are looking beyond those resumes and are doing all they can to change the narrative and put students on a better path.

We need teachers to see students' potential rather than perceived deficits because how we see students will determine how we interact with them. We cannot judge students for their current situations because they are not in control. Rather we must nurture them and help them see beyond their circumstances and feel optimistic about their future. Similarly, we cannot put all the blame on parents. Children do not come with a GPS, operation manual, or a how to book, but they should come with some basic instructions for developing a healthy brain, which impacts school success. Parents want what's best for their children and many may not know what that looks like; therefore, they place a lot of trust in the school system. What happens to children in the beginning of their lives matters and we know that if given the right experiences and opportunities, they will thrive. I am living proof that where you begin in life, does not dictate where you end. I stumbled out the blocks initially and had to fight harder than my peers but I never gave up and I continued to work hard towards my goals with my village in tow. We need medical experts to intentionally connect healthy brain development to school success and provide parents with strategies to grow their child's brain. I believe that when we know better, we should do better.

One of my goals for writing this book was to provide a clear understanding of the importance of brain development and school success. We need our legislators to work in concert with the school districts to open the purse strings and create more opportunities for children under eight years old. Opportunities like afterschool programs that are not only academically based, or camps during the school year and during the summer months, and opportunities for them to experience an environment different from the environment they live in. We need community members, church officials, and other stakeholders to give freely of their time and talent to tutor and mentor students and help them stay on a path towards greatness. We need champions for children to provide outside experiences and opportunities. The difference between children in under-resourced communities and their peers in more affluent communities is experience and opportunity. Yes, It Takes a Village to Raise a Reader! How can you become a Champion for a Child?

At the end of professional development sessions, a friend from Bank Street Education Center leaves participants with a reflective thought that I will share with each of you. After reading this book, fill in the blanks:

I used to think_____, but now I know_____.

"Once you learn to read, you will be forever free." Frederick Douglass

"A Covenant for Honoring Children"
We find these joys to be self-evident: That all children are created whole,
endowed with innate intelligence, with dignity and wonder, worthy of respect. The
embodiment of life, liberty, and happiness. Children are original blessings, here
to learn their own song. Every child is entitled to love, to dream, and belong to a
loving "village" and to pursue a life of purpose. Raffi

Thank you for taking this journey with me. I am not done yet...I am always
becoming. To whom much is given, much is required.

- Dr. Jacquelyn Bobien-Blanton

References

Adair, J. & Colegrove, K. (2021). *Segregation by Experience: Agency, Racism, and Learning in the Early Grades*. The University of Chicago Press. Chicago, Illinois.

Adams, M. J. (1990). *Beginning to Read: Thinking and Learning about Print.* Cambridge, MA: MIT Press.

Adler, C. R. (2001). Put reading first: The research building blocks for teaching children to read. *Pubs*, 47-56.

Alexander, B. (2014). Put down that cellphone! Study finds parents distracted by devices. NBCnews.com. Available at http://www.nbcnews.com/health/parenting/put-downcellphone-study-finds-parents-distracted-devices-n47431

Alexander, K.L., Entwisle, D.R., & Olson, L.S. (2007). Lasting consequences of the summer learning gap. *American Sociological Review, 72* (2), 167-180.

Alfieri, L., Brooks, P.J., Aldrich, N.J., & Tenenbaum, H.R. (2011). "Does discovery-based instruction enhance learning?" *Journal of Educational Psychology.* 103 (1): 1–18.

Anderson, E. (1999). What is the point of equality? Ethics, The University of Chicago Press. 109(2). 287-337

Andrew, M. (2014). The scarring effect of primary grade retention? A study of cumulative advantage in the educational career. Social Forces. 93(2) 653-685.

Ansari, A., & Purtell, K. M. (2017). What happens next? Delivering on the promise of preschool. *Early Childhood Research Quarterly, 45*, 177-182. https://doi.org/10.1016/j.ecresq.2018.02.015

Ansari, A. (2018). The persistence of preschool effects from early childhood through adolescence. *Journal of Educational Psychology, 110*(7), 952-973. https://doi.org/10.1037/edu0000255

Aronson, J., Zimmerman, J., & Carlos, L. (1998). Improving student a achievement by extending school: Is it just a matter of time? WestEd, 1–9. https://www2.wested.org/www-static/online_pubs/po-98-02.pdf

Ashby, R., Lee, P. J. & Shemil, D. (2005). Putting principles into practice: Teaching and practice. In M. S. Donovan & J. D. Bransford (Eds). How students learn: History in the classroom. Washington, DC: National Academies Press.

Atchison, B., & Pompelia, S. (2018). Transitions and alignment: From preschool to kindergarten. Special Report. *Education Commission of the States.*

Au, W. (2016). Meritocracy 2.0: High-stakes, standardized testing as a racial project of neoliberal multiculturalism. *Educational Policy, 30*(1), 39–62. doi:10.1177/0895904815614916

August, D., Branum-Martin, L., Cardenas-Hagan, E., & Francis, D. J. (2009). The impact of an instructional intervention on the science and language learning of middle grade English language learners. *Journal of Research on Educational Effectiveness*, 2(4), 345–376. doi:10.1080/ 19345740903217623

Austin, A. M. B., Blevins-Knabe, B., Ota, C., Rowe, T., & Lindauer, S. (2011). Mediators of preschoolers' early mathematics concepts. *Early Child Development and Care*, 181, 1181-1198. doi:10.1080/03004430.2010.520711

Austin, C., Vaughn, S., & McClelland, L. M. (2017). Intrinsic reading interventions for inadequate responders in grades K-3: A synthesis. *Learning Disability Quarterly, 40*(4), 191-210.

Babcock, P. & Bedard, K. (2011). The Wages of Failure: New evidence on school retention and long-run outcomes. *Association for Education Finance and Policy*.

Bailey, D., Duncan, G. J., Odgers, C. L., & Yu, W. (2017). Persistence and fadeout in the impacts of child and adolescent interventions. *Journal of Research on Educational Effectiveness, 10*(1), 7-39. https://doi.org/10.1080/19345747.2016.1232459

Baker, S.K., Fien, F., Nelson, N. J., Petscher, Y., Sayko, S., & Turtura, J. (2017). *Learning to read: The simple view of reading.* Washington, DC: U.S. Department of Education, Office of Elementary and Secondary Education, Office of Special Education Programs, National Center on Improving Literacy. Retrieved from http://improvingliteracy.org

Baker, T. L., Wise, J., Kelley, G., & Skiba, R. J. (2016). Identifying barriers: Creating solutions to improve family engagement. *School Community Journal, 26*(2), 161-184.

Bakken, L., Brown, N., & Downing, B. (2017). Early childhood education: The long-term benefits. *Journal of research in Childhood Education, 31*(2), 255-269.

Ball, D., & Bass, H. (2003). Making mathematics reasonable in school. I J. Kilpatrick, W. G. Martin & D. Schifter (Eds), A research companion to principles and standards for school mathematics (p. 27-44). Reston, VA: National Council of Teachers of Mathematics.

Bal, P. M., & Veltkamp, M. (2013). How does fiction reading influence empathy? An experimental investigation on the role of emotional transportation. *PloS one, 8*(1), e55341.

Bandura, A. (1977). *Social learning theory*. Englewood Cliffs, NJ: Prentice Hall.

Bandura, A. (1994). Self-efficacy. In V. S. Ramachaudran (Ed.), Encyclopedia of Human Behavior (Vol. 4, pp. 71–81). Academic Press

Baxter, J. A., Woodward, J., & Olson, D. (2005). Writing in mathematics: An alternative form of communication for academically low-achieving students. Learning Disabilities Research & Practice, 20(2), 119-135.

Bergen, D. 2001. Pretend play and young children's development. ERIC Digest ED4445805. Chicago: ERIC Clearinghouse on Elementary nd Early Childhood Education. www.eric.ed.gov/ERICWebPortal/ recordDetail?accno=ED458045.

Berkeley Media Studies Group. (2004). Making the case for early care and education: A message development guide for advocates. http://bmsg.org/sites/default/files/ bmsg_handbook_making_the_case_for_early_care_and_education.pdf

Berman, P., & Chambliss, D. (2000). Readiness of low-performing schools for comprehensive reform. Emeryville, CA: RPP International.

Birth to Five Policy Alliance. (2011). Advocacy toolkit: Promoting quality early childhood education. http://earlysuccess.org/sites/default/files/website_files/files/July-2011-B25-toolkitFINAL.pdf

Bloom, L. & Lahey, M. (1978). *Language, Development, and Language Disorders*, New York: Wiley.

Boaler, J., & Staples, M. (2008). Creating mathematical futures through an equitable teaching approach: The case of Railside School. *The Teachers College Record*, 110(3), 608-645.

Boerma, I. E., Mol, S. E., & Jolles, J. (2016). Reading pictures for story comprehension requires mental imagery skills. *Frontiers in psychology*, 7, 1630. https://doi.org/10.3389/fpsyg.2016.01630

Bohlmann, C., & Pretorius, E. (2002). Reading skills and mathematics. SAHE
6(3). Reading skills and mathematics : the practice of higher education (journals.co.za)

Brasof, M., & Spector, A. (2016). Teach students about civics through
schoolwide governance. *Phi Delta Kappan*, 97, 7, 63-68.

Brito, N. (2017). Influence of home linguistic environment on early language
development. *Policy Insights from the Behavioral and Brain Sciences*. doi.
org/10.1177/2372732217720699

Brown, D. F. (2004). Urban teachers' professed classroom management
strategies: Reflections of culturally responsive teaching. *Urban Education*, *39*(3), 266-289.

Bruya, B. (2010). "Two to tango: Automatic social coordination and the role of
felt effort." Effortless Attention: A New Perspective in the Cognitive Science of Attention and
Action. Cambridge, Mass: The MIT Press.

Burchinal, M., Peisner-Feinberg, E., Pianta, R., & Howes, C. (2002).
Development of Academic Skills from Preschool Through Second Grade: Family and
Classroom Predictors of Developmental Trajectories. *Journal of School Psychology*. 40. 415-436. 10.1016/S0022-4405(02)00107-3.

Cai, J., Moyer, J. C., & Wang, N. (1997). Parental roles in students' learning of
mathematics: An exploratory study. Paper presented at the annual meeting of the American
Educational Research Association, Chicago, IL.

Cairney, J., Bedard, C., Dudley, D., & Kriellaars, D. (2016). Towards a physical
literacy framework to guide the design, implementation and evaluation of early childhood
movement-based interventions targeting cognitive development. Annals of Sports Medicine
and Research 3(4): 1073.

Cantrell, S. C., Pennington, J., Rintamaa, M., Osborne, M., Parker, C., & Rudd,
M. (2017). Supplemental literacy instruction in high school: What students say matters for
reading engagement. *Reading & Writing Quarterly*, 33(1), 54–70. https://doi.org/10.1080/105
73569.2015.1081838

Caputo, C., & Estrovitz, C. (2017). More than just summer reading the shift to
"Summer Learning." *Association for Library Service to Children, 15*(1).
Carroll, B. (2019). Understanding the needs of children who are known to have experienced
neglect in the first years of life: The potential effects of early adversity on later self-regulation
skills and school functioning. *The Psychology of Education Review, 43*(2), 9-19.

Carson, V., Kuzik, N., Hunter, S., Wiebe, S. A., Spence, J. C., Friedman, A., ...
& Hinkley, T. (2015). Systematic review of sedentary behavior and cognitive development in
early childhood. *Preventive medicine*, *78*, 115-122.

Casey, A. (2010). Early Warning! Why Reading by the end of third grade
matters. Baltimore, MD: Annie E. Casey Foundation.

Castles, A., Rastle, K., & Nation, K. (2018). Ending the reading wars: Reading
acquisition from novice to expert. *Psychological Science in the Public Interest*, 19(1), 5-51.

Cassidy, J., Jones, J. D., & Shaver, P. R. (2013). Contributions of attachment
theory and research: A framework for future research, translation, and policy. *Development
and psychopathology*, *25*(4pt2), 1415-1434.
Center on the Developing Child. (n.d.-a). InBrief: The impact of early adversity on
children'sdevelopment [Video file]. http://developingchild.harvard.edu/resources/multimedia/
videos/inbrief_series/inbrief_impact_of_adversity

Center for Public Education. (2008). The Research on Pre-K. Alexandria, VA.

Center on the Developing Child—Harvard University (Producer). (2011b). InBrief: The science of early childhood development. http://developingchild.harvard.edu/resources/multimedia/videos/inbrief_series/inbrief_science_of_ecd/

Center on the Developing Child—Harvard University (Producer). (2015b). InBrief: The impact of early adversity on children's development [Video file]. http://developingchild.harvard.edu/index.php/resources/multimedia/videos/inbrief_series/inbrief_impact_of_adversity

Cervetti, G. N., Bravo, M. A., Hiebert, E. H., Pearson, P. D., & Jaynes, C. A. (2009). Text genre and science content: Ease of reading, comprehension, and reader preference. *Reading Psychology*, 30 (6), 487–511.

Chall, J. (1967). *Learning to Read: The Great Debate*. McGraw Hill.

Christensen, J. (2021). The science of reading: From research to instruction. Waterford Research Institute, LLC

Civil Rights Collection Data. (2014). https://www2.ed.gov/about/offices/list/ocr/docs/crdr-2013-14.html

Clay, M. M. (1989). Concepts about print in English and other languages. *The Reading Teacher, 42*(4), 268-276.

Cob, J. (2021). The man behind critical race theory. The New Yorker Annals of Equality. https://www.newyorker.com/magazine/2021/09/20/the-man-behind-critical-race-theory

Cobb, P. (2002). Reasoning with tools and inscriptions, *Journal of the Learning Sciences*, 11(2-3), 187-215.

Cohen L, Lehéricy S, Chochon F, Lemer C, Rivaud S, Dehaene S (2002). Language-specific tuning of visual cortex? Functional properties of the Visual Word Form Area. *Brain*. 125(5): 1054–1069. doi:10.1093/brain/awf094. PMID 11960895.

Colegrove, K. S. S., & Adair, J. K. (2014). Countering deficit thinking: Agency, capabilities and the early learning experiences of children of Latina/o immigrants. *Contemporary Issues in Early Childhood, 15*(2), 122-135.

Colker, L. J. (2014). The word gap: The early years make the difference. *Teaching Young Children, 7*(3), 26-28.

Cook-Sather, A. (2014). Student voice in teacher development. In Luanna Meyer (Ed.), Oxford bibliographies in education. New York: Oxford University Press.

Cooper, D. (2004). Professional Development: An Effective Research-Based Model. *Current Research Houghton Mifflin Harcourt Professional Development*. (pp. 97-134). Routledge.

Cooper, H., Nye, B., Charlton, K., Lindsay, J., & Greathouse, S. (1996). The effects of summer vacation on achievement test scores: A narrative and meta-analytic review. *Review of Educational Research, 66* (3), 227-268.

Cooper, P. (1996). In search of sufficient vocabulary: testing the vocabulary levels of undergraduate students. *South African Journal of Linguistics, Supplement* 26:25 37.

Cooper, R. (2017). How can educators best promote student agency? *Otterbox Business* How can educators best promote student agency? | K-12 Dive (k12dive.com)

Corson, D. (1983). Social dialect, the semantic barrier and access to curricular knowledge. *Language in Society*. 12(2), 213-222.

Cowan, C.D. (2016). What is structured literacy? *International Dyslexia Association*. https://dyslexiaida.org/what-is-structuredliteracy

Cozens, G. A. (1999). An investigation of the learning styles of ninth-grade public school students: Black and white, male and female, general level and gifted/magnet

(Unpublished doctoral dissertation). University of Georgia, Athens.

Cromley, J. G., Snyder-Hogan, L. E., & Luciw-Dubas, U. A. (2010). Reading comprehension of scientific text: A domain-specific test of the direct and inferential mediation model of reading comprehension. *Journal of Educational Psychology*, 102(3), 687.

Crosnoe, R. (2006). *Mexican roots, American schools: Helping Mexican immigrant children succeed*. Palo Alto, CA: Stanford University Press.

Cunningham, A. E., & Stanovich, K. E. (1997). Early reading acquisition and its relation to readingexperience and ability 10 years later. *Developmental Psychology*, 33, 934–945. doi:10.1037/0012-1649.33.6.934

Cypel, S. (2013). What happens in the brain as very young children learn. Early Childhood Matters. 13–17. http://earlychildhoodmagazine.org/wpcontent/uploads/2013/06/3-ECMnr120_What-happens-in-the-brain.pdf

Dabbs, L. (2013). The Power of the Morning Meeting: 5 steps toward changing your classroom and school culture. *Eutopia, George Lucas Educational Foundation*. https://www.edutopia.org/blog/morning-meeting-changing-classroom-culture-lisa-dabbs

Danish, J., Saleh, A., & Andrade, A. (2016). Observing complex systems thinking in the zone of proximal development. *Instructional Science*. https://doi.org/10.1007/s11251-016-9391-z

Davis, O. L., Jr. (1998). Beyond beginnings: From "hands-on" to "minds-on." *Journal of Curriculum and Supervision,* 13, 119–122.

Dehaene S, Le Clec'H G, Poline JB, Le Bihan D, Cohen L (2002). "The visual words in the fusiform gyrus". *NeuroReport*. 13 (3): 321–325 *CiteSeerX 10.1.1.10.7084. doi:10.1097/00001756-200203040-00015. PMID 11930131. S2CID 17598792.*

Dehaene, S., Cohen, L. (2007). "Cultural recycling of cortical maps." *Neuron*. 56 (2): 384–398. doi:10.1016/j.neuron.2007.10.004. PMID 17964253. S2CID 11364814.

Delpit, L. (2006). *Other people's children: Cultural conflict in the classroom*. New York: The New Press.

DeWitt, M. W., & Lessing, A. (2018). The Deconstruction and understanding of preliteracy development and reading acquisition. *Early Child Development and Care, 188*(12), 1843-1856. doi:10.1080/03004430.2017.1329727

Diakidoy, I., Kendeou, P., Ioannides, C. (2003). Reading about energy: The effects of text structure in science learning and conceptual change. *Contemporary Educational Psychology*. 28. 335-356. 10.1016/S0361-476X(02)00039-5.

Douglas, T.M., & Peck, C. (2013). Education by any means necessary: Peoples of African descent and community-based pedagogical spaces. *Educational Studies, 49*, 67-91.

Drose, J. (2019). Comprehending mathematical problem texts – Fostering subject-specific reading strategies for creating mental text representations. *Eleventh Congress of the European Society for Research in Mathematics Education*, Utrecht University, ffhal-02408765f.

Duke, N. K., & Pearson, P. D. (2009). Effective practices for developing reading comprehension. *Journal of Education, 189*(1–2), 107–122. https://doi.org/10.1177/0022057409189001-208

Dunlop, A., & Fabian, H., (2007). Informing transitions in the early years: *Research, Policy and Practice Berkshire, England*: Open University Press: 151.

Durkin, K., Lipsey, M. W., Farran, D. C., & Wiesen, S. E. (2022). Effects of a statewide pre-kindergarten program on children's achievement and behavior through sixth grade. *Developmental Psychology.* Advance online publication. http://dx.doi.org/10.1037/dev0001301

Edwards, S., Edick, N. (2013). Culturally responsive teaching for significant relationships. *Journal of Praxis in Multicultural Education*, (7)1.

Ehrlich, S. B., Gwynne, J. A., & Allensworth, E. M. (2018). Pre-kindergarten attendance matters: Early chronic absence patterns and relationships to learning outcomes. *Early Childhood Research Quarterly, 44*, 136-151. https://doi.org/10.1016/j.ecresq.2018.02.012

Eicher, J. D., Powers, N. R., Cho, K., Miller, L. L., Mueller, K. L., Ring, S. M., ... & Gruen, J. R. (2013). Associations of prenatal nicotine exposure and the dopamine related genes ANKK1 and DRD2 to verbal language. *PloS one, 8*(5), e63762.

Entwisle, D. R., Alexander K. L., Olson L. S. (2000). Summer learning and home environment. *A notion at risk: Preserving public education as an engine for social mobility* (pp. 9–30). New York, NY: Century Foundation Press.

Epstein, A. & Hohmann, M. (2012). High Scope's curriculum content areas and the KDIs. High Scope Extensions, High Scope Press.

Epstein, J. L. (2013). Ready or not? Preparing future educators for school, family, and community partnerships. Teaching Education, 24(2), 115–118.Epstein, T., Mayorga, E., & Nelson, J. (2011). Teaching about race in an urban history class: The effects of culturally responsive teaching. *Journal of social studies research, 35*(1), 2-21.

Evans, R. (2015). Why a school doesn't run or change like a business? Independent School Magazine Fang, Z. (2006). The language demands of science reading in middle school. *International Journal of Science Education*, 28(5), 491–520.

Fanguy, J., & Mathis, R. (2012). Psychosocial fallout from grade retention: Implication for educators. *Delta Journal of Education*, 2(2), 69-82.

Fang, Z. (2008). Going beyond the fab five: Helping students cope with the unique linguistic challenges of expository reading in intermediate grades. *Journal of Adolescent & Adult Literacy*, 51 (6), 476–487.

Fang, Z., & Wei, Y. (2010). Improving middle school students' science literacy through reading infusion. *The Journal of Educational Research*, 103(4), 262–273.

Fantuzzo, J. W., LeBoeuf, W. A., Chen, C., Rouse, H. L., & Culhane, D. P. (2012). The unique and combined effects of homelessness and school mobility on the educational outcomes of young children. *Educational Researcher*, 41(9), 393– 402.

Fergus, E. (2016). Social reproduction ideologies: Teacher beliefs about race and culture. In D. Connor, B. Ferri, & S. Annamma (eds), *DisCrit: Disability studies and critical race theory.* New York, NY: Teachers College Press.

Fountas, I.C. & Pinnell, G.S. (1996). Guided reading: Good first teaching for all children Heinemann. Portsmouth, NH.

Fowler, A. E. (1991). How early phonological development might set the stage for phoneme awareness. *Phonological Processes in Literacy: A tribute to Isabelle Y. Liberman* (pp. 97-117). Hillsdale, NJ: Lawrence Erlbaum Associates.

Fuchs, L., Compton, D., Fuchs, D., Hollenbeck, K., Craddock, C., & Hamlett, C. (2008). Dynamic assessment of algebraic learning in predicting third graders' development of mathematical problem solving. *Journal of Educational Psychology.* 100(4) 829-850.

Fuchs, L. S., Geary, D. C., Compton, D. L., Fuchs, D., Hamlett, C. L.,
Seethaler, P. M., . . . Schatschneider, C. (2010). Do different types of school mathematics
development depend on different constellations of numerical versus general cognitive
abilities? *Developmental Psychology*, 46, 1731-1746. doi:10.1037/a0020662

Fuhs, M. W., Nesbitt, K. T., & Jackson, H. (2018). Chronic absenteeism and
preschool children's executive functioning skills development. *Journal of Education for
Students Placed at Risk (JESPAR)*, 23(1-2), 39-52.

Fullan, M., Quinn, J. (2016). *Coherence: The right drivers in action for
schools, districts, and systems.* Corwin, SAGE Company. Thousands, Oaks, California.

Fuller, B. (2007) *Standardized Childhood: The political and cultural struggle
over early education.* Stanford, CA: Stanford University Press.

Gao, Q., Wang, H., Chang, F., An, Q., Yi, H., Kenny, K., & Shi, Y. (2020).
Feeling bad and doing bad: Student confidence in reading in rural China. *Compare: A
Journal of Comparative and International.* https://doi.org/10.1080/03057925.2020.1759027.

García, S. B., & Guerra, P. L. (2004). Deconstructing deficit thinking: Working
with educators to create more equitable learning environments. *Education and Urban
Society*, 36(2), 150-168.

Garcia, E. & Cuellar, D. (2006). Who are these linguistically and culturally
diverse students? *Teachers College Record*, 108(11), 2220-2246. http://dx.doi.org/10.1111/
j.1467-9620.2006.00780.x

Garcia, E. & Gonzales, D. (2006). PreK and Latina/os: The foundation for
America's future. Washington, DC: PreK Now.

Gay, G. (2002). Preparing for culturally responsive teaching. *Journal of
Teacher Education*, 53(2), 106-116.

Genishi, C. & Dyson, A.H. (2009). *Children, language, and literacy: Diverse
learners in diverse times.* New York: Teachers College Press and Washington, DC: The
National Association for the Education of Young Children

Gershenson, S., Holt, S., & Papageorge, N. (2016). Who believes in me?
The effect of student-teacher demographic match on teacher expectations. *Economics of
Education Review, 52*, 209-224. https://doi.org/10.17848/wp15-231

Gershenson, S. T., & Dee, T.S., (2017). "The Insidiousness of Unconscious
Bias in Schools." Brown Center Chalkboard. Brookings. https://www.brookings.edu/blog/
brown-center-chalkboard/2017/03/20/the-insidiousness-of-unconscious-bias-in-schools/

Gibbons, K. (2020). Literacy as a social justice issue: Why we must follow the
science of reading to give all students the skills and opportunity to succeed. *Illuminate
Education Science of Reading Play Book.*

Gilliam, W.S. 2014. "What could make less sense than expelling a preschooler?
Psychology Benefits Society (blog). American Psychological Association. https://
psychologybenefits.org/2014/12/13/preschoolexpulsions.

Gilmore, J. H., Knickmeyer, R. C., & Gao, W. (2018). Imaging structural
and functional brain development in early childhood. *Nature reviews. Neuroscience, 19*(3),
123–137. https://doi.org/10.1038/nrn.2018.1

Ginwright, S., & Cammarota, J. (2006). Youth activism in the urban
community: Learning critical civic praxis within community organizations. *International
Journal of Qualitative Studies in Education*, 20(6), 693-710.

Glanville, D. N., & Nowicki, S. (2002). Facial expression recognition and
social competence among African American elementary school children: An examination of

ethnic differences. *Journal of Black Psychology, 28*(4), 318-329.

Gonzalez, T. E., Hernandez-Saca, D. I., & Artiles, A. J. (2017). In search of voice: Theory and methods in k-12 student voice research in the US. *Educational Review, 69*(4), 451-473. https://doi.org/10.1080/00131911.2016.1231661

Gopnik, A. 2012. "Scientific thinking in young children: Theoretical advances, empirical research, and policy implications." *Science, 337*(6102), 1623–27.

Gottfried, M. (2019). Chronic absenteeism in the classroom context: Effects on achievement. *Urban Education, 54*(1), 3–34. https://doi.org/10.1177%2F0042085915618709

Gough, P.B. & Tunmer, W.E. (1986). Decoding, reading, and reading disability. *Remedial and Special Education*, 7, 6–10.

Graesser, A. C., León, J. A., & Otero, J. (2002). Introduction to the psychology of science text comprehension. *The Psychology of Science Text Comprehension* (pp. 1-15). Mahwah, NJ: Erlbaum.

Guskey, T. (2002). "Professional Development and Teacher Change." *Teachers and Teaching: Theory and Practice,* 381-391.

Hagopian, J., & Network for Public Education. (2015). Resistance to high stakes tests serves the cause of equity in education: A reply to "We oppose anti-testing efforts." http://www.networkforpubliceducation.org/2015/05/ resistance-to-high-stakes-tests-serves-the-cause-of-equity-in-education/

Halliday, M. A. K., & Martin, J. R. (1993). *Writing science: Literacy and discursive power*. London: Falmer Press.

Hamilton, L. G., Hayiou-Thomas, M. E., Hulme, C., & Snowling, M. J. (2016). The home literacy environment as a predictor of the early literacy development of children at family-risk of dyslexia. *Scientific Studies of Reading, 20*(5), 401-419.

Hammond (2015), Z. (2015). *Culturally Responsive Teaching and the Brain: Promoting Authentic Engagement and Rigor Among Culturally and Linguistically Diverse Students*. Corwin, California.

Hanford, E. (2019). What teachers should know about the science of reading. https://www.youtube.com/watch?v=1HGS9EG0HgU

Hanna, P. R. (1966). Phoneme-grapheme correspondences as cues to spelling improvement.

Hans, A. & Hans, E. (2014). Children acquire their mother tongue through various stages. *Scholars World, International Referred Multidisciplinary Journal of Contemporary Research*, 2(2).

Harry, B., & Klingner, J. K. (2006). *Why are so many minority students in special education? Understanding race and disability in schools*. New York, NY: Teachers College Press.

Harper, S. R., & Davis, C. H., III. (2012). They (don't) care about education: A counternarrative on Black male students' responses to inequitable schooling. *The Journal of Educational Foundations*, 26(1/2), 103.

Hart, B., & Risley, T. (2003). *Many languages, one classroom: Teaching dual and English language learners*. Silver Spring, Maryland, USA: Gryphon House, Inc.

Haslip, M. (2018). The effects of public pre-kindergarten attendance on first grade literacy achievement: A district study. *International Journal of Child Care and Education Policy, 12*(1), 1-19.

Hasbrouck J. & Glaser, D. (2012). Reading Frequently Does not mean reading fast. *International Literacy Association*, Newark, Delaware.

Hebbecker, K., Forster, N., & Souvignier, E. (2019). Reciprocal Effects
between reading achievement and intrinsic and extrinsic reading motivation. *Scientific Studies of Reading, 23*(5), 419-436. doi:10.1080/108884438.2019.1598413

Hecht, S. A., Torgesen, J. K., Wagner, R. K., Rashotte, C. A. (2001). The
relations between phonological processing abilities and emerging individual differences in mathematical computation skills: A longitudinal study from second to fifth grades. *Journal of Experimental Child Psychology*, 79, 192-227. doi:10.1006/jecp.2000.2586

Heckman, J. J. (2008). Schools, Skills, and Synapses. *Economic Inquiry, 46*(3),
289-324. https://doi.org/10.1111/j.1465-7295.2008.00163.x

Herba, C., & Phillips, M. (2004). Annotation: Development of facial expression
recognition from childhood to adolescence: Behavioral and neurological perspectives. *Journal of Child Psychology and Psychiatry, 45*(7), 1185-1198.

Herba, C. M., Benson, P., Landau, S., Russell, T., Goodwin, C., Lemche, E., ...
& Phillips, M. (2008). Impact of familiarity upon children's developing facial expression recognition. *Journal of Child Psychology and Psychiatry, 49*(2), 201-210.

Hilberg, R. S., Chang, J. M., & Epaloose, G. (2003). Designing effective
activity centers for diverse learners. *Center for Research on Education, Diversity & Excellence,* University of California, Santa Cruz.

Hippel, P. T., Workman, J., & Downey, D. B. (2018). Inequality in reading
and math skills forms mainly before kindergarten: A republican, and partial correction, of "Are schools the great equalizer?"*American Sociological Association, 9*(4), 323-357. doi:10.1177/0038040718801760

Holdaway, D. (2001). Shared Book Experience: Teaching Reading Using
Favorite Books. *Theory into Practice, 21*(4), 293-300.

Hooks, B. (2003). *Teaching community. A pedagogy of hope.* New York:
Routledge.

Hoover, W. A., & Gough, P. B. (1990). The simple view of reading. *Reading
and writing*, 2(2), 127-160.

Huettig, F., & Pickering, M. J. (2019). Literacy advantages beyond reading:
Prediction of spoken language. *Trends in Cognitive Sciences, 23*(6), 464-475.
Hulme, C., Snowling, M., West, G., Lervåg, A, and Melby-Lervåg, M. (2020). Children's language skills can be improved: Lessons from psychological science for educational policy. *Current Directions in Psychological Science, 29*(4), 372-377.

Iannelli, V. (2021). The importance of free play for kids: There are big payoffs
in letting kids be kids. Verywell Family. https://www.verywellfamily.com/the-importance-of-free-play-2633113

Iruka, L., Cuenton, S., Durden, T., & Escayq, K. (2020). *Don't Look Away:
Embracing Anti-Bias Classrooms.*

Gryphon House Inc., NC. Irvine, J.J. (2003). *Educating teachers for diversity:
Seeing with a cultural eye.* New York: Teachers College Press.

James, W. B., & Blank, W. E. (1993). Review and critique of available
learning-style instruments for adults. *New Directions for Adult and Continuing Education*, 59, 47-57.

Jenkins, J. M., Watts, T. W., Magnuson, K., Clements, D., Sarama, J.,
Wolfe, C. B., & Spitler, M. E. (2015). Preventing preschool fadeout through instructional intervention in kindergarten and first grade. *Society for Research on Educational Effectiveness*. Graduate School of Education, University of California, Irvine.

Jensen, E. (2005). *Teaching with the Brain in Mind.* (2nd Ed.). Alexandria, Va,

USA: Association for Supervision and Curriculum Development.

Jimerson, S. (2001). Meta-analysis of grade retention research: Implications for practice in the 21st century. *School of Psychology Review*, 30(3), 420-437.

Jimerson, S., Pletcher, S., & Kerr, M. (2005). Alternatives to grade retention. *Principal Leadership*, 5(6), 11-15.

Johnston, Peter H. 2004. *Choice Words: How Our Language Affects Children's Learning*. Portland, ME: Stenhouse.

Joseph, P. E. (2015). Why the Black church has always mattered. https://www.theroot.com/why-the-black-church-has-always-mattered-1790860217

Juel, C. (1988). Learning to read and write: A longitudinal study of 54 children from first through fourth grades. Journal of Educational Psychology, 80, 437–447. doi:10.1037/0022-0663.80.4.437

Kaeffer, T., Neuman, S., & Pinkham, A. (2015). Pre-existing background knowledge influences socioeconomic differences in preschoolers' word learning and comprehension. *Reading Psychology*. 36 203-231. DOI: 10.1080/02702711.2013.843064

Kalnay, E., Kanamitsu, M., Kistler, R., Collins, W., Deaven, D., Gandin, L., Iredell, M., Saha, S., White, G., Woollen, J., Zhu, Y., Chelliah, M., Ebisuzaki, W., Higgins, W., Janowiak, J., Mo, K. C., Ropelewski, C., Wang, J., Leetmaa, A., ... Joseph, D. (1999). The NCEP/NCAR 40-year reanalysis project. Bulletin of the American Meterological Society, 77(3), 437–471. https://doi.org/fg6rf9

Kemp, C. (2015). MRI shows association between reading to young children and brain activity. *American Academy of Pediatrics*. http://www.aappublications.org/content/early/2015/04/25/aapnews.20150425-4

Kennedy-Moore, E. (2014). Are you a distracted parent? How not to (smart) phone it in as a parent. *Psychology Today*. https://www.psychologytoday.com/blog/growing-friendships/210412/are-you-distracted-parent

Kennison, S. (2005). The latest offensive in the reading wars. Review of Dianne McGuinness's Language development and learning to read. *PsycCRITIQUES*. 51. np.

Khalifa, M., Dunbar, C., & Douglas, T. R. (2013). Derrick Bell, CRT, and educational leadership. *Race Ethnicity and Education*, 16(4), 489-513.

Kilpatrick, D. (2015). *Essentials of Assessing, preventing, and overcoming reading difficulties*. Hoboken, NJ. John Wiley & Sons.

Kohn, A. (2000). *The case against standardized testing: Raising the scores, ruining the schools*. Portsmouth, NH: Heinemann.

Krashen, S. (2011). *Free Voluntary Reading*. Santa Barbara, CA: Libraries Unlimited.

Kuhl, P. K. (2011). Early Language Learning and Literacy: Neuroscience Implications for Education. *Mind, Brain, and Education*, 5(3), 128-142.

Ladson-Billings, G. (2001). *Crossing over to Canaan: The journey of new teachers in diverse Classrooms*. San Francisco: Jossey-Bass, A Wiley Company.

Lanphear, B. P. (2015). The impact of toxins on the developing brain. *Annual review of public health*, *36*, 211-230.

Lee, G., McCreary, L., Breitmayer, B., Kim, M. J., & Yang, S. (2013). Promoting mother infant interaction and infant mental health in low-income Korean families: Attachment-based cognitive behavioral approach. *Journal for Specialists in Pediatric Nursing*, 18, 265–276.

Leerkes, E. M., & Zhou, N. (2018). Maternal sensitivity to distress and attachment outcomes: Interactions with sensitivity to non-distress and infant temperament.

Journal of Family Psychology. doi:10.1037/fam0000420

LeFevre, J. A., Fast, L., Skwarchuk, S. L., Smith-Chant, B. L., Bisanz, J., Wilger, M. (2010). Pathways to mathematics: Longitudinal predictors of performance. *Child Development*, 81, 1753-1767. doi:10.1111/j.1467-8624.2010.01508.x

Lemann, N. (1997). The tale of two schools. The challenge: history of the reading wars. *The Atlantic Monthly Magazine*. V280 n5 p128 (6). https://www.pbs.org/weta/twoschools/thechallenge/history/

Lemke, J. (1990). Talking science: Language learning and values. *Language in Society*. 21(1).123-128.

Leong, D. J., & Elena Bodrova. (2012). Why children need play. *Scholastic*. www.scholastic.com/teachers/article/why-children-need-play-0.

Lesnick, J., Goerge, R.M., & Smithgall, C. (2010). *Reading on grade level in third grade: How is it related to high school performance and college enrollment?* Chicago, IL: Chapin Hall at the University of Chicago.

Lillard, A.S., Lerner, M.D., Hopkins, E.J., Dore, R.A., Smith, E.D., & Palmquist, C.M. (2013). "The impact of pretend play on children's development: A Review of the Evidence." *Psychological Bulletin* 139 (1): 1–34.

Lindahl, M. (2001). Summer learning and the effect of schooling: Evidence from Sweden. Available at SSRN 267194.

Lin-Siegler, X., Dweck, S. & Cohen, G. (2016). "Instructional interventions that motivate classroom learning." *Journal of Educational Psychology*. 108(3): 295–99.

Lipman, P. (2013). *The new political economy of urban education: Neoliberalism, race, and the right to the city.* Routledge.

Lipsey, M. W., Farran, D. C., & Durkin, K. (2018). Effects of the Tennessee prekindergarten program on children's achievement and behavior through third grade. *Early Childhood Research Quarterly*, 1-22. https://doi.org/10.1016/j.ecresq.2018.03.005

Literacy Project (2019). *The Relationship between writing and literacy.* Newport Beach, California.

Lithner, J. (2008). A research framework for creative and imitative reasoning. *Educational Studies in Mathematics*. 67(3), 255-276.

Logan, S. (2018). *The Black family: Strengths, self-help, and positive change.* Routledge.

Lorimor-Easley, N.A. & Reed, D.K. (2019). An explanation of structured literacy, and a comparison to balanced literacy. Iowa Reading Research Center. https://iowareadingresearch.org/blog/structured-and-balanced-literacy

Love, B. (2019). *We want to do more than survive: Abolitionist Teaching and the pursuit of educational freedom.* Boston: Beacon.

Lynch, K., & Kim, J. S. (2017). Effects of a summer mathematics intervention for low-income children: A randomized experiment. *Educational Evaluation and Policy Analysis*, 39(1), 31–53.

Lynch, M. (2014). The true costs of social promotion and retention. *International Journal of Progressive Education*. 10(3).

Maniates, H. (2017). Teacher adaptations to a core reading program: Increasing access to curriculum for elementary students in urban classrooms. *Literacy Research and Instruction, 56*(1), 68-84. https://doi.org/10.1080/19388071.2016.1210706

Mantei, J., & Kervin, L. (2018). Examining literacy demands for children during teacher-led episodes of reading aloud across the transition from preschool to kindergarten. *Australian Journal of Language and Literacy, 41*(2), 82-92.

Manigo, C., & Allison, R. (2017). Does pre-school education matter? Understanding the lived experiences of parents and their perceptions of preschool education. *Teacher Educators' Journal, 10*, 5-42.

Mansfield, K. C. (2014). How listening to student voices can inform and strengthen social justice research and practice. *Educational Administration Quarterly*, 50, 3, 392-430.

Mastropieri. (1999). Strategies to increase reading fluency. *Intervention in School and Clinic, 34*(5), 278–283. https://doi.org/info:doi/

Massaro, D. (2017). Reading aloud to children: Benefits and implications for acquiring literacy before schooling begins. *The American Journal of Psychology, 130*(1), 63–72. https://doi.org/10.5406/amerjpsyc.130.1.0063

Matsumoto, D., & Hwang, H. S. (2011, May). Reading facial expressions of emotion. *Psychologica Science Agenda*. https://www.apa.org/science/about/psa/2011/05/facial-expressions

Mattson, S. N., Crocker, N., & Nguyen, T.T. (2011). Fetal alcohol spectrum disorders: neuropsychological and behavioral features. *Neuropsychology Review*, 21, 81-101. doi: 10.1007/s11065-011-9167-9.

McClanahan, M. M., Ennis, L. S., & Connell, P. H. (2016). The effects of reading engagement on literacy achievement for elementary students. *Asian Education Studies, 1*(2). http://dx.doi.org/10.20849/aes.v1i2.52

McClelland, M. M., Cameron, C. E., Connor, C. M., Farris, C. L., Jewkes, A. M., Morrison, F. J. (2007). Links between behavioral regulation and preschoolers' literacy, vocabulary, and math skills. *Developmental Psychology*, 43, 947-959. doi:10.1037/0012-1649.43.4.947

McLeod, S. A. (2016). Bandura - social learning theory. www.simplypsychology.org/bandura.html

McCombs, J., Augustine, C., Schwartz, H., Bodilly, S., McInnis, B., Lichter, D., & Cross, A. (2011). *Making summer count: How summer programs can boost children's learning*. RAND Corporation.

McDougal, S. (2007). An Afrocentric analysis of teacher/student style congruency and high school Black male achievement levels (Unpublished doctoral dissertation). Temple University, Philadelphia, PA

McFarlane, D. A. (2013). Understanding the challenges of science education in the 21st century: New opportunities for scientific literacy. *International Letters of Social and Humanistic Sciences*, 4(1), 35–44.

McGee, L. & Richgels, D. (2003). *Designing Early Literacy Programs: Strategies for At risk preschool and kindergarten*, Gullford Press, NY

McIntosh, R. & Curry, K. (2020). The role of a black church–school partnership in supporting the educational achievement of African American students. *School Community Journal*. 30(1).

McIntyre, L. L., Eckert, T. L., Fiese, B. H., DiGennaro, F. D., & Wildenger, L. K. (2007). Transition to kindergarten: Family experiences and involvement. *Early Childhood Education Journal*, 35, 83–88. doi:10.1007/s10643-007-0175-6.

McKinsey (2009). The Economic Impact of the Achievement Gap in America's Schools. The Economic Impact of the Achievement Gap in America's Schools.

McLear, C., Trentacosta, C. J., & Smith-Darden, J. (2016). Child self-regulation, parental secure base scripts, and at-risk kindergarteners' academic achievement. *Early Education and Development, 27*(4), 440-456. doi:10.1080/10409289.2016.1091972.

Miller, G. (1988). The challenge of universal literacy. *SCIENCE*. 241(4871). 1293-1299 10.1126/science.241.4871.1293

Miller, S. (2020). Showdown on the Kansas plains: The reading wars continue. *Kansas English*, 101(1).

Milner, R. H. (2013). Scripted and narrowed curriculum reform in urban schools. *Urban Education*, 48(2), 163–170. doi: 0.1177/0042085913478022.

Milteer, R. M., & Ginsberg, K. R. (2011). The importance of play in promoting healthy child development and maintaining strong parent-child bond: Focus on children in poverty. Pediatrics, 129(1), https://iths.pure.elsevier.com/en/publications/the-importance-of

Miura, I. T., Okamoto, Y. (2003). Language supports for mathematics understanding and performance. *The development of arithmetic concepts and skills: Constructing adaptive expertise* (pp. 229-242). Mahwah, NJ: Lawrence Erlbaum.

Moats, L. C. (1999). Teaching reading is rocket science: What expert teachers of reading should know and be able to do.

Moll, L., Amanti, C., Neff, D., & Gonzalez, N. (1992). Funds of knowledge for teaching: Using a qualitative approach to connect homes and classroom. *Theory into Practice*, 31(2), 132–141. http://dx.doi.org/10.1080/0040584920954353

Montessori, M. (1966). *The Secret of Childhood. Social learning theory*. Ballentine Books NY. Fides Publishers, Inc.

Morrison, V. & Wlodarczyk, L. (2009). Revisiting Read-Aloud: Instructional strategies that encourage students' engagement with texts. *The Reading Teacher*. 63. 10.1598/RT.63.2.2.

Music, G. (2017). *Nurturing Natures: Attachment and Children's Emotional, Sociocultural and Brain Development*. NY, New York: Routledge.

National Assessment of Education Progress. (2019). *NAEP Report Card: 2019 NAEP Reading Assessment*. United States Department of Education. Washington D.C.: The National Cengter for Education Statistics.

National Reading Panel (2000). *Teaching children to read: An evidence-based assessment of the scientific research literature on reading and its implications for reading instruction*. Washington, DC: NIH.

National Scientific Council on the Developing Child. (2015). Supportive Relationships and Active Skill-Building Strengthen the Foundations of Resilience: Working Paper 13. http://www.developingchild.harvard.edu

Nelson, S. W., & Guerra, P. L. (2014). Educator beliefs and cultural knowledge: Implications for school improvement efforts. *Educational Administration Quarterly, 50*(1), 67 –95. doi:10.1177/0013161X13488595.

Nevo, E., & Vaknin-Nusbaum, V. (2019). Enhancing motivation to read and reading abilities in first grade. *Educational Psychology*. doi:10.1080/01443410.2019.163568 0.

New Jersey Department of Education. (2019). NJ *Student Learning Assessment - English Language Arts*. Cranbury: Pearson Access Net.

Newmann, F. (1990). Higher order thinking in teaching social studies: A rationale for the assessment of classroom thoughtfulness. *Journal of Curriculum Studies*, 22, 41-56.

New York Daily News (2014). Education Pre K-12 Urban Policy NYC.
  https://www.manhattan-institute.org/html/fari%C3%B1as-upside-down-philosophy-4665.
  html

Nierenberg, C. (2014). Parents often glued to mobile phone while kids eat. *Live
  science*. http://www.livescience.com/43977-parents-glued-mobile-phonekids.html

Nieto, S. (2000). *Affirming diversity: The sociopolitical context of multicultural
  education* (3rd ed.). New York: Longman.

NICHD Early Child Care Research Network. (2005). Pathways to reading: The
  role of oral language in the transition to reading. *Developmental Psychology* 41(2), 428–442.

Oatley K. (2002). Emotions and the story world of fiction. *Narrative Impact.
  Social and Cognitive Foundations.* 39(69), 39–70.

Olson, L. (2007). Looking through a wider lens, executive summary of
  quality counts, from cradle to career: Connecting American education from birth through
  adulthood, *Education Week* https://www.edweek.org/ew/articles/2007/01/04/17execsum.h26.
  html.

Onyango, C., & Gakii, N. (2017). Influence of instructional strategies on
  pre-school children transition to lower primary school. A case of Kikuyu Sub-Urban, Kenya.
  International Journal of Law, Humanities & Social Science, 1(5), 39-45.

Ordetx, K. (2021). What is the science of reading: Our commitment to evidence
  based reading instruction aligning instruction with science and reading using structured
  literacy. Institute for Multisensory Education

Owings, W., & Kaplan, L. (2001). Standards, retention, and social promotion.
  NASSP Bulletin, 85(629), 57-66.

Ozek, V. (2015). Hold back to move forward? Early grade retention and student
  misbehavior. *Association for Education Finance and Policy* doi:10.1162/EDFP_a_00166.

Padilla, A. M. (1981). Competent communities: A critical analysis of theories
  and public policy. Institutional racism and community competence (pp. 20-29). Washington,
  DC: Government Printing Office.

Paradise, R. & Rogoff, B. (2009). "Side by Side: Learning by Observing and
  Pitching in." *Ethos*. 37(1) 102-138.

Patterson, A., Roman, D., Friend, M., Osborne, J., & Donovan, B. (2018).
  Reading for meaning: The foundational knowledge every teacher of science should have.
  International Journal of Science Education, 40(3), 291–307. doi:10.1080/09500693.2017.14
  16205.

Perry, B. D. (2013). Bonding and attachment in maltreated children. *The Child
  Trauma Center, 3*, 1-17.

Perry, B. D., & Winfrey, O. (2021). What happened to you? Conversations on
  trauma, resilience, and healing. NY: Flatiron Books.

Phillips, D., Lipsey, M. W., Dodge, K. A., Haskins, R., Bassok, D., Burchinal,
  M. R., Duncan, G., Dynarski, M., Magnuson, K., Weiland, C. (2017). Puzzling it out: The
  current state of scientific knowledge on pre-
  kindergarten effects: A consensus statement. Washington, DC: Brookings Institute.

Piccolo, L. R., Giacomoni, C. H., Julio-Costa, A., Oliveira, S., Zbornik, J.,
  Haase, V. G., & Salles, J. F. (2017). Reading anxiety in L1: Reviewing the concept. *Early
  Childhood Education Journal, 10*(3), 482-506.

Piscitelli, B. (2000). Practicing what we preach: Active learning in the
  development of early childhood professionals. *Promoting meaningful learning: Innovations
  in educating early childhood professionals*, 37-46.

Pizzolongo, P. J., & Hunter, A. (2011). I am safe and secure. *Young Children, 66*(1), 67-69.

Planty, M., Hussar, W. J., & Snyder, T. D. (2009). *Condition of education 2009.* Government Printing Office.

Plomin, R. 1990. *Nature and nurture: An introduction to human behavioral genetics.* Pacific Grove, CA: Brooks/Cole Publishing Co. https://doi.org/10.1007/s10643-016-0822-x

Powell, S. R., & Nelson, G. (2016). Influence of general vocabulary and mathematics knowledge on mathematics vocabulary. Manuscript submitted for publication.

Pullen, P. C., Justice, L. M. (2003). Enhancing phonological awareness, print awareness, and oral language skills in preschool children. *Intervention in School and Clinic, 39*, 87-98. doi:10.1177/10534512030390020401.

Purpura, D. J., Baroody, A. J., Lonigan, C. J. (2013). The transition from informal to formal mathematical knowledge: Mediation by numeral knowledge. *Journal of Educational Psychology, 105*, 453-464. doi:10.1037/a0031753.

Purpura, D. J., Hume, L. E., Sims, D. M., Lonigan, C. J. (2011). Early literacy and early numeracy: The value of including early literacy skills in the prediction of numeracy development. *Journal of Experimental Child Psychology, 110*, 647-658. doi:10.1016/j.jecp.2011.07.004.

Purpura, D. J., Napoli, A. R. (2015). Early numeracy and literacy: Untangling the relation between specific components. *Mathematical Thinking and Learning, 17*, 197-218. doi:10.1080/10986065.2015.1016817

Radesky, J. S., Kistin, C.J., Zuckerman, B., Nitzberg, K., Gross, J., Kaplan-Sanoff, M., Augustyn, M., & Silverstein, M. (2014). Patterns of mobile device use by caregivers and children during meals in fast food restaurants. *Pediatrics, 133*(4): 843-9.

Ramirez, G., Fries, L., Gunderson, E., Schaeffer, M. W., Maloney, E. A., Beilock, S. L., & Levine, S. C. (2019). Reading anxiety: An early affective impediment to children's success in reading. *Journal of Cognition and Development, 20*(1), 15-34. https://doi.org/10.1080/15248372.2018.1526175.

Ransaw, T. 2016. Closing the education achievement gaps for African American males. http://ebookcentral.proquest.com.

Rasinki, T. (2017). Readers who struggle and a modest proposal for improving their reading. *The Reading Teacher* 70(5), 519-524.

Rasoal, C., Eklund, J., & Hansen, E. M. (2011). Toward a conceptualization of ethnocultural empathy. *Journal of Social, Evolutionary, and Cultural Psychology, 5*(1), 1.

Ravitch, D. (2016). *The death and life of the great American school system: How testing and choice are undermining education.* Basic Books.

Restak, R. M. (1979). *The other differences between boys and girls. Student learning styles: Diagnosing and prescribing programs* (pp. 75–80). Reston, VA: National Association of Secondary School Principals.

Reyhner, J. (2020). The reading wars: Phonics versus whole language. https://jan.ucc.nau.edu/~jar/Reading_Wars.html.

Rojas, S. P., Meneses, A., & Miguel, E. S. (2019). Teachers' scaffolding science reading comprehension in low-income schools: How to improve achievement in science. *International Journal of Science Education, 41*(13), 1827-1847. doi:10.1080/09500693.2019.1641855.

Rokeach, M. (1968). Beliefs, attitudes, and values: A theory of organization and change. San Francisco: Jossey-Bass.

Román, D., & Busch, K. C. (2015). Textbooks of doubt: Using systemic functional analysis to explore the framing of climate change in middle-school science textbooks. *Environmental Education Research.* 10.1080/13504622.2015.1091878.

Robinson, C., Lee, M., Dearing, E., & Rogers, T. (2018). Reducing student absenteeism in the early grades by targeting parental beliefs. *American Educational Research Journal, 55*(6), 1163–1192. https://doi.org/10.3102%2F0002831218772274.

Romero, M. & Lee, Y. 2007. *A National Portrait of Chronic Absenteeism in the Early Grades*, New York, NY: National Center for Children in Poverty: The Mailman School of Public Health at Columbia.

Rose, M. (2014). School reforms fails the test. https://theamericanscholar.org/school-reform-fails-the-test/#.W8yoWNMrLOQ

Roseberry-McKibbin, C. (2012). The impact of poverty and homelessness on children's oral and literate language: Practical implications for service delivery. Paper presented at ASHA Schools Conference, Milwaukee, WI. http://www.asha.org/uploadedFiles/Poverty-Homelessness-Childrens-OralLiterate-Language.pdf.

Rubie-Davies, C., & Peterson, E. (2016). Relations between teachers' achievement, over- and underestimation, and students' beliefs for Maori and Pakeha students. *Contemporary Education Psychology, 47*, 72-83. https://doi.org/10.1016/j.cedpsych.2016.01.001.

Salisbury, J., Rollins, K., Lang, E., & Spikes, D. (2019). Creating spaces for youth through student voice and critical pedagogy: The case of RunDSM. *International Journal of Student Voice*, 4. https://ijsv.psu.edu/?article=creating-spaces-for-youth-through-studentvoice-and-critical-pedagogy-the-case-of-rundsm.

Saluja, G., D.M. Early, & R.M. Clifford. (2002). "Demographic characteristics of early childhood teachers and structural elements of early childcare and education in the United States." *Early Childhood Research and Practice, 4*(1). http://ecrp.uiuc.edu/v4n1/saluja.html.

Saracho, O. N. (2017). Parents' shared storybook reading - learning to read. *Early Child Development and Care, 187*(3-4), 554-567. doi:10.1080/03004430.2016.1261514.

Sawchuk, S. (2021). An action plan for confronting chronic absenteeism in the fall. Education Week. An Action Plan for Confronting Chronic Absenteeism This Fall. https://edweek.org

Scarborough, H.D. & Dobrich, W. (1994). On the efficacy of reading to preschoolers. Developmental Review, 14, 245-302.

Schaffner, E., Philipp, M., Schiefele, U. (2016). Reciprocal effects between intrinsic reading motivation and reading competence? A cross-lagged panel model for academic track and nonacademic track students. *Journal of Research in Reading.* 39. 19-36. 10.1111/1467-9817.12027.

Schaughency, E., Suggate, S., & Reese, E. (2017). Links between early oral narrative and decoding skills and later reading in a New Zealand sample. *Australian Journal of Learning Difficulties, 22*(2), 109-132. doi:10.1080/19404158.2017.1399914.

Schunk, D. H., & Pajares, F. (2009). Self-efficacy theory. *Handbook of motivation at school* (pp. 35-54). New York, NY: Routledge. 3, pp. 657-700. Hoboken, NJ: John Wiley & Sons.

Schwerdy, G., West, M., & Winters, M. (2017). The effects of test-based detention on student outcomes overtime : Regression discontinuity evidence from Florida. National Bureau of Economic Research. Working Paper 2509.

Scott, J. (2014). Parenting while distracted – it's an epidemic: Don't push your kids away to grab another minute of screen time. *Pittsburgh Post-Gazette*. http://www.post-gazette.com/opinion/2014/09/04/Parenting-whiledistracted/stories/201409040159.

Segerby, C. (2014). Reading strategies in mathematics: A Swedish example. *Nottingham: British Society for Research into Learning Mathematics.* https://bsrlm.org.uk/BCME8/BCME8-Full.pdf

Seidenberg, M. (2017). *Language at the speed of sight: How we read, why so many can't, and what can be done about it*, New York, NY: Basic Books.

Shanahan, T., & Shanahan, C. (2008). Teaching Disciplinary literacy to Adolescents: Rethinking content-area literacy. *Harvard Educational Review* 78(1), 40-49.

Shields, C., Bishop, R., & Mazawi, A. (2005). Pathologizing practices. The impact of deficit thinking on education. New York, NY: Peter Lang.

Shinwell, J., & Defeyter, M. A. (2017). Investigation of summer learning loss in the UK? Implications for holiday club provision. *Frontiers in Public Health*, 5, 270.

Shonkoff, J. P., Phillips, D. A., & National Research Council. (2000). The developing brain. *In From neurons to neighborhoods: The science of early childhood development*. National Academies Press (US).

Simmons, F., & Singleton, C. (2007). Do weak phonological representations impact on arithmetic development? A review of research into arithmetic and dyslexia. *Wiley InterScience*. DOI: 10.1002/dys.341.

Sleeter, C. E. (2011). An agenda to strengthen culturally responsive pedagogy. *English teaching: Practice and critique, 10*(2), 7-23. Southern Early Childhood Association. (2001). Brain development and its implications for early childhood programs. http://www.southernearlychildhood.org/upload/pdf/Brain_Research__Its_Implications.pdf.

Solity, J. & Vousden, J. (2009). Real Book vs Reading Schemes: A new perspective from instructional psychology. *Education Psychology*. 29(4). 469-511 10.1080/01443410903103657.

Stanovich, K. E. (1986). Matthew effects in reading: Some consequences of individual differences in the acquisition of literacy. *Reading Research Quarterly*, 21, 360-407.

Stanovich, K. (1994). "Romance and Reading" *The Reading Teacher*. 47, 280-291.

Starck, J. G., Riddle, T., Sinclair, S., & Warikoo, N. (2020). Teachers are people too: Examining the racial bias of teachers compared to other American adults. *Educational Researcher, 49*(4), 273–284. https://doi.org/10.3102/0013189X20912758.

Stires, S. & Genishi, C. (2008). Learning English in school: Rethinking curriculum, relationships, and time.

Stover, K., Sparrow, A., & Siefert, B. (2017). "It ain't hard no more!" Individualizing instruction for struggling readers. *Alternative Education for Children and Youth, 61*(1), 14-27. https://doi.org/10.1080/1045988X.2016.1164659.

Strickland, D. S. (1990). Emergent Literacy: How young children learn to read. *Educational Leadership*, 18-23.

Strickland, D. & Schickedanz, J. (2004). *Learning about print and preschool: Working with letters, words, and beginning links with phonemic awareness*. International Reading Association. Newark, Delaware.

Stuckey, S. (2013). Slave culture: Nationalist theory and the foundations of Black America. Oxford University Press.

Suggate, S., Schaughency, E., McAnally, H., & Reese, E. (2018). From Infancy to adolescence: The longitudinal links between vocabulary, early literacy skills; oral narrative, and reading comprehension. *Cognitive Development, 47*, 82-95. doi:10.1016/j.cogdev.2018.04.005.

Sussman, F. (2012). Let's Pretend: The relationship between play and theory of mind in typical children and children with ASD. *The Hanen Centre Web site:* http://www. hanen. org/SiteAssets/Helpful-Info/Articles/pretend-play. aspx.

Sutton-Smith, B. 2001. *The Ambiguity of Play*. Rev. ed. Cambridge, MA: Harvard University Press.

The National Assessment of Education Progress. (2019). *NAEP Report Card: 2019 NAEP Reading Assessment.* United States Department of Education. Washington D.C.: The National Cengter for Education Statistics. https://www.nationsreportcard.gov/highlights/reading/2019/.

The Urban Child Institute. (2015). Baby's brain begins now: Conception to age 3. http://www.urbanchildinstitute.org/July-0-3/baby-and-brain.

Thompson, C., & Cunningham, E. (2000). Retention and social promotion: Research and implications for policy. New York: ERIC Clearinghouse on Urban Education. Accessed 14 July 2010. Available at https://www.eric.ed.gov/PDFS/ED449241.pdf

Tierney, A., & Nelson, C. (2009). Brain Development and the Role of Experience in the Early Years. *National Institute of Health.* 30(2) 9-13.

Timmermans, A. C., Boer, H. d., & Werf, M. P. (2016). An investigation of the relationship between teachers' expectations and teachers' perceptions of student attributes. *Social Psychology of Education, 19*, 217–240. https://doi.org/10.1007/s11218-015-9326-6.

Tomlinson, C. A. (2017). *How to Differentiate Instruction in Academically Diverse Classrooms* (3 ed.). Alexandria, VA: Association for Supervision and Curriculum Development.

Toub, T.S., B. Hassinger-Das, H. Ilgaz, D.S. Weisberg, K.T. Nesbitt, M.F. Collins, K. Hirsh-Pasek, R.M. Golinkoff, D.K. Dickinson, & A. Nicolopoulou. (2016). "The Language of Play: Developing Preschool Vocabulary Through Play Following Shared Book-Reading." Manuscript submitted for publication.

Trelease, J. (2001). The Read-aloud Handbook. https://books.google.com/books?id=fkImAQAAIAAJ.

Turnbull, K. L., & Justice, L. M. (2017). *Language Development from Theory to Practice.* Upper Saddle River, New Jersey: Pearson.

University of Arizona. (2011). How the brain strings words into sentences. https://uanews.arizona.edu/story/how-brain-strings-words-sentences

Valencia, R. R. (2010). *Dismantling contemporary deficit thinking: Educational thought and practice*. NewYork: Routledge.

Vaughn, M. (2019). Making Sense of Student Agency in the Early Grades. *Phi Delta Kappan*, 99(7).

Voss, P., Thomas, M. E., Cisneros-Franco, J. M., & de Villers-Sidani, E. (2017). Dynamic brains and the changing rules of neuroplasticity: Implications for learning and recovery. *Frontiers in psychology, 8*, 1657.

Wanless, S., & Crawford, P. (2016). Reading your way to a culturally responsive classroom. YC Young Children. 71. 8-15.

Weisberg, D.S., K. Hirsh-Pasek, R.M. Golinkoff, A.K. Kittredge, & D. Klahr. (2016). "Guided Play: Principles and Practices." *Current Directions in Psychological Science* 25 (3): 177–82.

Weisman, E., & Garza, S. (2002). Preservice teacher attitudes toward diversity: Can one class make a difference? Equity & Excellence in Education, 35(1), 28-34.

Welsch, J. (2008). Playing within and beyond the classroom. *Texas Child Care Quarterly*, 36(3), Childcarequarterly.com story: Encouraging book-related play. *The Reading Teacher*. 62 (2). Retrieved Dec. 27, 2011, EBSCOHost Academic Search Elite Database.

Wexler, N. (2019). *The Knowledge Gap: The Hidden Cause of America's Broken Education System – And how to Fix it.* Penguin Random House LLC, NY.

Whitehurst, G. J., Lonigan, C. J. (1998). Child development and early literacy. *Child Development*, 69, 848-872. doi:10.1111/j.1467-8624.1998.tb06247.x.

Willerman, L. 1979. *The psychology of individual and group differences.* San Francisco: W.H. Freeman and Company

Williams, P. (2019). Student agency for powerful learning. *American Library Association*, 45(4).

Wlodkowski, R. J., & Ginsberg, M. B. (1995). Diversity and motivation: Culturally responsive teaching. San Francisco: Jossey-Bass.

Workman, S. & Ullrich, R. (2017). Quality 101: Identify the core components of a high quality early childhood program. Center for American Progress.

Yoshikawa, H., Weiland, C., & Brooks-Gunn, J. (2016). When does preschool matter? *The Future of Children*, 21-35.

Yoshikawa, H., Weiland, C., Brooks-Gunn, J., Burchinal, M., Espinosa, L., Gormley, W., … Zaslow, M. J. (2013). Investing in our future: The evidence base for preschool education. Policy brief, Society for Research in Child Development and the Foundation for Child Development. Foundation for Child Development website: fcd-us. org/sites/default/files/Evidence Base on Preschool Education FINAL.pdf.

Zamosky, L. (2011). How boys and girls learn differently. *WebMD*. http://www. webmd.com.

Zeiser, K., Scholz, C., Cirks, V. (2018). Maximizing Student Agency: Implementing and measuring student-centered learning practices. American Institute for Research.

Zeng, N., Ayyub, M., Sun, H., Wen, X., Xiang, P., & Gao, Z. (2017). Effects of physical activity on motor skills and cognitive development in early childhood: A systematic review. *BioMed research international, 2017*.

Zhao, Y. (2018). What works may hurt: Side effects in education. New York, NY: Teachers College Press.

www.ingramcontent.com/pod-product-compliance
Lightning Source LLC
Chambersburg PA
CBHW051313020426
42333CB00028B/3315